ACHIEVING
YOUR FINANCIAL
POTENTIAL

ACHIEVING YOUR FINANCIAL POTENTIAL

A COMPREHENSIVE GUIDE TO
APPLYING BIBLICAL PRINCIPLES
OF FINANCIAL SUCCESS

SCOTT KAYS, CFP

President, Kays Financial Advisory Corporation

DOUBLEDAY
NEW YORK LONDON TORONTO SYDNEY AUCKLAND

To Lisa,
whose encouragement has brought out the best in me;
and to Elizabeth, Eric, Seth, and Rachel:
The book is finished;
Daddy can play now.

PUBLISHED BY DOUBLEDAY
a division of Random House, Inc.
1540 Broadway, New York, New York 10036

DOUBLEDAY and the portrayal of an anchor with a dolphin are trademarks of
Doubleday, a division of Random House, Inc.

Scripture taken from the NEW AMERICAN STANDARD BIBLE ®, copyright ©
The Lockman Foundation 1960, 1962, 1963, 1968, 1971, 1972, 1973, 1975, 1977
Used by permission.

Library of Congress Cataloging-in-Publication Data
Kays, Scott, 1960–
Achieving your financial potential: a comprehensive guide to applying
biblical principles of financial success / by Scott Kays.
p.   cm.
1. Finance, Personal.   2. Finance, Personal—Religious aspects.
I. Title.
HG179.H387 1999
332.024—dc21   98-39088
                                                                   CIP

ISBN 0-385-49345-2

98 99 00 01 10 9 8 7 6 5 4 3 2 1

ACKNOWLEDGMENTS

I owe many thanks to several people who helped make this book a reality:

Charles Hampton, Esq., partner of the Atlanta law firm Thrasher, Whitley, Hampton, and Morgan, for critiquing the section on estate planning and providing me with his technical expertise in this area;

David Brown, president of David Brown Accounting and Tax Service, Inc., for his assistance on income tax related issues and retirement plans;

Dave Lanier, State Farm agent, who reviewed the chapter on insurance and provided me with several ideas which were incorporated into the book;

Janice Meadows, my office manager, who spent endless overtime hours typing revisions without complaint. I can never adequately express my gratitude for her unwavering faith in this project—she truly treated it as if it were her own;

Robin Gant, a friend and writer whose advice and suggestions were indispensable;

Deidre Knight, president of the Knight Agency, my agent, who introduced me to Doubleday. Her expert counsel has been invaluable;

Eric Major, vice president of Doubleday and my editor for this work. His expertise and insight have added immensely to the quality of this book.

I would especially like to thank my parents, Ancil and Rose Mary Kays, for their support and for becoming my first clients in 1985.

Finally, I am greatly indebted to Dr. Oliver Welch, J.D., CPA, CFP, former chairman of the board of the IBCFP, for giving me my start in this great profession. His example of integrity and professionalism has left a permanent imprint on my life and career.

CONTENTS

SECTION IV

PROTECTING WHAT YOU HAVE

SECTION V

TRUE WEALTH

GETTING STARTED

## CHAPTER 1

KNOWLEDGE—THE KEY TO FINANCIAL SUCCESS

Ken and Toni approached me in church and asked if I could meet with them to help them with their finances. As a Certified Financial Planner®[1] practitioner and president of my own Atlanta financial advisory firm, it is not unusual for church members to request such an appointment with me. I enjoy helping others get their financial households in order, so I gladly set up a time to meet with Ken and Toni.

As they walked into my office, it was obvious that something was very wrong. Normally affable, friendly people, who looked more like Ken and Barbie than Ken and Toni, they were looking at the floor and hardly speaking. They sat down in the chairs across from my desk. I offered them some coffee, but neither was interested.

Ken began the conversation. "We need help," he said. "Our debt is killing us."

He had put together a list of everybody to whom they owed money, along with the balance, interest rate, and monthly payment for each obligation. Even with the several years of experience I had under my belt, I was surprised at what I saw. Ken had a good salary, earning $50,000 per year. Uncontrolled spending, however, had sent them into a financial tailspin. Reality was starting to set in, and they realized that it was time to pay the price for their irresponsible spending habits.

Ken and Toni had accumulated more than $50,000 in short-term debt. Almost $32,000 of this was credit card debt, with interest rates ranging between 18 to 21 percent. As their debt piled up, so did their debt payments. Once they finally admitted they had a problem, they cut their living expenses to the bone in a vain effort to make ends meet. But it was too late.

Their monthly financial outflow still exceeded their income. Each month they were going further into debt.

The strain of the financial pressure was taking its toll. Not only had their finances fallen apart but now their marriage was beginning to crumble as well. Their once happy and loving relationship was coming apart at the seams. They were fighting more and more, even arguing on the way to my office.

As a professional financial adviser, I can often spot things about people's financial situations that they may not see themselves. I frequently can suggest solutions they hadn't previously considered. It is similar to going to a doctor thinking you have a major health problem. Untreated, the problem may kill you. But, if treated in time, a week's worth of medicine may heal you.

Ken and Toni needed more than a week's worth of medicine, but there was a solution to their problem. It would take discipline and time, but at least they had a fighting chance to recover from their past mistakes.

WHY?

That's a question you cannot help but ask after a counseling session with people like Ken and Toni. God tells us in the early verses of Deuteronomy 28 that ". . . The Lord will make you abound in prosperity. . . ." He goes on to say ". . . and you shall lend to many nations, but you shall not borrow. . . ." If God's promises are true, and they are, *then why do so few Christians walk in financial freedom?* If God means what He says, *why are so many Christians floundering in a sea of debt?* What does it take for a Christian to experience the financial blessings that God has promised to His people?

WHAT CAUSES ABUNDANCE?

The Bible tells us that when Solomon took over as king of Israel, "God was with him and exalted him greatly." Then one night, still early in Solomon's reign, the Lord appeared to him and said, "Ask what I shall give you." Instead of asking for something self-centered, such as riches or honor, Solomon asked for wisdom and an understanding heart. God told

Solomon that because he had asked for these things, He would grant his request and give him riches and honor as well.

On the surface, it looks as though God did something special just for Solomon—that Solomon did something that pleased God, and God was rewarding him for his deed of unselfishness. The king, however, later realized that he had tapped into a financial principle that applies to anyone who makes acquiring wisdom and knowledge his or her lifelong pursuit. Solomon writes in Proverbs 3:

13 How blessed is the man who finds wisdom, and the man who gains understanding.

14 For its profit is better than the profit of silver, and its gain than fine gold.

16 Long life is in her right hand; in her left hand are riches and honor.

What Solomon discovered was an immutable law of God: financial success and honor spring from wisdom and knowledge. Knowledge is the accumulation of facts, while wisdom is knowing how to apply those facts to accomplish an objective. Without wisdom, knowledge is fruitless. True wisdom results in decisive action. Knowing how to solve a problem is worthless unless you actually apply what you know to solve the problem.

The Bible is filled with principles of wisdom, especially in the book of Proverbs, that tell us how to handle our financial affairs in a responsible manner. God has carefully detailed for us ways to increase our income, further our careers, gain favor with our employers, and preserve assets once we have successfully accumulated them.

Because they think the pursuit of financial abundance is worldly, many Christians are not willing to say that God wants them to be blessed financially. However, the pursuit of success in the financial realm does not have to be an exercise in carnality. Deuteronomy 28 tells us that God's blessings come upon us as we obey His word. *Pursuing financial prosperity means that we order our financial affairs in such a way that they are pleasing to God.*

Jesus, during His earthly ministry, spoke frequently about money. He understood that every person has an innate desire to live in financial abundance. That desire is actually placed in us by our Creator, and as long as it is kept in subjection to God's will, and is not allowed to get out of control, there is nothing wrong with the desire. Be honest with your feelings and ask yourself the question, "If I had the opportunity, would I like to experience greater financial blessing than I am experiencing right now?" I believe virtually every person would answer that question with a resounding "yes!"

THE GOODNESS OF GOD!

As we learn about God and discern His will for our lives, we must keep in mind that He is a good God. I recently heard Gregg Harris, a leader in the home school movement, speak about this issue. He said if there are things in life that God has created as His will for us, then a good God would give us desires for those things and make their fulfillment a pleasurable experience. For instance, God created us to reproduce. Though God could have made the reproductive act painful and distasteful, because He is good, He made the fulfillment of His will in this area to be a source of great pleasure.

Gregg continued his point with another analogy. God created us in such a way that we must eat to be energized. If God was not good, He could have created a process of reenergizing us that was painful, such as sticking one of our fingers into an electric socket. But because God is good, He created us to be energized by eating, which He made to be a pleasurable experience (at least until fast food came along!).

In the same way, God created man to rule and placed within him corresponding desires. He told Adam and Eve in the Garden of Eden to subdue the earth. Notice that He placed man in a garden of abundance, where all of his needs were met, to live his life. He did not create man in His image and then house him in a garbage dump. Rather, He first placed in man the desire to have abundance, and then He created an environment of abundance to be man's home. Only when man sinned and fell did he begin to suffer lack. Deuteronomy 28 lists the curses that came into the earth as a result of man's sin, one of which was the "lack of all things," i.e., poverty. God did not create man to live in lack. Neither did He place in man a desire for lack, but rather He placed in man a desire for plenty. Anything can be abused, but this basic, innate desire for financial abundance was placed in man by God.

THE MONEY ADDICTION

Unfortunately, another result of man's fall is the tendency to become obsessed with money and the pleasures it can buy. Yes, God places desires in our hearts, and, yes, God has created pleasure for us to enjoy. However, people frequently err by allowing the blessings of God to replace God Himself as the focus of their lives! Sex, food, and money—all designed by God for our enjoyment—when out of balance, or impulsively or excessively pursued, all lead to sin. Only the person who maintains the lordship of Christ in his life is truly free to delight himself in the goodness of God!

Why is money addictive?

God created man in a state of perfection. He was in union with God and lacked nothing, inwardly or outwardly. He was not lonely, depressed, or empty-feeling. He did not struggle with his self-image. The presence of God fulfilled him, and his happiness flowed from the inside out.

Then man sinned; he rebelled against God and chose to go his own way. His outward circumstances crumbled as the curse took hold. Even worse, however, he lost the inner peace and sense of personal fulfillment he had always known. Emptiness filled his soul as he realized he was no longer one with God.

Ever since man's fall, he has tried to fill his inward emptiness from outside sources. He could no longer simply enjoy the things for their own sake with which God provided him, but instead used them to try to fill his inner void. Since only the presence of God can meet this need, attempts to find fulfillment in external things are futile. This is why people become addicted to sex, drugs, pornography, and other things. The thrill that is so satisfying at first no longer gratifies after a few times. A greater stimulation is needed and sought after. Eventually, no level of excitement is enough. Before people realize it, they are hooked.

Money is the same way. Material things were created by God to be enjoyed. But, when a person looks to those material things for fulfillment, they become addictive. One starts by seeking only enough wealth to be comfortable, believing that will satisfy him. When people attain that level, however, they realize that their desire for more is not abated. What they thought would satisfy them does not, but they are sure just a little more would. This vicious cycle repeats itself endlessly, and, before they realize it, they are hooked.

There is an old saying in financial planning circles that rich is always just a little more than what you have.

If you feel caught in the money addiction cycle, the key to freedom is to realize that the problem is an internal one. You will never be able to accumulate enough "stuff" to fill your inner void. Enough will never be enough. Only the presence of God, through a personal relationship with Jesus Christ, can bring peace and personal fulfillment. Once this relationship with God has been established, however, you will gain the freedom to enjoy material things as God intended, without being in bondage to them.

UNDERSTANDING GOD'S WILL

There are two key reasons why most Christians would hesitate to say that it is God's will for His people to live in abundance. First, just the thought of such a statement conjures up a vision of television evangelists telling viewers that they can become rich by simply sending money to the evangelist's ministry. In many people's minds, teaching abundance has become associated with eccentric charlatans using God's word to abuse His people and enrich themselves.

A second reason that Christians hesitate to proclaim it is God's will to succeed in the financial realm is they fear that those who are experiencing financial problems will feel condemned for not experiencing the fullness of God's will. Far from ministering condemnation to such people, my purpose in making this statement is to minister hope to these individuals. Telling someone that the financial problems they are experiencing is God's desire for them does not help them, but rather it prevents them from taking those actions that will lead to financial freedom, for taking such actions would be fighting against the will of God! Only when someone is assured of God's will can they begin to take those steps that will allow them to achieve His will for their lives.

GUIDING PREMISES

As we embark on our journey to financial independence, there are four guiding premises upon which this book will be based:

- God wants His people to experience blessing.

- God's blessings come as we obey His principles.

- Financial problems are not normally due to a lack of money, but rather are a result of mishandling our money.

- For most people, obtaining financial freedom takes time and is the result of executing a carefully designed plan.

> **PREMISE #1**
>
> **God wants His people to experience blessing.**

Psalm 35:27 says, "Let them shout for joy and rejoice, who favor my vindication; and let them say continually, 'The Lord be magnified, who delights in the prosperity of His servant.'" The word translated "prosperity" is the Hebrew word *"shalom."* According to *Strong's Enhanced Lexicon,* this word has several meanings, including "safety," "soundness," "welfare," "health," "peace," and "prosperity." It speaks of the all-encompassing blessings of God. According to this verse, God actually takes pleasure in blessing His people, financially and otherwise.

WHY GOD WANTS TO BLESS US

Why does God want to bless us financially? In Genesis 12, God spoke to Abraham and made a covenant with him. He told Abraham to leave his country and his father's house and to travel to a land that God would show him. He promised Abraham that if he would obey Him, He would make him a great nation. Then He told him, "And I will bless you, . . . and so you shall be a blessing; . . ." Contained in this covenant that God made with Abram are the two main reasons why God wants to bless His people.

9

First, *God loves us and simply wants to bless us.* All too often I think the Church has forgotten how good God is and how much He loves His people.

I have heard numerous ministers comment, as they were teaching about finances, that the only reason God blesses us financially is so that we will be able to give more money to the gospel. While I do believe that this is one reason God blesses us financially, it is not accurate to say this is the *only* reason that God blesses us financially. To find God's original intent for man, we must go back to the creation of man in the Garden of Eden.

Here there was no one with whom Adam needed to share the gospel. He didn't need to minister salvation to Eve. There were no missionaries to support, no church programs requiring money. Yet, in the midst of these circumstances, God provided Adam with everything he could want. He did not give Adam just enough to get by; He gave Adam abundance. Why? For no other reason than that He loved Adam and wanted to bless him. He took delight in the prosperity of His servant.

It is odd to me how so many people think they are more loving than God is. Does a father need a reason to buy a new doll for his little girl? Of course not! He buys his daughter a doll just because he knows the pleasure she will get from it. He looks forward to the look on her face when he gives it to her. Does this same father need a reason to buy his son a new bicycle? Does he tell his son that the only reason he is getting him the bicycle is so he can ride it door to door to preach the gospel to the neighbors? Of course not! He buys his son the bicycle because he loves his son and knows that his son wants the bicycle. It delights the father to see his children blessed!

How much more does God want to bless His children simply because He loves us and takes delight in seeing us blessed. Does God need any other reason than this to bless His children? I should say not! Just the pleasure alone He receives from giving a good gift to His children is reason enough for Him to bless us. Why? Because God is more loving than any earthly father could ever hope to be.

However, there is a second part to this covenant that God made with Abram. He said "And so you shall be a blessing." *Part of the reason God blesses us is so that we will be a blessing to other people.* There *are* people who are lost and need to hear the gospel; there *are* missionaries who need to be supported; and there *are* church programs that require finances in order to reach out to those in need.

We are the only hands that God has to minister to the poor. God's desire is to channel blessings to those in need through His people. We do not need to be selfish with the blessings that God gives us, but rather we need to be open to letting Him use us to bless others.

Ephesians 1:3 says, "Blessed be the God and father of our Lord Jesus Christ, *who has blessed us with every spiritual blessing in the heavenly places in Christ*" (emphasis mine). Note that the word "blessed" is in the past tense. When you commit your life to Christ, God's blessing is a part of your life from that moment forward. Yet, we would all have to admit that there are areas of our lives in which we do not seem to be experiencing His favor. Why? What is it that brings God's blessing into our everyday affairs?

> **PREMISE #2**
>
> **God's blessings come as we obey His principles.**

WISE ACTIONS, THE KEY TO PROSPERITY

"So David went out wherever Saul sent him, and prospered; . . ." I Samuel 18:5.

Prosperity means more than just making a lot of money. In the above passage of scripture, the Bible is not telling us that David made a lot of money every time he went out to war. Rather it is telling us that he was successful in his endeavors.

To prosper means just that—to be successful in your ventures. God desires that you prosper in every area of your life. He wants your marriage to be strong and your children to be godly; He desires that you be fulfilled in your career; He wants you to be emotionally healthy and happy; and He wants you to prosper financially. *The blessings of God are all-encompassing; do not limit them to just the financial realm, but do not exclude finances either.*

David was a man of war. The above passage was written about him shortly after his victory over the giant Goliath. Because of the bravery that David displayed in fighting and defeating Goliath, Saul pressed David into his service and made him a military leader. Everywhere that David was sent by Saul to conquer, God saw to it that David was successful. But there was more to David's success than just God's blessing. David played a very important role also.

A word study on the word "prosper" reveals some interesting facts. The word translated "prosper" is the Hebrew word "sakal." According to Strong's concordance, "sakal" can also be translated "have good success" or "behave wisely." In other words, David *acted wisely* in his affairs. His wise actions resulted in success in his endeavors! To prosper means to have success in those activities in which we are engaged. The biblical equivalent of success was to act wisely. It was commonly understood that success was brought about by wise actions!

I believe very strongly in the blessing of God that abides in the life of Christians. The Bible tells us in Deuteronomy 28 that God's blessings will overtake us if we will be diligent to obey Him. The same chapter tells us that God will bless whatever the righteous man puts his hands to. However, if the blessing of God was all that was necessary to experience God's

> **KEY POINT**
>
> **David experienced success wherever he went because David *acted wisely* wherever he went. In other words, *success in any area of life is brought about by taking wise actions in those areas.***

abundance in our lives, then all Christians would be walking in abundance, and there would be no lack within the Church!

If we are to have a successful marriage, we must act wisely with our spouse; if we are to have a successful career, then it is essential that we take wise actions in our career; and if we are to succeed in financial matters, *we must make wise financial decisions and act in a wise manner with our money.* The failure to do so will result in the failure to achieve our financial potential!

After fourteen years of experience as a professional financial counselor, I have had the opportunity to counsel with literally hundreds of individuals and couples concerning their financial affairs. If I asked those who were experiencing financial difficulties to name the source of their problems, most would respond that they make too little money. Yet, I can tell you in reality that *most financial problems are not caused by making too little money, but rather by handling the money that we do have in an unwise manner.*

For instance, if you buy a bigger house than you can afford with an income of $40,000 per year, you would probably do the same if your annual income were $80,000. The problem is not the level of your income, but that you purchased a house that was too expensive relative to your income. If you buy a bigger car than you can afford with an annual income of $40,000, you would likely buy an even more expensive car if you had an annual income of $80,000. I could go on and on, but I think you get the picture. I have seen people with large incomes who have financial problems just as serious as people with smaller incomes, the only difference being that the

KEY POINT

Very few financial problems are caused by a lack of income. To the contrary, most money problems are caused by a lack of discipline to make appropriate decisions relative to your existing financial circumstances. The problem is internal, not external, and would exist regardless of your level of income. Therefore, the solution must begin internally. You must decide to begin spending and saving in a responsible manner now, not when your income increases.

numbers were bigger. On the other hand, I have seen people with smaller incomes who handled their money wisely and were quite comfortable financially as a result.

Many people have the attitude that they would not overspend if they only had more money. While this sounds good, it simply is not true. In the parable of the talents, which I will examine in detail later, Jesus makes it very clear that you will be faithful with much only if you were faithful with little. The failure to recognize this fact will result only in greater financial problems as your income increases. Indeed, this parable also makes it clear that God will bless only those with much who were faithful with little.

Finances are more important to people's lives than many Christians are willing to admit. Studies show that the majority (I have heard as high as 80 percent) of marriage problems are financially related. Many emotional and physical problems have their roots in financial problems. The fact is, money is a very important part of our lives, and it is time that we begin talking openly and frankly about it in the Church.

Too often it seems that the only time finances are discussed in the Church is during a stewardship campaign, when the leadership is asking the congregation to increase their level of giving. The only teachings we normally hear concerning money regard either charitable giving or getting out of debt. This must change because handling our money responsibly encompasses so much more than just these two areas. The Bible is full of principles on how to properly handle our finances. It may not say which mutual fund to buy, but it does give principles of investing. The scriptures may not tell us how much money to set aside each pay period for retirement, but they do give us principles about saving.

Why does the Bible talk so much about money? Because money pervades almost everything we do. Most of our time is spent in activities that involve money in some way or another. We work forty hours each week earning money to live on during the other hours of our lives. We spend leisure time on activities that cost money. It takes money to spread the gospel of salvation. God knows that if our money and our attitude about it are brought under His lordship, then our hearts will be brought under His lordship as well.

> **PREMISE #4**
>
> **For most people, obtaining financial freedom takes time and is the result of executing a carefully designed plan.**

For most people, achieving financial freedom will not happen overnight. It will take place over a period of time, normally many years, so be patient. It occurs as the result of consistently applying God's principles. Observe what the Lord said in the following verses from Mark 4:

26 And He was saying, "The kingdom of God is like a man who casts seed upon the ground;

27 and goes to bed at night and gets up by day, and the seed sprouts up and grows—how, he himself does not know.

28 The earth produces crops by itself; first the blade, then the head, then the mature grain in the head.

29 But when the crop permits, he immediately puts in the sickle, because the harvest has come."

This passage of scripture illustrates the seed principle, one of the key principles in scripture. It is both a physical and a spiritual principle. Normally, when God accomplishes something in a person's life, it does not happen instantaneously, but rather over time. Just as seeds do not sprout immediately, neither is God's will for your life accomplished overnight.

Not only does a seed not sprout overnight but it sprouts in stages. It is not a seed one day and a fully grown plant the next. First, the blade of the plant begins to develop and show forth. Next, the head of the plant forms on top of the blade. Finally, the mature grain grows in the head, and then the plant is ready for harvest.

As there are phases to the growth of a plant, there are phases of development in almost any endeavor, including obtaining financial freedom. Instead of getting discouraged because we don't see the ultimate fruit of our endeavor immediately, we should rejoice with each stage of growth, recognizing that it is simply another milestone on our path to success.

SUCCESS IS PROGRESSIVE

There is a godly progression in the attainment of wealth. Proverbs 20:21 tells us that "An inheritance gained hurriedly at the beginning, will not be blessed in the end." When many people give their hearts to Jesus and learn the biblical principles of financial success, they expect God to

> **KEY POINT**
>
> **Financial abundance involves more than just the blessing of God in our lives. If that were all that was involved, every Christian would be prospering, because the Bible tells us that every Christian is blessed. In addition to the blessing of God, there are principles the Bible gives that must be followed in order for us to experience financial success. It is up to us whether or not we follow these principles. The more closely we follow these principles, the more we will experience God's blessing in our lives.**

make them rich overnight. Though I'm sure there are occasional exceptions, this is not generally how God works.

It takes time to learn to obey God, just as it takes time to learn His word and His principles. Sometimes we disobey God out of sheer rebellion; other times we don't do God's will simply because of an ignorance of what His will is. We don't become instantly mature the second we become Christians. It takes time.

If God manifested every blessing He has for us the moment we became Christians, it would destroy us. Having not learned the principles that result in blessing, we would not be able to follow all those principles at first and would quickly lose the blessings that God gave us. We would experience a level of wealth well beyond what we were capable of handling and probably deny God within moments of giving our hearts to Him.

It is not always easy to obey God and apply His principles. Sometimes we must deny our flesh and worldly desires, forcing ourselves to do what is right when it would be much easier to do what is wrong. It is in this struggling against sin and learning to obey God against our natural inclinations that we develop a godly character. In other words, it is in struggling to faithfully apply God's principles that we develop the character that will allow us to keep, and not lose, God's blessings during periods of testing. This process takes time. There is no alternate route. It is the people who make obeying God a *lifestyle* rather than an *event* who will experience God's best for their life. Begin your journey today, but understand it is a journey that will last the rest of your life.

## CHAPTER 2

OVERVIEW
OF THE FINANCIAL
PLANNING PROCESS

When Pete first came to me for counsel, his finances were an absolute mess. He had been through a business failure in another state and was just getting established in Atlanta. He and his wife worked for the same organization, and together they made a reasonable income. Income wasn't their problem, however. Debt was their problem.

Pete, because of his business failure, owed the IRS many thousands of dollars. He owed money on credit cards. He owed money on his car. The monthly payments on all of Pete's debt consumed a major portion of his cash flow.

After reviewing Pete's financial situation with him, I told him he had two choices, the first of which was to declare bankruptcy. This was a legitimate choice that many financial advisers would have recommended to Pete because of his level of debt. Although I did not want to see Pete go that route because of the problems it would create for him down the road, he needed to know that it was an available option.

Pete's second option was to put himself on a very disciplined budget, cut his expenses to the bone, and pay off his debts in an accelerated fashion. If he chose not to declare bankruptcy, but did not pay down his debts at an accelerated pace, debt payments would strap him financially for many years to come. When people have debt problems of the magnitude that Pete was experiencing, I highly recommend taking drastic actions to pay the debt off as quickly as possible. Otherwise, they tend to get discouraged and lose their financial discipline. On the other hand, after people have been on a Spartan budget for a period of time, even increasing their spending budget ever so slightly as things loosen up makes them feel good about their situation. Once they are out of debt and are relieved of large monthly payments, they feel rich.

Pete chose the second option, and his life began to epitomize the principles discussed in this book. He cut his expenses, gave faithfully to the Lord, and took advantage of every opportunity God opened up for him to increase his income. As his income increased, he paid even more on his debts to further accelerate their liquidation. The process of becoming financially free took time; actually, it took a few years. But today Pete is free.

God blessed Pete as he chose to obey God. But what set the whole restorative process in motion was Pete developing a plan that put him in control of his finances. He decided in advance how he would spend his money, based on a knowledge of his financial status, rather than spend impulsively and pay the price for his irresponsibility later. Pete also set up a schedule for paying down his debts, and he followed his strategy in strict fashion. Planning allowed Pete to efficiently utilize his resources to attain his goal.

WHY PLAN?

The term "financial planning" has become such a buzzword in recent years that we often fail to recognize what the phrase itself means. During the 1980s, it seemed that everyone involved in any way with financial products became a "financial planner." Stockbrokers were no longer stockbrokers; they became financial planners. Insurance agents were no longer simply insurance agents; they became financial planners. I even met an undertaker who called himself a financial planner because he helped people plan

---

KEY POINT

Financial planning in the literal sense means deciding *in advance* how we will conduct our financial affairs; that is, how we will spend, save, and invest our money. Instead of just reacting to every circumstance that places a demand on our finances, we take a *proactive* approach to our money.

the financing of their funeral in advance. Everybody who pushed any sort of financial product was a "financial planner."

Proverbs 20:5 reads "A plan in the heart of a man is like deep water, but a man of understanding draws it out." Deep water represents potential, but it remains only potential until it is drawn out and put to use. In the same manner, a plan represents the potential for success. Drawing the water out is a picture of acting on our plan, which is essential for our plan to be effective. Without having a plan to act on, however, there is little, if any, potential for success.

A PLAN

A plan is the *blueprint* for the successful accomplishment of an objective. It tells how a goal will be accomplished by outlining those actions that must be performed for a task to be brought to completion. There are several reasons why one should plan, but three are key:

- A plan gives you a direction in which to head.
- A plan gives you an organized series of action steps leading to the achievement of your goal.
- A plan allows you to measure your progress against benchmarks and make necessary adjustments.

DIRECTION

First, *a plan gives you a direction in which to head.* It helps you channel your energy and efforts in the most efficient manner, and keeps you from wasting time and resources on unproductive activities.

Because the purpose of a plan is to accomplish one's goals, a plan, by definition, starts with the setting of meaningful goals. Keep in mind that the principles of planning are universal; they are the same whether you are planning a two-week vacation, the start of a new business, or how to conduct your financial affairs.

How do you set goals? A good idea is to start in broad, general terms, and then boil the general goals down to *specific* terms. Years ago, I heard one man put it this way: visualize yourself as having already achieved your goals; then describe in detail the circumstances that exist in your mental image. The process of setting financial goals is no different. Begin in broad, general terms; then reduce your goals to very specific details.

When I am conducting one of my public seminars, I will often ask people to give examples of financial goals. Common answers are "retirement," "education," "getting out of debt," "buying a house," and "providing for an elderly parent."

Let's take a look at the first goal mentioned, that of retirement. This goal stated in a general sense might read "I want to retire in financial comfort." While this is an excellent starting point, there is not much that you can do with the goal as stated. When do you want to accomplish this goal? What does "financial comfort" mean to you? How will you know if you have accomplished this goal or not? Reducing this goal to specific terms might be stated as "I would like to retire at age sixty-two with a combined annual income of forty thousand dollars from my pension, Social Security benefits, and personal investments." This specific statement gives you something concrete to work toward. You can tell if you have reached this goal or not. In other words, the details of this goal are *measurable*.

Let's examine the example of the educational goal. A general stating of this goal might read, "I would like to provide a college education for my two children." Again, this is an excellent starting point, but it is incomplete as stated. What kind of college would you like your children to be able to attend? How long is it until they will attend college? How many years will their formal education take? A more specific goal might be, "I would like to provide eight thousand dollars per year of college-related expenses for four consecutive years, beginning at age eighteen, for each of my two children." A simple spreadsheet can then be designed that will tell you how much money you need to be saving for this goal based on the rate of return you expect to receive on your investments.

KEY POINT

To bring a goal from general terms down to specific terms often involves adding a time frame and a dollar amount to the general goal.

ACTION STEPS

Second, *a plan gives you an organized series of action steps that, when completed, bring about the achievement of your goal.* It is very important that these action steps be written down.

The accomplishment of any goal requires that certain actions be taken. Generally, these actions must be accomplished in a specific order and often within a given time frame. A plan outlines those actions that must be taken and then lays them out in an organized sequence, allowing you to see the order of the steps as well as any time constraints involved. By laying the steps out in advance, you do not waste time wondering what to do next after an action has been completed.

Normally, the steps that must be taken in order to accomplish a goal are too numerous to be kept in one's mind. When we fail to write the steps down, we tend to waste time trying to remember what the next step is, rather than being able to focus clearly on completing the task at hand. God designed our mind for more important jobs than being file cabinets. Writing your action steps in consecutive order frees your mind to think creatively about how to best accomplish the current task.

Writing down your action steps also serves as a reminder of those activities on which you should be focusing. It is easy to get distracted and lose your focus when your plan is kept only in your mind. Having a piece of paper to look at serves as a focal point to help you direct your mind and efforts in the right direction.

MEASURING OUR PROGRESS

*The third benefit of a plan is that it allows us to **measure** our progress against a benchmark and **adjust** our actions.* Any well-thought-out plan will have milestones that lead to the achievement of our ultimate goal. We can, therefore, tell by the progress we have made in achieving our milestones if we are on track for achieving our goal. If we are not on track, we may need to adjust our actions. We do not set a goal of becoming financially independent in twenty years and then check twenty years later to see if we made it or not. Rather, we know that to be in a certain financial position twenty years from now requires that we reach certain milestones within one year. We can check our progress at the end of that first year to see if we are on schedule to reach our twenty-year goal in a timely fashion. If we are not on target, it is better to realize it with nineteen years left than to reach the end of our time frame and find that we are nowhere near the achievement of our goal.

Checking our progress and making necessary adjustments is an essential part of the planning process.

WHAT IS FINANCIAL PLANNING?

Having discussed some of the basics of the planning process, let's define the term "financial planning." I have heard several good definitions, but my favorite is *allocating a limited amount of available financial resources in the most efficient manner among an unlimited number of financial needs and desires.*

All of us have an unlimited number of alternatives to which we can allocate our finances. We have things we would like to do, ministries to which we would like to give, and items we would like to buy, all of which cost money. When helping clients formulate financial goals, one of the first questions I will normally ask is "When would you like to retire?" The typical response is "Yesterday."

The problem that the vast majority of us share is that we have a limited amount of financial resources with which to meet these financial desires. This creates the necessity of using our limited resources as efficiently as possible. To do so, we must determine which of our goals are the most important to us. If I cannot do everything I would like to do, I should at least strive to accomplish the objectives that are most important to me.

There are three general steps and six specific steps involved in the preparation of a personal financial plan.

THREE GENERAL STEPS IN THE PLANNING PROCESS

1. SET GOALS—The first step in developing any plan is to set goals. Determine what it is that you want to accomplish. This defines the reason for the very existence of the plan itself. Financial goals should be reasonable, and, very important, they should be measurable. If goals are not stated in

measurable terms, then they are vague, and it will be difficult to know when they have been accomplished. Vague goals will not provide the proper motivation for their achievement.

Years ago I heard of a study that had been conducted to determine what it is that makes financially successful people successful. The researcher interviewed hundreds of people from various walks of life and socio-economic backgrounds. After conducting extensive research, he stratified people into three categories. He classified approximately 58 percent of the subjects as having achieved average levels of financial success. Next, he delineated an upper 13 percent of participants, who he classified as having attained above average levels of financial success. Of that top 13 percent, he deemed the top 3 percent to be extremely successful.

His first task was to determine the most prevalent characteristics of the top 13 percent of subjects. He discovered that one of the most common qualities of that group was they were goal-setters. They knew what they wanted to accomplish in life. They were living life with a purpose, instead of just existing from day to day. As a result, they expended their efforts in directions that led to the achievement of their goals.

He determined that the second most prevalent characteristic of the upper 13 percent was that they were planners. They not only had concrete goals defining what they wanted to accomplish but they took the time to plan how they would achieve those goals. Each morning when they woke up, they had a reason for living that day; they had specific tasks they needed to carry out.

The researcher's next duty was to determine, out of the 13 percent above average group, what characteristics separated the top 3 percent (extremely successful people) from the remaining 10 percent. What was it that allowed them to go beyond their colleagues and achieve levels of success about which most people only dream? The primary characteristic he discovered these people shared was that they wrote their goals down!

The power of goal setting is awesome! When we take the extra time to write our goals down and let these written goals serve as a constant visual reminder of where our efforts need to be focused, the power of goal setting becomes even greater!

2. DETERMINE YOUR CURRENT POSITION—Determining where you want to go and setting specific goals are critical to the development of a plan, but equally important is determining your starting point. This step answers the question, "What do you have to work with that is going to help you achieve your objectives?"

For most people, the two primary resources available to them are their current income and their current assets. Their discretionary income should be directed into those areas that will help them attain their goals most efficiently. Discretionary income, by the way, is one's income after all his or her obligatory payments are made, such as taxes, mortgage payments, and other debt payments.

The same is true for one's assets. All too often I meet people in my office who state that their primary desire is to grow their assets for retirement purposes, and, yet, when I examine their current assets, most of their investments are designed to generate income, not growth. When your assets are not lined up with your goals, this results in inefficient money—money that does not work hard for you; its potential is not being fully utilized. Successfully achieving financial independence requires the elimination of inefficient money. We must get all of our current assets to work their hardest for us, as well as direct a portion of our income stream into investments that will help us achieve our goals most efficiently.

3. DEVELOP A STEP-BY-STEP WRITTEN PLAN—Once you know where you are and where you want to go, the next phase is to develop a step-by-step written plan to get you from point A to point B. This written plan should outline the action steps necessary to achieve the desired goal, as well as specify a time frame within which each step should be taken. Milestones should be built into the plan so that your progress can be measured on a regular, periodic basis.

These are the same three steps that you would follow in planning a two-week vacation. You would take out a map, circle your destination, circle your starting point, and then map out the shortest route from the starting point to the destination. The sad truth is that most people will take more time to plan a two-week vacation than they will to plan their entire life's financial affairs.

The first financial planning case I ever worked on was for a group of doctors preparing for retirement, all of whom had been making six-digit incomes for many years. I would have expected that they could have retired anytime they wanted to. The results of their financial analyses were so startling to me that the need for planning was indelibly etched into my consciousness.

One doctor, who was in his early sixties and desirous of retiring immediately, was told that he would have to continue practicing medicine a few more years in order to enjoy the retirement lifestyle he desired. Another was forced to sell his home and move to a smaller residence in order to reduce his living expenses to a level that would allow him to quit working. Why would doctors who had maintained such a high level of income for so many years be subject to such disappointing news regarding their goals for retirement? Because, in spite of their substantial incomes, they had never taken the time to ensure they were setting aside enough assets to support them in their retirement years.

SIX SPECIFIC STEPS IN PREPARING A FINANCIAL PLAN

1. IDENTIFY SPECIFIC GOALS AND OBJECTIVES—One's financial goals and objectives can be divided into two primary categories:

a. **Living goals**—Living goals will be discussed in more detail in an upcoming section. These are obviously goals that you want to accomplish while you are still alive.

b. **Postmortem goals**—"Postmortem" is Latin and means "after death." These goals, to be accomplished after one's passing, fall primarily into the category of estate planning, to which I devote a full chapter later in this book.

If you are typical, your primary postmortem goal involves the distribution of your estate to your heirs upon your death. In addition to the monetary aspect, this is your opportunity to let your personal wishes be known, such as bequests to family members and donations to charitable organizations that are special to you. You want to accomplish two things here: (1) To pass your assets on to your heirs in the manner you desire, and (2) To pass as little of your estate as possible to Uncle Sam in the form of estate taxes. Techniques for achieving these objectives will be discussed in detail under the section on estate planning.

2. GATHER INFORMATION AND PREPARE PERSONAL FINANCIAL STATEMENTS—
In order to determine your current position, it will be necessary to complete some personal financial statements, including:

a. **Net worth statement**—Your net worth is the difference between your assets and your liabilities—what you own versus what you owe. You should prepare a net worth statement every six to twelve months in order to ensure that this figure is growing on a regular basis.

b. **Income/cash flow statement**—It is absolutely essential that you have an accurate picture of how much money you are spending each month relative to your income. There is not a successful business in the country that does not track how much money it is spending and where it is spending it, as well as the amount of its incoming cash flow. Businesses that fail to do this do not survive very long. Yet, individuals think that they can successfully run their household financial affairs without the same information. It cannot be done.

   In this area you want to track actual income and expenditures versus budgeted income and expenditures. The actual income and expenditure figures will let you know how much discretionary cash flow is available for investing, paying off debt, etc. Comparing the actual figures to budgeted figures will alert you to any problem areas where you are overspending and which threaten the achievement of your financial goals.

c. **Tax return/tax projection**—A dollar saved on taxes is as valuable as an extra dollar of revenue earned. Review your last couple of tax returns to see if there are any areas where you can increase deductions. Consider having an accountant review your latest tax return to see if there are steps you can take in order to reduce your income tax burden. There are many tax-saving techniques available. The challenge is to know what they are and to determine which ones you are eligible to use. Along these same lines, develop a projection of this coming year's tax return to spot any areas of opportunity for reducing your projected tax liability.

d. **Inventory of insurance policies**—Most people are not even aware of all the types of insurance coverage they carry, much less the levels of coverage on each of their insurance policies. Often it is too late, after a claim has been filed, when they discover they did not have a type of coverage they thought they had, or the limits of coverage they carried were woefully inadequate. Maintaining an inventory of your various insurance policies will help you stay organized and ensure that you maintain the appropriate types and levels of insurance coverage.

3. ANALYSIS OF PRESENT POSITION WITH RESPECT TO YOUR GOALS—Analyzing where you are with respect to your goals in each area will help you determine areas of strength and areas of weakness. This also helps you prioritize which areas will require the most attention and resources and which areas will require less attention and resources.

4. DEVELOP A PLAN TO GET FROM YOUR CURRENT POSITION TO YOUR GOAL IN THE ALLOTTED PERIOD OF TIME—This plan must be step by step and it must be written. This is the portion of your financial plan that will require the most time and thought. Here you strategize, using many of the tools presented in this book to determine how you will actually allocate your resources in order to achieve your goals most efficiently. Your plan must be step by step so that as you complete one action step you know exactly the next action step to be accomplished. Your plan must be written so that you can focus your attention on performing each action rather than trying to remember each step.

5. IMPLEMENT THE PLAN—This is the most important phase of the entire planning process. The most carefully designed plans are a waste of time and totally worthless if they are not implemented. In my professional practice, one of my greatest frustrations has been for clients to pay my firm to prepare a financial plan for them, only to come to this phase of the process and then procrastinate or never execute the plan at all.

Change is a very difficult thing for most people to embrace. The problem is that, by definition, growing involves changing. In fact, growth is a type of change!

Excuses not to change are a dime a dozen. One case, in particular, stands out in my mind. Years ago, a gentleman paid my firm a goodly sum of money to prepare a financial plan for him. When it came time to take the first step of implementation, he had to wait because his mother-in-law was visiting. When I called back after his mother-in-law had left, he couldn't do anything because his children were getting ready to go back to school. Then something came up at work. Then it was the holiday season. Then it was . . . well, you get the picture. The bottom line is that months went by, and he never took the first step to effect the necessary changes in his financial affairs. My efforts to prod him into implementing the plan eventually ceased because I got tired of hearing his latest excuse. The plan we developed is probably still sitting in his desk drawer collecting dust.

Do yourself a favor. Make a *commitment* to yourself to implement your plan, no matter how uncomfortable the change may be. Make this commitment up front, or don't waste your time preparing a plan.

6. PERIODIC REVIEW—Once a financial plan has been put into place, it is not carved in stone. Tax laws change, your personal circumstances change, economic circumstances change, all of which necessitate that your plan be reviewed and updated periodically. I recommend reviewing it about every six months to determine if any changes in your circumstances warrant adjustments to your plan.

AREAS OF NEED

Now that you know the basics of the financial planning process, the next logical question is: what areas should a financial plan address?

Your financial plan should cover six basic areas:

- Risk Management
- Savings
- Education Planning
- Estate Planning
- Tax Planning
- Investment Planning

PRIORITIES OF OBJECTIVES

As you embark on your journey of preparing and executing a financial plan, you will discover, if you are like most people, that you have more goals than money. Most people simply do not have all the resources needed to meet every one of their goals. Because of this limitation, it becomes necessary to prioritize your goals and objectives.

KEY POINT

You must determine which of your goals are the most important and which of them are less important. If you cannot achieve all of your goals, you want to make sure that you at least achieve the most important ones.

Two areas of financial planning, risk management and savings, are more critical than others and, therefore, should be the top priorities in almost everyone's financial plans. Beyond these universal priorities, however, you must determine for yourself the order of importance of your other goals. Someone who is fifty-five, is retired, and has $2 million in assets, will want to place estate planning at or near the top of his list. On the other hand, a younger couple with three children, the oldest of whom is fourteen, will likely give saving for education expenses a higher place of priority. Regardless of your situation, what is critical is that you take the time to think about what is important to you and what you want to accomplish financially. Prioritize your objectives so that you know which goals will be given the most attention and allocated the most resources.

1. RISK MANAGEMENT PROGRAM—The first priority in your financial plan is your risk management program. Risk management refers to the various types of insurance coverage you need. Simply stated, this part of your plan is designed to protect you and your loved ones financially in the event that a calamity of some sort occurs.

Let's take the example of a family where the husband is the breadwinner and the wife stays home to raise their three children. This couple has put together a wonderful savings plan that, with a reasonable rate of return on their investments, will allow the husband to retire by age fifty-five. A savings plan is also in place for the children's college education. They have arranged their affairs in such a way that they consistently owe the minimum amount of income taxes legally possible. Everything seems to be in order. Then tragedy strikes, and the breadwinner dies. The rest of the financial plan is worthless if provisions have not been made for the surviving family in the event of such a tragedy.

Similar consequences could arise if the breadwinner became disabled, or if the couple was sued for injuries someone sustained in an auto accident that was the fault of either of them. Therefore, the foundation of your financial plan is your risk management program.

I will tell you up front that I do not believe in loading up on expensive insurance policies. Your objective is to make sure that you are adequately insured against unexpected events while not wasting money on insurance you don't really need. There are several different types of insurance policies of which you should be aware:

- Life
- Disability income
- Health
- Homeowners
- Auto
- Umbrella liability

In addition to the above standard types of insurance coverage, there are also numerous miscellaneous types of insurance policies designed to provide protection for very specific situations. Some insurance policies cover you for liability that you incur as a result of your professional activities. An example of this type of coverage would be a surgeon's malpractice liability policy. Professional athletes sometimes acquire insurance coverage that provides protection for them in the event they incur a career ending injury. During the 1990–91 recession, some insurance companies even went so far as to offer policies that continued paying policyholders their salaries in the event they were laid off from their jobs!

2. SAVINGS PLAN—If you are going to reach your financial goals, it is essential that you establish a systematic savings plan. A portion of each paycheck must be set aside after satisfying bills and routine living expenses to help you advance your financial situation. Savings have five basic purposes:

a. **Liquid/emergency reserves**—Every person needs a level of liquid funds set aside so that if an emergency, opportunity, or other unexpected expense arises, you will not need to borrow or dip into your long-term savings in order to meet this need. Build some liquidity into your financial affairs, i.e., cushion yourself against the unexpected.

   For this money, you may use several different types of savings vehicles. Bank savings accounts are very safe and are insured by the Federal Deposit Insurance Corporation (FDIC) up to $100,000 per account. However, they generally pay a lower rate of interest than other types of savings accounts.

   Generally, a money market account offered by a mutual fund or brokerage firm is a better choice for accumulating liquid funds than a bank savings account. These money market accounts normally offer free check-writing privileges and typically pay a higher rate of interest than a bank savings account.

   A third possible vehicle for these funds is a short-term certificate of deposit. Interest rates paid on various instruments like money market accounts and CD's vary over time. If we experience a period where short-term CD's pay a significantly higher rate of interest than money market accounts, then CD's may be a viable choice for some of your liquid funds. Generally, I do not recommend using a maturity date beyond six months. Remember that the purpose of this account is to provide liquidity for emergencies. You will not get rich on the interest this account earns, but getting rich is not the purpose of these funds.

   The amount of money that should be placed in a liquid savings account will vary from person to person. It really depends on what amount makes you comfortable. Conventional wisdom says to set aside six months' worth of expenses in a liquid savings account. Personally, I think this is too much for most people. If you have a salary of $40,000 per year, I don't think it is wise to have $20,000 liquid *and* earning a low rate of interest.

For most people, the need to have a lot of money set aside in a liquid savings account is not as great today as it was ten or twenty years ago. As long as you have liquid investments, such as mutual funds, that could be liquidated in a reasonably short period of time without paying a significant penalty, you can afford to meet most short-term emergencies with cash on hand, a cash advance on a credit card, or by drawing on a home equity loan. The liquid investments could then be sold to meet the need, and the short-term loan can be immediately repaid.

I have clients who are comfortable with as little as $2,000 in savings. On the other end of the spectrum, I had one lady in my office who told me she could not sleep at night if she had less than $100,000 in her checking account. Realistically, unless you have extenuating circumstances that require a high level of liquidity, one to three months of salary set aside in a liquid savings account is adequate for most people.

b. **Liquidate debt**—One of the biggest financial problems with which most people struggle is the level of debt they carry. High interest payments on credit card balances consume a significant portion of their cash flow, putting them under financial pressure and preventing them from using their income to grow their net worth. While I do not believe it is a sin to carry debt, as some teach, neither do I believe it is necessarily smart. It may not be a sin to pay 18 percent interest on a credit card, but neither does it make sense. Most people would be wise to set aside a sum of money over and above their required monthly payments to accelerate the liquidation of their debts.

c. **Big-ticket purchases**—Big-ticket purchases are those large expense items that we must purchase on a regular, but infrequent basis. Included in this category would be items such as cars, appliances, furniture, etc. Normally, people do not plan ahead for the acquisition of these items, forcing them to borrow in order to purchase them.

Once you have achieved the level of liquid reserves that you desire, continue setting money aside in either the same or another liquid account, but have this additional money pegged for future purchases of big-ticket items. Let's say, for instance, that you want $5,000 in liquid reserves. Once you have achieved this level of savings, continue contributing money to this account that will be earmarked for the future purchases of furniture, appliances, etc. By budgeting in advance for the acquisition of these items, you will eventually reach the point where you are paying cash even for cars!

Next to a house, a car is most people's largest expense item. When someone makes the last payment on an automobile, they often breathe a sigh of relief because they now have additional cash available for spending. Unfortunately, when the time comes to buy another car, they are forced to finance the purchase because they lack the reserves needed to pay cash. Why not, instead of spending the extra cash flow, continue to make your normal monthly payment—only now make the "payments" into a savings account in anticipation of your next auto purchase. You will be earning interest on your car payments instead of paying interest on them. What a concept!

Perhaps you will need a new car before you have saved enough money to pay cash for it. At least now you will be able to put more down on the purchase of the auto than you would have been able to otherwise. Because you will be making a larger down payment, you may be able to negotiate a lower interest rate with the finance company. You should also be able to make the loan for a shorter time period, say two years instead of four years. By paying this car off quicker than the previous one and then continuing to make car payments into your savings account, you should be able to save even more money in advance of your next auto purchase. Eventually, you should be able to pay cash for your cars.

d. **Long-term investments**—The fourth recipient of your savings plan is your long-term investment account. This is the account that will increase your net worth over time. It is this account in which you will systematically accumulate wealth.

Having this type of savings account is a foreign thought to many Americans. They are depending on their employers and Social Security to meet their retirement income needs. But now I hope you understand the fallacy of such thinking, and realize that we have the responsibility to provide for our own retirement needs. I am not saying to not include Social Security or pension benefits in your planning, but do not depend solely on these to meet your needs. Think of your personal investments as the third leg on a stool, upon which you will be supported during your retirement years. Remember, however, that the goal that we are striving to attain is financial independence. There is no law that says you must wait until retirement for this to take place. Dream big! Shoot for financial independence at an earlier age than retirement.

Once you have developed an adequate liquid savings account, a portion of every paycheck should be set aside into some type of long-term investment account. In a later section, we will discuss appropriate investment vehicles that can be used for these funds. Your attitude toward this account should be that you will not touch it until you are financially independent and are ready to draw income from it. This money is available for emergencies, but use these funds only as a last resort. If you must withdraw some of these funds prior to achieving financial independence, purpose to pay back what you remove.

e. **Special savings**—Over time, there will be specific things or events for which you want to save. An example in this category might be a daughter's wedding or a dream vacation. The whole point of this discussion on savings is that you will be much better off having planned and saved for these special expenditures in advance, rather than scrambling to find the money when the expenditures occur, or going into debt to meet the need.

3. EDUCATION PLANNING—College education expenses have historically risen somewhat faster than the inflation rate. Depending on where your child goes to college, tuition, room and board, books, and other expenses can easily run over $10,000 per year. Many parents do not think about

planning for these college costs until just a few years before the oldest child reaches college age. At that point, parents generally look at funding the expenses through either one or more of various loan programs that are available, placing either themselves and/or the college student in debt, or from assets that have been designated for retirement or other purposes. Some parents try to fund the costs from their cash flow, often placing themselves and the rest of their family under a tremendous financial strain.

Paying for a child's education need not be the nightmare that it often is if parents would only take the time to plan for it far enough in advance. Immediately after a child's birth, parents should begin setting money aside on a regular basis in anticipation of funding the child's college education. *Time can be a parent's biggest ally.* If a parent would regularly set aside only a little money from the time a child is born, that money would have eighteen years to grow. Compound interest is the eighth wonder of the world!

4. WILLS AND ESTATE PLANNING—Estate planning is an often-ignored area of one's financial affairs. A well-designed will is typically the primary vehicle through which your estate plans will be executed.

5. TAX PLANNING—Some Christians feel that it is wrong to try to arrange their financial affairs in such a way as to reduce their income tax burden, since Romans 13:7 says to "Render tax to whom tax is due. . . ." While this verse makes an important point, it is not telling us to avoid legally *lessening the amount* of tax that is due.

It is wrong not to pay taxes for which you are legally liable. However, there is absolutely nothing wrong with taking actions designed to minimize the tax burden for which you are legally liable. Doing so is good stewardship.

There are two terms with which you need to be familiar: *tax evasion* and *tax avoidance.* At seminars I tell people that the difference between the two is about twenty years in prison. *Tax evasion* is not paying taxes you legally owe. *Tax avoidance* is reducing your income tax burden by using any or all of several techniques allowed by the government. A dollar saved in taxes is the equivalent of earning an extra dollar of income. A dollar not sent to the Internal Revenue Service is a dollar that can now work hard to help you achieve your financial objectives.

6. INVESTMENT PLANNING—The amount of money you invest each pay period plays a large role in determining how much wealth you will accumulate during your lifetime. However, how that money is invested plays an equally big role. The difference in the rate of return between two investments may be small, but a small percentage compounded over many years adds up to some big numbers. Take the time to choose your investments carefully.

One of the major principles of successful investing is to decide on a strategy and then to follow that strategy in a very disciplined fashion. The long-term benefits of consistently following sound investment principles can be enormous.

## CHAPTER 3

GETTING STARTED

SETTING GOALS

The first step in preparing your personal financial plan is to set goals in each of the six areas we discussed earlier. Remember to make the goals as specific as possible. You may also have special goals that are not included in the six standard categories, such as saving for a dream vacation, or increasing your level of giving to the church. Write these goals down, and you will have the basis from which you can prepare your plan.

FINANCIAL INDEPENDENCE—THE ULTIMATE FINANCIAL GOAL!

Our ultimate financial goal is financial independence. Financial independence is defined as reaching that point where you no longer have to be gainfully employed in order to maintain a desired lifestyle. For most people who achieve this, it occurs at retirement. However, it can certainly occur earlier.

I remember years ago, when I was much younger in the profession of financial planning, listening to a talk by another financial planner who had achieved financial independence.

He was encouraging us to make sure that we executed our own financial plan with the same level of diligence that we expected from our clients, i.e., not to be the cobbler whose children had no shoes. Then he made a statement I have never forgotten, a statement that sparked a powerful vision inside me. Reflecting on his own experience, he said, "I will never forget the day when it hit me that I no longer had to work in order to make it financially. My work took on a whole new meaning when I realized I didn't *have* to work anymore." I have not arrived at that point yet, but I look forward to having that same experience.

Surveys consistently show that only about 3 to 7 percent of Americans who retire each year are financially independent. This means that at least 93 percent of Americans retiring each year are forced to depend on Social Security, family members, or charity of some sort in order to meet their retirement income needs, or else they are forced to continue working during their retirement years. The primary reason for this sad state of affairs is poor planning on the part of individuals during their financially productive years.

SIX CATEGORIES OF GOALS

To help me illustrate several of the concepts of financial planning, I will be using Tom and Mary Sue Smith, a fictitious couple, as an example. Many of the financial forms I use will be completed based on Tom and Mary Sue's data. Blank forms, which can be photocopied for your personal use, will be provided at the end of their respective chapters. My goal in writing this book is not just to tell you how to manage your money, but also to provide you with the tools necessary to accomplish the job.

Tom, thirty-five, is a computer programmer and has a pretax annual salary of $35,000. Mary, thirty-four, is a part-time nurse and earns $20,000 annually. They have two sons, Thomas, age five, and Billy, age two.

After discussing their financial desires together and praying for God's direction, they have established the following goals:

1. SAVINGS—Tom and Mary Sue have determined that a $2,000 liquid savings account would be adequate. They have already achieved this objective.

They have several debts that they want to liquidate as quickly as possible. The elimination of their debts would free up a significant amount of cash flow that could then be utilized to increase their net worth and to help them achieve other goals.

An important decision to be made regarding debt liquidation is whether or not you want to pay your mortgage off early. Several factors must be considered in making this decision, which I discuss in detail in chapter 6. The Smiths have decided not to pay their house off in an accelerated fashion, at least for the time being.

Once they are out of debt, Tom and Mary Sue would like to increase their savings level to prepare for the future purchase of big-ticket items.

They would eventually like to set aside an adequate amount of their cash flow into long-term investments so that they can both retire when Tom turns fifty-five. In order to retire comfortably, they want to maintain 70 percent of their present income during their retirement years.

2. RISK MANAGEMENT PROGRAM—Tom and Mary Sue want to make sure they are adequately protected in all the major areas of risk management. Due to their limited cash flow, they want to keep their insurance premiums as low as possible.

3. EDUCATION PLANNING—They must also save for the education of their two sons, ages five and two. They would like to provide $5,000 (before taking inflation into account) per year for four years, beginning at age eighteen, for each child.

4. ESTATE PLANNING—If Tom and Mary Sue were to die in a common accident, it is important to them that Mary Sue's sister and her husband raise their two sons. They want the greatest amount possible of their hard-earned estate to go to their children and the least possible amount to be consumed by estate taxes. They also want their assets to be used as necessary to provide for their children's education expenses and other essential living needs. Once both children have graduated from college, they want their estate assets to be equally distributed to their sons in three separate installments over a ten-year period.

5. TAX PLANNING—Tom and Mary Sue want to utilize every legal option available to them to keep their tax burden at a minimum. They understand, however, that some tax saving techniques may entail a level of investment risk and/or illiquidity that they are not willing to assume.

6. INVESTMENT PLANNING—Tom and Mary Sue want to grow their invested assets aggressively. They do not need current income from their investments, so they can reinvest any dividends and interest that they earn. They

would like to maintain at least a moderate level of liquidity with their investments.

MISCELLANEOUS: The Smiths, knowing the value of giving financially to the Lord's work, have determined to give a tenth of their gross income to the Church. They would like to be able to increase their giving, both in absolute terms and as a percentage of their incomes, as their financial situation improves.

A question that often arises in this area is whether or not our giving should be based on our gross income (before taxes) or our net income (after taxes). Without a doubt, gross income is the appropriate choice. First, the Bible says to give from our "first fruits." Beyond this, however, once you have decided what percentage of your income to give, whether your giving is based on gross or net income often does not affect your bottom line *at all*. What is does affect is what percentage of your income goes to Uncle Sam versus the Church.

Let me illustrate this with an example. Suppose that you have an annual income of $50,000. Let's assume that your combined federal and state tax bracket is 30 percent. You have decided to give 10 percent of your net income to your church. Because you pay $15,000 in taxes, your after-tax income is $35,000, so you make a $3,500 donation. Your combined out-of-pocket cost for taxes and giving is $18,500.

Suppose, instead, that you decided to give 10 percent of your gross income to the Church. Your donation would be $5,000. Since charitable donations are tax-deductible, your taxable income is reduced to $45,000. At a 30 percent rate, your tax on this amount is $13,500. Once again, your combined cost for taxes and giving is $18,500, only this time your gift to the church is $1,500 greater!

Once you have determined your financial goals, the next step will be to gather information about yourself so that you can determine your current financial position, i.e., what you have to work with in order to achieve your goals.

NET WORTH STATEMENT

Let's begin by preparing a net worth statement. A net worth statement is designed to show what you own (your assets) as well as detail what you owe others (your liabilities). The difference between the two is your net worth. Exhibits 3-1 through 3-5 illustrate Tom's and Mary Sue's net worth information.

ASSETS

Exhibit 3-1 shows a completed assets inventory for Tom and Mary Sue. A blank statement is provided at the end of the chapter for you to complete.

First, list your assets, beginning with your fixed return assets. Fixed return assets, in the sense that I am using the term, refers to those assets that pay you interest. With these interest-bearing assets, your principal amount remains constant (if held to maturity), but the interest rate paid may be adjusted periodically. Examples of such assets would be checking accounts, savings and money market accounts, certificates of deposit, bonds, and annuities.

For each asset listed, write down its current value, as well as who owns it. Since the balance of your checking account is not stable, but will move up and down on almost a daily basis as checks you have written and deposits you have made clear the bank, write down an average balance for your checking account. For CD's and bonds, complete the blank form "Bonds/CD's Supplemental Detail." For bond mutual funds that you own, complete the blank form "Stocks and Mutual Funds Supplemental Detail."

Next, in the process of listing your assets, list your variable return assets. These are investment assets that *do not* pay a specified interest rate and in which your principal fluctuates in value. Examples of such assets would be individual common stocks, stock mutual funds, interests in limited partnerships, business interests (for self-employed individuals, this may be one of your largest assets), and real estate (including your residence). Again, list the most recent value you have available for each asset and who owns it. For stocks and mutual funds, also complete the blank form "Stocks and Mutual Funds Supplemental Detail." For real estate assets, complete the blank form "Real Estate Supplemental Detail."

EXHIBIT 3-1

ASSETS
TOM AND MARY SUE SMITH

FIXED	CURRENT VALUE	OWNERSHIP CODE[1]
Checking	$ 1,560	J
Savings	$ 2,019	J
Money Market	$	
CD's[2]	$ 5,000	W
Municipal Bonds[2]	$	
Corporate Bonds[2]	$	
Treasury Bonds[2]	$	
Bond Funds[3]	$ 10,988	J
Annuity	$	
Other	$	
Other	$	
Other	$	
TOTAL FIXED	$ 19,567	

VARIABLE	CURRENT VALUE	OWNERSHIP CODE[1]
Common Stocks[3]	$ 6,450	H
Stock Mutual Funds[3]	$ 22,789	J
Limited Partnerships	$	
Business Interests	$	
Real Estate[4]		
(Direct Ownership)	$ 112,000	J
Other	$ 33,478	401(k)-H
Other	$	
Other	$	
TOTAL VARIABLE	$ 174,717	

| **TOTAL ASSETS** | $ 194,284 | |

[1]H=Husband, W=Wife, J=Joint, OT=Other, IRA, 401(k), OR=Other Retirement
[2]Complete **Bonds/CD's Supplemental Detail.** (Exhibit 3-3)
[3]Complete **Stocks and Mutual Funds Supplemental Detail.** (Exhibit 3-4)
[4]Complete **Real Estate Supplemental Detail.** (Exhibit 3-5)

You will notice that missing from the list of assets are items such as televisions, stereo systems, autos, and other personal effects. The reason is that these personal assets, while perhaps necessary, will not help you achieve your goal of financial independence. Therefore, you are not interested in listing them for the purpose of your financial plan.

The final step in developing your statement of assets is to compute

EXHIBIT 3-2

LIABILITIES
TOM AND MARY SUE SMITH

CREDIT CARDS	CREDITOR NAME	BALANCE	OWNERSHIP CODE[1]	PAYMENT AMOUNT	INTEREST RATE
Card #1	ABC Credit Card	$ 1,428	J	45	18 %
Card #2	XYZ Credit Card	$ 2,019	J	61	21 %
Card #3	Department Store	$ 655	J	20	19 %
Card #4		$			%
TOTAL CREDIT CARDS		$ 4,102			

OTHER LIABILITIES	CREDITOR NAME	ORIGINAL LOAN AMT.	BALANCE	OWNERSHIP CODE[1]	1ST PYMT. DATE	LOAN PERIOD	FREQUENCY OF PYMTS.[2]	PAYMENT AMOUNT	INTEREST RATE
Mortgage	Bank	$ 105,000	$102,437	J	07/93	30 yrs.	M	$ 734	7.5 %
Home Equity		$	$		/			$	%
Bank Notes		$	$		/			$	%
Auto #1	Acme Credit	$ 10,000	$ 6,441	H	03/94	4 yrs.	M	$ 246	8.5 %
Auto #2	Dealer Credit	$ 8,750	$ 3,602	W	04/93	4 yrs.	M	$ 213	7.75 %
Notes to others		$	$		/			$	%
Taxes Payable		$	$		/			$	%
Cash Value Life									
Insurance Loan		$	$		/			$	%
Other		$	$		/			$	%
Other		$	$		/			$	%
TOTAL OTHER LIABILITIES			$112,480						
TOTAL LIABILITIES			$116,582						
NET WORTH			$ 77,702						

[1]H=Husband, W=Wife, J=Joint, OT=Other, IRA, 401(k), OR=Other Retirement   [2]M=Month, Q=Quarter, S=Semiannual, A=Annual

EXHIBIT 3-3

BONDS/CD'S
SUPPLEMENTAL DETAIL
TOM AND MARY SUE SMITH

INVESTMENT NAME	CURRENT VALUE (TOTAL)	OWNERSHIP CODE[1]	INTEREST RATE	MATURITY DATE
Metro Bank	$ 5,000	W	4.7 %	07/09/04
	$		%	/ /
	$		%	/ /
	$		%	/ /
	$		%	/ /
	$		%	/ /
	$		%	/ /
	$		%	/ /
	$		%	/ /
	$		%	/ /
	$		%	/ /
	$		%	/ /
	$		%	/ /
	$		%	/ /
	$		%	/ /
	$		%	/ /
	$		%	/ /

[1]H=Husband, W=Wife, J=Joint, OT=Other, IRA, 401(k), OR=Other Retirement

the combined total value of your fixed return and variable return assets.

LIABILITIES

The next step in developing your net worth statement is to detail your liabilities. Exhibit 3-2 has been completed for Tom and Mary Sue. As you begin the process of getting out of debt, this sheet will serve as your periodic score card.

First, begin by listing your credit card debts on the blank form. If the space allowed is not adequate, feel free to make copies of the form. For each credit card, list the creditor's name, your current balance, the cardholder, the minimum monthly payment amount, and the interest rate. Total the balance figures.

Next, list any other liabilities you have. Notice that I separate these liabilities from credit cards. I do this for two reasons. First, credit cards gen-

EXHIBIT 3-4 STOCKS AND MUTUAL FUNDS
SUPPLEMENTAL DETAIL
TOM AND MARY SUE SMITH

INVESTMENT NAME	DATE ACQUIRED	CURRENT PRICE PER UNIT	NUMBER OF UNITS	CURRENT VALUE (TOTAL)	OWNERSHIP CODE[1]
General Bond Fund	06/19/96	$14.95	735	$10,988	J
XYZ Technology	04/16/96	$64.50	100	$6,450	H
ABC Growth Fund	05/12/95	$22.79	1,000	$22,789	J
	/ /	$		$	
	/ /	$		$	
	/ /	$		$	
	/ /	$		$	
	/ /	$		$	
	/ /	$		$	
	/ /	$		$	
	/ /	$		$	
	/ /	$		$	
	/ /	$		$	
	/ /	$		$	
	/ /	$		$	

[1]H=Husband, W=Wife, J=Joint, OT=Other, IRA, 401(k), OR=Other Retirement

erally do not have set monthly payments. The payment amount varies from month to month based on the balance at the end of each month. Liabilities listed in this second section will normally have set payment amounts that do not vary from month to month.

The second reason that I segregate these two sections of liabilities is because credit cards tend to be the main culprits in people's debt problems. By separating the credit cards into their own section, you can readily see if you have a major problem in this area. While Tom and Mary Sue have some credit card debts that need to be eliminated, they do not appear to be out of control. They simply need a plan to become debt-free.

For each liability in this second section, list the creditor's name, original loan amount, current balance, and the person responsible for paying the debt. Also list when the payments began, the term of the loan (is it a three-year loan, thirty-year loan, etc.), the frequency with which payments

EXHIBIT 3-5

REAL ESTATE
SUPPLEMENTAL DETAIL
TOM AND MARY SUE SMITH

PROPERTY DESCRIPTION: RESIDENCE

CURRENT VALUE	PURCHASE PRICE	PURCHASE DATE	OWNERSHIP CODE[1]	CAPITAL IMPROVEMENTS	MONTHLY RENTAL AMOUNT	TAX BASIS (DEPRECIATED)
$112,000	$111,000	06/93	J	$ —	$ —	$ —

MORTGAGE INFORMATION

	ORIGINAL LOAN AMOUNT	BALANCE	FIRST PAYMENT DATE	LOAN PERIOD[2]	FREQUENCY OF PAYMENTS[3]	PAYMENT AMOUNT (P&I ONLY)	INTEREST RATE
1st Mortgage	$105,000	$102,437	07/93	30 yrs.	M	$734	7.5 %
2nd Mortgage	$	$	/			$	%

PROPERTY DESCRIPTION:

CURRENT VALUE	PURCHASE PRICE	PURCHASE DATE	OWNERSHIP CODE[1]	CAPITAL IMPROVEMENTS	MONTHLY RENTAL AMOUNT	TAX BASIS (DEPRECIATED)
$	$	/		$	$	$

MORTGAGE INFORMATION

	ORIGINAL LOAN AMOUNT	BALANCE	FIRST PAYMENT DATE	LOAN PERIOD[2]	FREQUENCY OF PAYMENTS[3]	PAYMENT AMOUNT (P&I ONLY)	INTEREST RATE
1st Mortgage	$	$	/			$	%
2nd Mortgage	$	$	/			$	%

[1] H=Husband, W=Wife, J=Joint, OT=Other   [2] 15 yrs., 30 yrs., etc.   [3] M=Month, Q=Quarter, S=Semiannual, A=Annual

are due (normally monthly), the amount of each payment, and the interest rate. Once again, total the amount of these liabilities. Adding this total
to the credit card total gives you the sum of your total liabilities.

The final step is to subtract your total liabilities figure from your total
assets figure, the result being your net worth. Tom and Mary Sue have a net
worth of almost $78,000.

I recommend updating your net worth statement at least every six
months in order to stay on top of what is happening to your financial status. This figure is critical to your financial health, and it is important that
it be growing each time you update this statement. The only exceptions to
this are if you have just paid cash for a big-ticket personal item that is not
reflected on the asset column of the net worth statement, or if a substantial portion of your assets are of the variable return type and experience a
temporary drop in value.

ASSETS

FIXED	CURRENT VALUE	OWNERSHIP CODE[1]
Checking	$	
Savings	$	
Money Market	$	
CD's[2]	$	
Municipal Bonds[2]	$	
Corporate Bonds[2]	$	
Treasury Bonds[2]	$	
Bond Funds[3]	$	
Annuity	$	
Other	$	
Other	$	
Other	$	
TOTAL FIXED	$	

VARIABLE	CURRENT VALUE	OWNERSHIP CODE[1]
Common Stocks[3]	$	
Stock Mutual Funds[3]	$	
Limited Partnerships	$	
Business Interests	$	
Real Estate[4]		
(Direct Ownership)	$	
Other	$	
Other	$	
Other	$	
TOTAL VARIABLE	$	

TOTAL ASSETS	$	

[1]H=Husband, W=Wife, J=Joint, OT=Other, IRA, 401(k), OR=Other Retirement
[2]Complete **Bonds/CD's Supplemental Detail.** (Exhibit 3-3)
[3]Complete **Stocks and Mutual Funds Supplemental Detail.** (Exhibit 3-4)
[4]Complete **Real Estate Supplemental Detail.** (Exhibit 3-5)

LIABILITIES

CREDIT CARDS	CREDITOR NAME	BALANCE	OWNERSHIP CODE[1]	PAYMENT AMOUNT	INTEREST RATE
Card #1		$		$	%
Card #2		$		$	%
Card #3		$		$	%
Card #4		$		$	%
TOTAL CREDIT CARDS		$			

OTHER LIABILITIES	CREDITOR NAME	ORIGINAL LOAN AMT.	BALANCE	OWNERSHIP CODE[1]	1ST PYMT. DATE	LOAN PERIOD	FREQUENCY OF PYMTS.[2]	PAYMENT AMOUNT	INTEREST RATE
Mortgage		$	$		/			$	%
Home Equity		$	$		/			$	%
Bank Notes		$	$		/			$	%
Auto #1		$	$		/			$	%
Auto #2		$	$		/			$	%
Notes to others		$	$		/			$	%
Taxes Payable		$	$		/			$	%
Cash Value Life									
Insurance Loan		$	$		/			$	%
Other		$	$		/			$	%
Other		$	$		/			$	%
TOTAL OTHER LIABILITIES			$						
TOTAL LIABILITIES			$						
NET WORTH			$						

[1]H=Husband, W=Wife, J=Joint, OT=Other, IRA, 401(k), OR=Other Retirement [2]M=Month, Q=Quarter, S=Semiannual, A=Annual

BONDS/CD'S
SUPPLEMENTAL DETAIL

INVESTMENT NAME	CURRENT VALUE (TOTAL)	OWNERSHIP CODE[1]	INTEREST RATE	MATURITY DATE
_____	$ _____	_____	____ %	/ /
_____	$ _____	_____	____ %	/ /
_____	$ _____	_____	____ %	/ /
_____	$ _____	_____	____ %	/ /
_____	$ _____	_____	____ %	/ /
_____	$ _____	_____	____ %	/ /
_____	$ _____	_____	____ %	/ /
_____	$ _____	_____	____ %	/ /
_____	$ _____	_____	____ %	/ /
_____	$ _____	_____	____ %	/ /
_____	$ _____	_____	____ %	/ /
_____	$ _____	_____	____ %	/ /
_____	$ _____	_____	____ %	/ /
_____	$ _____	_____	____ %	/ /
_____	$ _____	_____	____ %	/ /
_____	$ _____	_____	____ %	/ /

[1]H=Husband, W=Wife, J=Joint, OT=Other, IRA, 401(k), OR=Other Retirement

STOCKS AND MUTUAL FUNDS
SUPPLEMENTAL DETAIL

INVESTMENT NAME	DATE ACQUIRED	CURRENT PRICE PER UNIT	NUMBER OF UNITS	CURRENT VALUE (TOTAL)	OWNERSHIP CODE[1]
_____	/ /	$ _____	_____	$ _____	_____
_____	/ /	$ _____	_____	$ _____	_____
_____	/ /	$ _____	_____	$ _____	_____
_____	/ /	$ _____	_____	$ _____	_____
_____	/ /	$ _____	_____	$ _____	_____
_____	/ /	$ _____	_____	$ _____	_____
_____	/ /	$ _____	_____	$ _____	_____
_____	/ /	$ _____	_____	$ _____	_____
_____	/ /	$ _____	_____	$ _____	_____
_____	/ /	$ _____	_____	$ _____	_____
_____	/ /	$ _____	_____	$ _____	_____
_____	/ /	$ _____	_____	$ _____	_____
_____	/ /	$ _____	_____	$ _____	_____
_____	/ /	$ _____	_____	$ _____	_____

[1]H=Husband, W=Wife, J=Joint, OT=Other, IRA, 401(k), OR=Other Retirement

REAL ESTATE
SUPPLEMENTAL DETAIL

PROPERTY DESCRIPTION:

CURRENT VALUE	PURCHASE PRICE	PURCHASE DATE	OWNERSHIP CODE[1]	CAPITAL IMPROVEMENTS	MONTHLY RENTAL AMOUNT	TAX BASIS (DEPRECIATED)
$	$	/		$	$	$

MORTGAGE INFORMATION

	ORIGINAL LOAN AMOUNT	BALANCE	FIRST PAYMENT DATE	LOAN PERIOD[2]	FREQUENCY OF PAYMENTS[3]	PAYMENT AMOUNT (P&I ONLY)	INTEREST RATE
1st Mortgage	$	$	/			$	%
2nd Mortgage	$	$	/			$	%

PROPERTY DESCRIPTION:

CURRENT VALUE	PURCHASE PRICE	PURCHASE DATE	OWNERSHIP CODE[1]	CAPITAL IMPROVEMENTS	MONTHLY RENTAL AMOUNT	TAX BASIS (DEPRECIATED)
$	$	/		$	$	$

MORTGAGE INFORMATION

	ORIGINAL LOAN AMOUNT	BALANCE	FIRST PAYMENT DATE	LOAN PERIOD[2]	FREQUENCY OF PAYMENTS[3]	PAYMENT AMOUNT (P&I ONLY)	INTEREST RATE
1st Mortgage	$	$	/			$	%
2nd Mortgage	$	$	/			$	%

[1]H=Husband, W=Wife, J=Joint, OT=Other   [2]15 yrs., 30 yrs., etc.   [3]M=Month, Q=Quarter, S=Semiannual, A=Annual

## CHAPTER 4

GAINING CONTROL
OF YOUR CASH FLOW

If I want to see noses crinkle at a seminar, all I have to do is mention the word "budget." I may as well have told people that we were going to discuss the bubonic plague. Budgets have unfortunately developed a bad reputation over the years. When most people think of a budget, they think of something telling them that they cannot spend any money on anything that brings pleasure to them; money can be spent only on absolute necessities. Everything above that must go into savings. In reality, properly prepared and followed, a budget does just the opposite. It does not put you in bondage; it liberates you. It does not tell you what you *cannot* spend, but rather it tells you what you *can* spend.

The main purpose of a budget is to put you in control of your spending—in a proactive mode rather than a reactive mode with your money. When I review recent expenditures with clients during the process of helping them establish a budget, it is not unusual to hear them exclaim, "If I had known how much I was spending in that area, I wouldn't have spent so much." Most people's cash flow problems develop because they do not know how much they are spending. A budget does not tell you how much you can or cannot spend on various items. Rather, a budget lets *you* decide how and where to spend your money, and then it tells you how closely your actual expenditures match your goals.

By the way, I recognize that there are some other very good budgeting systems on the market that you may like better than the one presented here. If that is the case, by all means use one of these other systems. Many of the paper systems that I have seen are more comprehensive than the one I am proposing, but they are so detailed that I doubt most people will take the time to prepare and follow them on a regular basis. I have designed my system with enough simplicity to be used consistently, yet with enough functionality to accomplish its objective.

As an alternative, I highly recommend the budgeting modules of some of the commercially available money management software packages. I personally use one of these programs and have found it to be easy to work with and extremely helpful. Computer budgeting systems allow you to run reports automatically that would take a long time to compute by hand. They also allow you to maintain your checkbook, track your investments, and perform other helpful functions in a time saving and efficient manner. If you have a personal computer, consider purchasing one of these software packages.

MONTHLY PAYMENTS

The budgeting worksheets for the Smiths begin with Exhibit 4-1. Blank forms for your use are once again provided at the end of the chapter. The first page of the budget should be completed at the beginning of each month. Begin by listing all of your monthly bills. Some of these, such as your car and house notes, have consistent amounts due each month, while other payments, such as utilities, will vary from month to month.

Make your best guess for each payment due in the "Estimated Amounts" column. A suggested method for making this estimate for non-fixed payments is to use the figure for the same month from the previous year plus a little extra to account for inflation. For payments that do not vary from month to month, you can go ahead and complete the "Actual Amounts" column at the same time. For payments that vary each month, complete the "Actual Amounts" column once the bill comes in. Comparing the estimated amounts with the actual amounts will let you see if there is a surplus or deficit in your budget for the month based on the amount you budgeted for each payment. Comparing these amounts will also help you make better estimates for the following months. For variable payments, be conservative in your estimates. It is better to budget for more than the actual amounts rather than less in order to prevent a shortfall in your cash flow for the month.

EXHIBIT 4-1

BUDGET FOR THE
MONTH OF <u>OCTOBER</u>
TOM AND MARY SUE SMITH

MONTHLY FINANCIAL COMMITMENTS	ESTIMATED AMOUNTS	ACTUAL AMOUNTS
Car Payments	$ 459	$ 459
Charitable	$ 458	$ 458
Credit Cards	$ 126	$ 126
Debt Repayment	$ 150	$ 150
Electricity	$ 90	$ 81
Gas	$ 58	$ 67
House Payments	$ 734	$ 734
Insurance (Auto, Life, Disability, Etc.)	$ 309	$ 309
Permanent Investments[3]	$ 150	$ 150
Phone	$ 55	$ 60
Rent	$	$
Savings[1]	$	$
Special Savings[2]	$ 50	$ 50
Water	$ 35	$ 35
Other	$	$
Other	$	$
Other	$	$
Other	$	$
TOTAL MONTHLY FINANCIAL COMMITMENTS	$ 2,674	$ 2,679

NET CASH INFLOW (AFTER TAXES)		
Salary	$ 3,437	$ 3,437
Commissions	$	$
Interest	$	$
Dividends	$	$
Other	$	$
Other	$	$
Other	$	$
TOTAL NET CASH INFLOW	$ 3,437	$ 3,437

MARGIN:

Total Estimated Inflow – Total Estimated Commitments =	$ 763

WEEKLY MARGIN:

Margin divided by weeks in the month (4.333) =	$ 176

[1]Liquidity
[2]Big-Ticket Items
[3]Long Term

GIVING

Notice that I place charitable giving in this section of the budget. The Bible says in Proverbs 3:9 to "honor the Lord from your wealth, and from the first of all your produce." Too many times we pay all of our creditors first and then try to give to the Lord's work from what is left over. As a result, we often give less than we had intended. According to this scripture, God wants the first of our fruits. We should determine the amount we want to give and then treat our giving with the same level of commitment as a bill. Our giving is not a bill; it is not a debt we are trying to pay back to God. Our giving is just that—a gift! It is an expression of love and worship. It is free will and from our hearts.

Let me make another comment while I am on the subject of giving. I know many people who pray before each offering and ask God how much they should give. This is not biblical. Paul tells us in II Corinthians 9:7 to give what we have purposed in our hearts to give. In other words, God wants us to prayerfully determine in advance how much we want to give and then follow through by giving that amount.

My wife and I determine our annual budget at the beginning of each year. It is at this time that we pray and determine our level of giving for the coming year. Now, if God impresses on us during the year to give special offerings, we are open to His leading. But if He does not minister something out of the ordinary to us, we have determined in advance what we will give.

Determining our giving in this manner allows us to make deliberate decisions about our giving instead of being subject to our emotions during an offering. It allows us to make a commitment during times when we are at peace and thinking clearly instead of having to make a separate decision each time the plate is passed. Though necessary adjustments can be made, advance decisions act as an anchor to our giving during times of financial testing, preventing us from being blown about by every little wind of adversity.

God instructs us to give as we have determined in our hearts. By making our giving one of the monthly commitments in our budget, we honor the Lord from the *first* of all our produce, not the last of our produce. Our giving becomes a deliberate decision, not a haphazard response to our circumstances. This is what pleases God.

SAVINGS

You will also notice that there are three categories of savings in this section of the budget. As well as paying God before we pay everybody else, we should also pay ourselves before we pay everybody else. We need to treat our savings with the same level of commitment with which we treat our other monthly bills. If we do not do this, then we will not achieve our financial goals. Therefore, you will notice that there are spaces for building a liquid account, saving for big-ticket items, and for making long-term investments. I also give you a line for committing an extra sum of money each month to paying off debt at an accelerated pace, as well as several spaces for any "other" monthly commitments you may have.

You will notice that the Smiths are paying $585/month in debt payments, not including their house. This represents over 10 percent of their gross income. You can see what a dramatic impact it will have on their net cash flow to liquidate their debts and eliminate their monthly debt payments. These large payments are currently preventing the Smiths from saving as much as they need to in order to reach their retirement goal.

Total the "Estimated Amounts" column. Use this figure for preparing the rest of the budget. After all the bills have come in, total the "Actual Amounts" column to see how close your estimates were.

CASH INFLOW

In the next section of the budget, enter your net cash inflow, typically on an after-tax basis. The majority of people are paid in such a way that taxes are already taken out of their paychecks, so computing this figure on an after-tax basis is very convenient. However, if you are self-employed and are paid on a pretax basis, you may want to list your gross level of income and use one of the "other" columns in the above portion of the budget for taxes.

A question naturally arises at this point for those who are not paid on a monthly basis. Since each month does not divide neatly into four weeks, how do you determine your monthly income? No problem. Simply multiply your typical paycheck amount times the number of paychecks you receive in a year, then divide the result by twelve.

A second question arises for those who are self-employed or paid on a commission basis: how do you project your income for a given month when your income varies each pay period? Unfortunately, there is no perfect solution to this problem. Make your best guess as to what your average income is for a particular month of the year, and then reduce it slightly to be conservative. If your income is higher, you can save the extra or apply it to the next month's budget. If your income is less, you may need to reduce your expenditures the following month to make up for it.

Once again, complete the "estimated" lines as you plan your budget and the "actual" lines once your income is received. Total your net cash inflow.

On the line after "Margin," subtract your total estimated commitments from your total estimated inflow to arrive at your monthly margin amount. Monthly margin is defined as the discretionary amount of money available to spend each month after all of your obligations have been met. Dividing this figure by the number of weeks in the month will yield your weekly margin. Once again, a problem occurs because all months do not contain the same number of weeks. Neither do months always begin on a Sunday and end on a Saturday. Solve this problem by dividing your monthly margin by 4.333, the average number of weeks in a month, to arrive at your weekly margin.

Tom and Mary Sue are paid $1,586.40 (after taxes) every other week. Following the above instructions gives Tom and Mary Sue an average monthly margin of $763. Dividing this figure by 4.333 gives them a weekly margin of $176.

Congratulations! You are halfway through the planning stage of your new budget. Once you have worked through this exercise a time or two, the figures will generally not change much from month to month. This part of computing your budget should go much faster after the first time.

ROUTINE LIVING EXPENSES

Now turn to Exhibit 4-2, entitled "Routine Living Expenses." This sheet helps you determine your weekly and monthly budget for specific cate-

EXHIBIT 4-2

ROUTINE LIVING EXPENSES
TOM AND MARY SUE SMITH

MONTH OF _____ October

ITEM	MONTHLY GOAL	WEEKLY GOAL	WEEK 1	WEEK 2	WEEK 3	WEEK 4	WEEK 5	MONTHLY TOTAL
Auto Fuel	$70	$14	$14	$17	$13	$12	$5	$61
Auto Maintenance	$45	$9	$	$	$	$45	$	$45
Charitable Donations	$	$	$	$	$	$	$	$
Child Care	$	$	$	$	$	$	$	$
Children—Extracurricular	$20	$4	$20	$	$	$	$	$20
Christmas	$25	$5	$	$14	$	$	$14	$28
Clothing	$115	$23	$23	$23	$23	$23	$23	$115
Dining Out	$40	$8	$	$16	$10	$14	$	$40
Dry Cleaning	$	$	$	$	$	$	$	$
Entertainment	$20	$4	$	$	$	$25	$	$25
Food	$	$	$	$	$	$	$	$
Furniture/Furnishings	$	$	$	$	$	$	$	$
Gifts	$	$	$	$	$	$	$	$
Groceries	$355	$71	$90	$70	$56	$75	$54	$345
Home Repair & Maintenance	$40	$8	$	$55	$	$	$	$55
Housecleaning	$	$	$	$	$	$	$	$
Household Other	$15	$3	$	$	$	$20	$	$20
Laundry	$	$	$	$	$	$	$	$
Medical & Dental	$45	$9	$	$	$23	$	$30	$53
Miscellaneous	$35	$7	$	$3	$14	$9	$10	$36
Toys	$20	$4	$	$	$25	$	$	$25
Vacation	$35	$7	$7	$7	$7	$7	$7	$35
Other	$	$	$	$	$	$	$	$
Other	$	$	$	$	$	$	$	$
TOTAL:	$880	$176	$154	$205	$171	$230	$143	$903

gories and then allows you to compare your actual expenditures to your budget. I have divided expenditures into several standard categories. Begin by determining your average spending goals by category for each week. I suggest taking a look at your checkbook and credit card registers for the last two or three months to get an accurate idea of how much you normally spend by category. Budget based on your best guess. Undoubtedly, after using this system for a few months, you will find some areas that need adjusting based on your actual spending habits.

When you translate your weekly goals into monthly figures, the problem of dividing months into four or five weeks appears again. You determined your average weekly margin based on months having 4.333 weeks. However, you must track your actual expenditures by complete weeks. Therefore, you must determine at the beginning of each month whether it will be considered a four- or five-week month. Multiply the weekly margin figures by the number of weeks in the month to arrive at monthly margin figures for each category.

One challenge that people face in this part of the budget planning process is that they do not spend the same amount each month on each item. For example, expenditures for items like groceries tend to be fairly consistent. But clothing is typically another matter. A man may buy suits once or twice a year. Clothing expenditures will be very heavy during those months in which he buys suits, but very light, or nonexistent, in other months. How do you handle this on the budget?

Budget each month based on your *average monthly expenditures* for each of these types of categories. Visualize the monthly budget for this type of expense category as a savings account. If you do not spend the total amount budgeted for a given month, "save" the excess for future purchases. Keep track of the total amount saved. Some people go so far as to designate an envelope for each of these expense categories and then deposit cash for the saved amount each month in the appropriate envelope. When they go shopping for items in that category, they limit their purchases to the amount of cash available. A simple ledger system that tracks your accruals accomplishes the same objective while allowing you to earn interest on your money.

Total your monthly and weekly goal columns.

The right-hand side of the "Routine Living Expenses" page will be used to keep track of your actual expenditures for each week by category. Use Exhibit 4-3 to help you accomplish this.

TRACKING ACTUAL EXPENDITURES

Exhibit 4-3 is titled "Daily Expense Sheet." Complete a separate sheet for each week of the month. Write down every expenditure you make each day. Lisa and I used to keep one of these sheets on our dresser so that we could record our expenditures as we went to bed each night. Some people carry an index card with them to log purchases made during the day and then transfer them to this sheet at night. Others obtain a receipt for all of the purchases that they make and then use these to recall their daily expenditures. However you do it, keep track of your expenditures each day on this sheet. Don't worry about pennies, unless you're an engineer or accountant; round all expenditures to the nearest dollar. Rounding to the nearest dollar is too frustrating for engineers and accountants, however, so they can track everything to the nearest penny.

At the end of each week, transfer your actual expenditures from the "Daily Expense Sheet" to the appropriate weekly column on the "Routine Living Expenses" page, totaled by category. Put a "✓" by each expense as it is transferred. Keeping track of your expenses like this will do two things for you. First, it will let you compare your estimated expenditures to your actual expenditures. This will let you see if you have made a bad estimate for a given category, or if you have a spending problem in a particular area.

Second, this will help you make appropriate spending choices during the week. Not only can you tell at the end of the week if you kept within your budget, but you can make expenditure decisions as the week progresses to keep you from overspending.

For instance, let's say that it's a Friday night and you and your spouse are deciding what to do for entertainment. You check your budget and see that if you spend more than three dollars, you will be over budget for the week. So you run down to the video store, rent a movie, and pop popcorn at home.

Conversely, let's say it's the same scenario, only this time your budget tells you that you have a hundred dollars available for entertainment that

DAILY EXPENSE SHEET

EXHIBIT 4-3

TOM AND MARY SUE SMITH

MONTH OF _____ OCTOBER _____

WEEK 1

DATE	AMOUNT	ITEM	✓
10/1	$ 9	Fuel	✓
10/1	$ 97	Groceries	✓
10/1	$ 7	Refill gas tank for grill	✓
10/2	$ 3	Magazine	✓
10/2	$ 33	Boys' clothes	✓
10/2	$ 10	Vacation savings	✓
10/3	$ 25	Karate	✓
10/3	$ 10	Groceries	✓
10/4	$ 9	Fuel	✓
10/4	$ 7	Car wash supplies	✓
10/4	$ 7	Pet treats	✓
10/5	$ 7	Gift—video	✓
10/6	$ 15	Bowling	✓
10/7	$ 8	Groceries	✓
/	$		
/	$		
/	$		
/	$		
/	$		
/	$		
/	$		
/	$		

DATE	AMOUNT	ITEM	✓
/	$		
/	$		
/	$		
/	$		
/	$		
/	$		
/	$		
/	$		
/	$		
/	$		
/	$		
/	$		
/	$		
/	$		
/	$		
/	$		
/	$		
/	$		
/	$		
/	$		
/	$		
/	$		

has not been spent yet. You go to a nice restaurant for dinner, catch a movie, and don't feel the least bit guilty about spending a hundred dollars.

People often live under a load of guilt about spending money. They feel as if they should be saving every penny that they do not absolutely have to spend. This can cause problems in a marriage if both spouses do not think the same way. Major conflicts of the kind that result in divorces can occur when one spouse is a miser and the other is a spendthrift. A budget is very helpful in these situations because the couple can agree in advance on a spending and savings plan. There is no reason for either spouse to feel guilty about spending money on "nonessential" items as long as it is accounted for in the budget. Indeed, some of this type of spending is emotionally healthy.

It is wonderful therapy for a married couple to have a heart-to-heart talk at the beginning of the budget planning process. They should each communicate very openly about what is important to them regarding the spending and saving of money. By communicating in this way, each person can begin to understand why the other person behaves as he or she does. Compromises can be worked out, and the couple can agree in advance on the goals they will work toward achieving. As long as the budget is followed, neither spouse can blame the other for any financial problems that may arise, and, thus, many arguments are avoided. This process can help a couple go to the next level and develop a genuine unity on their finances. This is powerful when it occurs. What used to be a sore spot in their marriage becomes a true strength.

Husbands, in particular, tend to be bad about blaming their wives for overspending, when many times the husband is the guilty party. I would be embarrassed to tell you how many times I have accused my wife of putting us over the budget, only to look at the record of actual expenditures and find that it was I who had committed the crime of overspending. Numerous fights were avoided because the record was available to speak for itself. Adult conversations, where meaningful communication occurred, gradually took the place of heated arguments. Our finances increased, and our marriage grew stronger.

BUDGET FOR THE MONTH OF _____ 19___

MONTHLY FINANCIAL COMMITMENTS	ESTIMATED AMOUNTS	ACTUAL AMOUNTS
Car Payments	$_____	$_____
Charitable	$_____	$_____
Credit Cards	$_____	$_____
Debt Repayment	$_____	$_____
Electricity	$_____	$_____
Gas	$_____	$_____
House Payments	$_____	$_____
Insurance (Auto, Life, Disability, Etc.)	$_____	$_____
Permanent Investments[3]	$_____	$_____
Phone	$_____	$_____
Rent	$_____	$_____
Savings[1]	$_____	$_____
Special Savings[2]	$_____	$_____
Water	$_____	$_____
Other	$_____	$_____
Other	$_____	$_____
Other	$_____	$_____
Other	$_____	$_____
TOTAL MONTHLY FINANCIAL COMMITMENTS	$	$

NET CASH INFLOW (AFTER TAXES)		
Salary	$_____	$_____
Commissions	$_____	$_____
Interest	$_____	$_____
Dividends	$_____	$_____
Other	$_____	$_____
Other	$_____	$_____
Other	$_____	$_____
TOTAL NET CASH INFLOW	$	$

MARGIN:
Total Estimated Inflow – Total Estimated Commitments= $_____

WEEKLY MARGIN:
Margin divided by weeks in the month (4.333)= $_____

[1]Liquidity
[2]Big-Ticket Items
[3]Long Term

ROUTINE LIVING EXPENSES

MONTH OF _____

ITEM	MONTHLY GOAL	WEEKLY GOAL		WEEK 1	WEEK 2	WEEK 3	WEEK 4	WEEK 5	MONTHLY TOTAL
Auto Fuel	$	$		$	$	$	$	$	$
Auto Maintenance	$	$		$	$	$	$	$	$
Charitable Donations	$	$		$	$	$	$	$	$
Child Care	$	$		$	$	$	$	$	$
Children—Extracurricular	$	$		$	$	$	$	$	$
Christmas	$	$		$	$	$	$	$	$
Clothing	$	$		$	$	$	$	$	$
Dining Out	$	$		$	$	$	$	$	$
Dry Cleaning	$	$		$	$	$	$	$	$
Entertainment	$	$		$	$	$	$	$	$
Food	$	$		$	$	$	$	$	$
Furniture/Furnishings	$	$		$	$	$	$	$	$
Gifts	$	$		$	$	$	$	$	$
Groceries	$	$		$	$	$	$	$	$
Home Repair & Maintenance	$	$		$	$	$	$	$	$
Housecleaning	$	$		$	$	$	$	$	$
Household Other	$	$		$	$	$	$	$	$
Laundry	$	$		$	$	$	$	$	$
Medical & Dental	$	$		$	$	$	$	$	$
Miscellaneous	$	$		$	$	$	$	$	$
Toys	$	$		$	$	$	$	$	$
Vacation	$	$		$	$	$	$	$	$
Other	$	$		$	$	$	$	$	$
Other	$	$		$	$	$	$	$	$
TOTAL:	$	$		$	$	$	$	$	$

DAILY EXPENSE SHEET

WEEK _____

MONTH OF _____

DATE	AMOUNT	ITEM	✓
/	$		
/	$		
/	$		
/	$		
/	$		
/	$		
/	$		
/	$		
/	$		
/	$		
/	$		
/	$		
/	$		
/	$		
/	$		
/	$		
/	$		
/	$		
/	$		
/	$		
/	$		
/	$		
/	$		

DATE	AMOUNT	ITEM	✓
/	$		
/	$		
/	$		
/	$		
/	$		
/	$		
/	$		
/	$		
/	$		
/	$		
/	$		
/	$		
/	$		
/	$		
/	$		
/	$		
/	$		
/	$		
/	$		
/	$		
/	$		
/	$		
/	$		

GAINING
YOUR
FREEDOM

## CHAPTER 5

THE DEBT TRAP

As I stated earlier, I do not believe the Bible teaches that borrowing money is a sin. However, rarely is it wisdom, either. Because excessive debt is one of the worst problems that people struggle with financially, getting out of debt and staying out of debt is a worthy and profitable goal.

Why do many Christian financial planners teach that it is a sin to borrow money? In Deuteronomy 28:12, as God is rehearsing the blessings that will come upon the Israelites for obeying Him, He states emphatically ". . . and you shall lend to many nations, but you shall not borrow." Lifting this verse out of its context, many Bible teachers interpret this to mean that it is a sin to borrow money for any reason from anyone. However, that is not at all what God is saying here. The context of the statement "but you shall not borrow" is not one of a commandment, but rather God is telling the Israelites that He will bless them so abundantly that they will not *need* to borrow money. Indeed, they were to have such an overflow of finances that they would be in a position to lend to others.

Just the fact that God is telling the Israelites that they will lend money to others makes it clear that it is not a sin to borrow money. By definition, if you are lending something to someone, then they are borrowing from you. If it were a sin to borrow, would God tell you to help that person sin? Of course not! However, God's perfect will is to reach a point where we do not need to borrow. This will take time, but by following the instructions in this book, you can get there.

BIBLICAL DEBT

Another passage of scripture people use to teach that debt is sin is Romans 13:8, which says to "Owe nothing to anyone except to love one another. . . ." As I have studied this scripture and others concerning debt, I am convinced that the Bible is not referring to debt as a transaction where one person borrows money from someone else in return for collateral and/or the promise to repay the money. Biblical debt, which the Bible says is wrong, is when you have promised to give something to someone in return for something they have done for you, and then you refuse to honor your word. You owe that person and should pay them what you owe. To not do so is sin.

For example, if I tell you that I will pay you $100 for typing several letters for me, once you have typed those letters, I owe you $100. That is a debt I owe, and God says I must pay it. If I do not pay this debt, I have sinned. I either made a promise to you that I was not in a position to keep from the beginning, or I am not keeping my word to you. Both are wrong. Proverbs 11:24 says "There is one who scatters, yet increases all the more, and there is one who *withholds what is justly due* [emphasis mine], but it results only in want." Debt that is sin is the withholding of what is justly due to someone. When you incur an obligation to another person, you should pay that obligation in a timely fashion.

This kind of debt extends beyond money. It can refer to a service you have promised to provide someone. It can be honor that is due an individual. Romans 13 refers specifically to the payment of taxes as an obligation for which we are responsible. Anything we owe someone, for which payment is due, is covered by this biblical concept. With regard to financial debt specifically, it is not a sin to borrow money for the purchase of an item. However, it is a sin not to make each payment as it comes due.

THE DEBT TRAP

Even though it may not be a sin to carry debt, the reality of the matter is that debt is a downward spiral for most people. They see something they want, but do not have the money to pay cash for it, so they charge it. They justify the purchase by telling themselves that they can afford the monthly payment. Generally, most people do not realize how much money they are spending or borrowing because they do not keep an account of their expenditures. Their monthly payments grow larger and larger with the passage of time. They keep telling themselves that everything is okay since they can still afford the monthly payments. Credit card payments at 18 percent interest begin consuming an ever-higher percentage of their monthly cash flow. At some point, they begin to feel the emotional strain of their tight financial situation. Their fiscal problems begin to dominate their thinking. At this point, they often become irritable and less productive at work.

I have seen numerous marital problems arise at this stage in the debt cycle. The husband blames the wife for her overspending, forgetting about the set of new golf clubs he bought last month on credit. The exasperated wife angrily reminds the husband of his unnecessary expenditures. Their marriage suffers as they react to the pressure and blame each other for their financial woes. Communication shuts down, making impossible any logical discussion on how to resolve their situation.

Then it happens! The unexpected emergency occurs that puts them over the edge. Now they can no longer afford their monthly payments. They begin borrowing just to pay the interest on other debts. Few individuals or couples recover once they reach this point. Many file for bankruptcy. At this stage in the cycle, countless marriages are destroyed by the financial pressure. The real dilemma here, apart from the obvious problems associated with a poor credit record, is that if the individuals involved do not correct the habits that led to their debt problems in the first place, they are destined to repeat this cycle again in a few years.

If you find yourself being sucked down the debt trap, declare war on it and fight with everything you have to get out of debt. Seek professional counsel. There is an organization called the Consumer Credit Counseling Service that specializes in helping people get out of debt. They do not charge for their services and are an excellent resource for people with serious debt problems.

Perhaps you are in debt, but are not at the point of desperation. Nevertheless, as a financial professional I recommend that you strive to pay off your debts, except possibly the mortgage on your house (I will discuss this possible exception later). I believe that you will go further financially by living debt-free. Later in this book I give specific advice on how to accomplish this.

DEBT IS BONDAGE

Why should we strive to be free from debt? Proverbs 22:7 states "The rich rules over the poor, and the borrower becomes the lender's slave." In the first half of this verse we have the golden rule stated: "He who has the gold makes the rules." Ever since the beginning of time, rich people have, with few exceptions, ruled over poor people. Generally speaking, it is accurate to say that the rich determine how the game is to be played by everybody else.

The second half of this verse states an interesting truism. When somebody borrows money from another person or an institution, they have, in some form or fashion, made themselves subservient to the lender. For instance, many people are not aware that on virtually every bank loan there is a clause in the contract stating that the bank can call the loan at any time. This means that you can borrow money to start a business, make tremendous progress on your business plan, and then experience the trauma of the bank calling your loan, possibly destroying what you have taken years to build. Is this likely? No. But it is possible.

If you are forced to borrow money, the lender sets the terms on how the money will be repaid. The terms of the loan may contain very restrictive provisions regarding the types of activities that you or your company may engage in during the term of the loan. For whatever reasons, borrowing money can restrict your freedom based on the conditions the lender places on your obtaining the loan, and, in some sense, you become the lender's servant.

If you are not able to repay debt in a timely fashion, according to the terms of the loan, the noose becomes even tighter. At that point, the lender may have legal recourse against you. If the lender is willing to work with you to remedy the situation, then you must oblige whatever conditions the lender poses or suffer the legal consequences. You really do fall into slavery at that point.

Many friendships have been destroyed by one friend borrowing money from another friend, especially when the loan is not repaid on time. The lender feels taken advantage of if he does not receive his money back. He may try to exact a price from the borrower by laying on a guilt trip, which the borrower may either accept or come to resent. The lender often assumes the right to tell his friend what to do because of the debt owed, and every visible purchase may be scrutinized. Eventually the friendship is torn apart by the guilt, anger, and bitterness that develops.

Debt is an obligation that impedes your ability to obey God and to make choices with your money. Money being used to make loan payments is money for which you have no choice how to spend. Your financial freedom is hindered.

Many people want to give more money to the Church, but cannot because their monthly debt payments are too high. Sometimes a wife is forced into the workplace against her wishes in order to meet the monthly obligations of accumulated consumer debt. Yes, debt is a bondage from which you do well to get free.

SURETY

One of the most foolish things you can do is to co-sign on a loan for someone else. When you do so, you are assuming the responsibility for repaying the debt if they do not. The tendency, especially if the borrower is a friend, is to assume they will pay back the loan, and your co-signing won't really mean anything. The opposite is actually true. The lender would not be requiring a co-signer for the loan if it felt the borrower was capable of repaying the loan on his or her own.

The Bible is very plain on the subject of co-signing, or becoming surety, for someone else's debts:

Proverbs 6:1 My son, if you have become surety for your neighbor, have given a pledge for a stranger,

2 if you have been snared with the words of your mouth, have been caught with the words of your mouth,

3 do this then, my son, and deliver yourself; since you have come into the hand of your neighbor, go, humble yourself, and importune your neighbor.

4 Do not give sleep to your eyes, nor slumber to your eyelids;

5 deliver yourself like a gazelle from the hunter's hand, and like a bird from the hand of the fowler.

Proverbs 11:15 He who is surety for a stranger will surely suffer for it, but he who hates going surety is safe.

Proverbs 17:18 A man lacking in sense pledges, and becomes surety in the presence of his neighbor.

If you are approached by a friend to co-sign a loan for him, be emphatic in saying "no!" Explain to him that even though you value his friendship, you have a personal policy of never co-signing a loan for others. I would rather lose a friend than become surety for his debt. It is foolish for you to come into financial bondage because of someone else's problems.

BEING DEBT-FREE IS A TESTIMONY TO GOD'S BLESSINGS

In Deuteronomy 28, God tells Israel the blessings that would come as a result of obeying Him. Note the following verses:

11 "And the Lord will make you abound in prosperity, in the offspring of your body and in the offspring of your beast and in the produce of your ground, in the land that the Lord swore to your fathers to give you."

12 "The Lord will open for you His good storehouse, the heavens, to give rain to your land in its season and to bless all the work of your hand; and you shall lend to many nations, but you shall not borrow."

13 "And the Lord shall make you the head and not the tail, and you shall only be above, and you shall not be underneath, if you will listen to the commandments of the Lord your God, which I charge you today, to observe them carefully . . ."

In verse 11, God tells the Israelites that He will make them abound in prosperity. Remember that Israel was primarily an agricultural society, so when God spoke of blessing them financially, He would often speak of blessing their land and their cattle. The first half of verse 12 further states that God will bless their labor so that it will produce much fruit. In this context, God then tells the Israelites that His blessing on them will be so great that they will no longer need to borrow money. Instead, they will have such a surplus of finances that they will actually lend to other nations.

Being debt-free is a testimony to God's blessings. God said He would bless His people to the point that they would not need to borrow money. When we experience that level of blessing, and others ask us how we manage to live above debt, it is an opportunity to witness about the blessings of God in our lives. When others around us are stressed out over financial problems, and we are at ease financially because we are free from the burden of debt, it is evidence that God's word is true and that God is indeed a good God.

## CHAPTER 6

THE DEBT LIQUIDATION SYSTEM

Just as in any other area of finances, successful debt liquidation will not come overnight, but over an extended period of time. It is the result of diligently executing a carefully constructed plan. There is a process involved in becoming debt-free that, when followed, will allow for the orderly disposition of our liabilities.

The process of getting out of debt is very simple, yet very effective. First, begin by setting aside an amount of money over and above your required monthly payments that will be dedicated to accelerating the liquidation of debt. Apply this entire sum to the smallest debt, in addition to that debt's regular payment. Since you are attacking the smallest debt first, hopefully it will be completely paid off in a short period of time.

Once the first debt is paid off, take its monthly payment, plus the extra amount you have set aside for accelerating the liquidation of your debts, and apply this entire amount each month to your next smallest debt, in addition to that debt's regular payment. In other words, whenever you pay off a debt, don't assume that the payment for that liability is then available as part of your normal cash flow. Keep that obligation's payment dedicated to eliminating debt, applying it to the next largest debt each time.

Let me illustrate this process with an example. The following table represents Tom and Mary Sue Smiths' debt situation (see Exhibit 3-2).

Tom and Mary Sue have determined that they can apply an extra $150 each month to the liquidation of their debt. They begin the process of becoming debt-free by making a monthly payment of $170 on their department store credit card. This amount consists of the regular monthly

CREDITOR	BALANCE	MONTHLY PAYMENT
ABC Credit Card	$1,428	$45
XYZ Credit Card	$2,019	$61
Department Store	$655	$20
Acme Credit Company	$6,441	$246
Dealer Credit Company	$3,602	$213

payment of $20, plus the extra $150 that they have set aside each month for debt liquidation. As you can tell, they pay this obligation off in four payments. Any amount of the final payment that exceeds the remaining balance is applied that month to the next smallest debt.

Next, Tom and Mary Sue will pay off the ABC Credit Card. However, instead of making the normal $45 payment on this card each month, they add to that $45 the $170 they were paying on the debt that was just liquidated, yielding a total monthly payment of $215. This debt is eliminated within seven months. In less than one year, the Smiths have successfully liquidated two of their debts.

Now the Smiths are starting to get excited. They can see the light at the end of the tunnel. During the eleven months in which the Smiths have paid off the department store card and one of their credit cards, they have also continued making the regular monthly payments on their other obligations. As a result, their auto loan from the Dealer Credit Company now has a balance of only $1,450, making it the next smallest debt (see Exhibit 6-1). Instead of making monthly payments of only the required $213, they can now make monthly payments of $428, i.e., the normal $213 payment plus the $215 they were paying on the previous debt. This obligation is paid off within four months.

The Smiths, after only fifteen months on their debt liquidation program, have only two debts remaining: their XYZ Credit Card, with a balance of $2,019, and their Acme Credit Company car loan, with a remaining balance of $3,274.

Adding the $428 payment that was being applied to the previous debt to XYZ's $61 regular monthly payment allows Tom and Mary Sue to make

EXHIBIT 6-1 APPROXIMATE PAYMENT SCHEDULE
DEALER CREDIT COMPANY
TOM AND MARY SUE SMITH

PAYMENT #	PAYMENT AMOUNT	PRINCIPAL	INTEREST	BALANCE
				$8,750.00
1	$212.59	$156.08	$56.51	$8,593.92
2	$212.59	$157.09	$55.50	$8,436.83
3	$212.59	$158.10	$54.49	$8,278.73
4	$212.59	$159.12	$53.47	$8,119.61
5	$212.59	$160.15	$52.44	$7,959.46
6	$212.59	$161.19	$51.40	$7,798.27
		↓		
30	$212.59	$188.12	$24.47	$3,601.50
31	$212.59	$189.33	$23.26	$3,412.17
32	$212.59	$190.55	$22.04	$3,221.62
33	$212.59	$191.78	$20.81	$3,029.84
34	$212.59	$193.02	$19.57	$2,836.81
35	$212.59	$194.27	$18.32	$2,642.55
36	$212.59	$195.52	$17.07	$2,447.02
37	$212.59	$196.79	$15.80	$2,250.24
38	$212.59	$198.06	$14.53	$2,052.18
39	$212.59	$199.34	$13.25	$1,852.84
40	$212.59	$200.62	$11.97	$1,652.22
41	$212.59	$201.92	$10.67	$1,450.30
42	$428.00	$418.63	$ 9.37	$1,031.67
43	$428.00	$421.34	$ 6.66	$ 610.33
44	$428.00	$424.06	$ 3.94	$ 186.27
45	$187.47	$186.27	$ 1.20	$ 0.00

$489 payments on this card. Its balance disappears in just four months. By the time they begin liquidating the Acme Credit Company debt, regular monthly payments have reduced its balance to $2,372 (see Exhibit 6-2). They now attack it with monthly payments of $735 (the $489 used to liquidate the XYZ obligation and the regular Acme payment of $246). This debt is eliminated in four payments, with enough money left over from the last payment for the Smiths to enjoy a very nice evening together, celebrating their new debt-free status.

Using this simple system, the Smiths have eliminated their entire debt burden in only twenty-three months—less than two years! They also have

EXHIBIT 6-2 APPROXIMATE PAYMENT SCHEDULE
ACME CREDIT COMPANY
TOM AND MARY SUE SMITH

PAYMENT #	PAYMENT AMOUNT	PRINCIPAL	INTEREST	BALANCE
				$10,000.00
1	$246.48	$175.65	$70.83	$9,824.35
2	$246.48	$176.89	$69.59	$9,647.46
3	$246.48	$178.14	$68.34	$9,469.32
4	$246.48	$179.41	$67.07	$9,289.91
5	$246.48	$180.68	$65.80	$9,109.24
6	$246.48	$181.96	$64.52	$8,927.28
		↓		
19	$246.48	$199.44	$47.04	$6,441.17
20	$246.48	$200.86	$45.62	$6,240.32
21	$246.48	$202.28	$44.20	$6,038.04
22	$246.48	$203.71	$42.77	$5,834.33
23	$246.48	$205.15	$41.33	$5,629.18
24	$246.48	$206.61	$39.87	$5,422.57
25	$246.48	$208.07	$38.41	$5,214.50
26	$246.48	$209.54	$36.94	$5,004.96
27	$246.48	$211.03	$35.45	$4,793.93
28	$246.48	$212.52	$33.96	$4,581.41
29	$246.48	$214.03	$32.45	$4,367.38
30	$246.48	$215.54	$30.94	$4,151.83
31	$246.48	$217.07	$29.41	$3,934.76
32	$246.48	$218.61	$27.87	$3,716.15
33	$246.48	$220.16	$26.32	$3,496.00
34	$246.48	$221.72	$24.76	$3,274.28
35	$246.48	$223.29	$23.19	$3,050.99
36	$246.48	$224.87	$21.61	$2,826.12
37	$246.48	$226.46	$20.02	$2,599.66
38	$246.48	$228.07	$18.41	$2,371.60
39	$735.00	$718.20	$16.80	$1,653.40
40	$735.00	$723.29	$11.71	$ 930.11
41	$735.00	$728.41	$ 6.59	$ 201.70
42	$203.13	$201.70	$ 1.43	$ 0.00

an additional $735/month cash flow available to help them reach their other financial objectives. The key to their success was having the discipline to develop and follow a sound debt liquidation plan.

This debt liquidation system has two key advantages. First, it is psychologically healthy to see yourself actually eliminating debts early in the process. If it takes two years to pay off the first obligation, it can be very discouraging. Conversely, if you can drop two debts from your list of liabilities within the first few months, it is very encouraging.

Second, when you begin liquidating your larger debts, you are able to make significantly larger payments toward them. Again, trying to pay down a $10,000 debt with $200 payments is depressing. You may feel as if you are fighting a forest fire with a water pistol. But that is not the situation with this system. Because of the increasing amount you are able to apply to each successive debt, you have the pleasure of seeing substantial progress being made each month. The keys are to budget carefully and to execute your plan faithfully.

Once you have liquidated all your debts, which may take some time, you will likely have a substantial amount of extra monthly cash flow available. What should you do with this cash flow? The temptation will be to spend this money. Instead, because you are used to living without this money anyway, you should use most, or even all, of this money to build your liquid savings account, your big-ticket items savings account, and then ultimately your long-term investment account. In Tom and Mary Sue's situation, they should set some of it aside, say an additional $150/month, in their big-ticket savings account, in preparation for their next auto purchase. The remainder, as we will see in a later chapter, should be invested to help the Smiths achieve their longer-term goals of retirement and educating their children.

The point is, after you have struggled so faithfully to get out of debt, it would be a shame to find yourself wrestling with debt problems again two years later. By following this strategy, debt should become a part of your past.

SELLING INVESTMENTS TO PAY OFF DEBT

Paying off a debt is in some respects the equivalent of making an investment that yields the same rate of return as the interest rate of the debt. A dollar of interest saved improves my net worth as much as a dollar earned from investments. For instance, paying off a $1,000 credit card balance with an 18 percent interest rate is equivalent to making a $1,000 investment that returns 18 percent. Since I don't know of any investments that can guarantee me anything close to an 18 percent return, it makes a lot of sense to pay off the credit card instead of investing the $1,000.

Normally, the lowest interest rate you will be able to obtain on a loan will be for the mortgage on your house. This is because the loan is fully collateralized by what is normally an appreciating asset. The equity in your house tends to grow over time as the value of your house increases and the balance of your mortgage declines. Mortgages are relatively safe loans for a lender to make. If you fail to make your payments in a timely fashion, the lender can generally foreclose on the loan, sell your house, and recover the amount of his loan. Thus, because of the high probability that the lender will get his funds back one way or another, the loan is considered to be relatively low risk, and the lender charges a low interest rate.

The same is not true for a car, which depreciates in value over time. Many times a new auto drops 10 percent in value the moment you drive it off the lot. As a result, you do not build much, if any, equity in your automobile. As your loan balance declines, so does the value of your car. If you fail to make timely payments on your loan, the car could be repossessed and sold by the lender, but the likelihood of them getting all of their money back is somewhat lower than for a home loan. As a result, lenders are generally going to charge you a higher interest rate for an auto loan than for a mortgage on your residence. Higher interest rates are used to compensate lenders for higher levels of risk.

Credit card debts are the worst. Lenders charge very high interest rates because there is no collateral for them to sell in order to recover their money if you fail to make your payments. The lender can not repossess a dress you bought at the department store and sell it on the courthouse steps to the highest bidder. Credit card debt is *not collateralized*. Repayment is based solely on the integrity of the borrower. Since the risk of not getting their money back is the highest for this type of loan, lenders will place lower borrowing limits on credit cards than on collateralized debts, and they will charge significantly higher interest rates.

With these principles in mind, you may find it advantageous to liquidate lower yielding assets and use the proceeds to pay off higher interest debts. In making this decision, compare the returns you are earning on your investments to the interest rates you are being charged for loans. For stock and stock mutual fund investments, which do not pay a steady return, use 11 percent, the long-term average return of the stock market,[2] as the comparison return. If an asset is earning significantly less than the rate a loan is charging, you should liquidate the asset to pay off the loan.

If the Smiths were really financial planning clients of mine, I would have recommended that they sell their CD and shares of their bond mutual fund to pay off all their debts other than their mortgage. Had I done this, however, then you would have lost the benefit of seeing how the debt liquidation system works.

PAYING OFF YOUR MORTGAGE

One of the few possible exceptions to accelerating the liquidation of debt may be paying off your home mortgage. The primary advantage to paying your house off early is the security of owning your home outright. If your house is debt-free, you do not have to worry about the lender foreclosing on it if you experience a period of financial hardship. Also, the burden of making the monthly payments goes away once the house is paid for. Much can be said for the emotional well-being that comes from owning your house free and clear.

Financially, however, it may be smarter not to pay your house off early. Because the interest rate on home mortgages tends to be low, it is often possible to invest money at a higher rate of return than the interest rate on your home loan. This is a major point to be considered. For instance, as I said earlier, the average annual rate of return of the stock market has been about 11 percent since 1925.[3] If you have a mortgage at 7 percent, you could profit an additional 4 percent on your principal each year by investing that money in the stock market (assuming you continue to average 11 percent annually on your stock investments) as opposed to paying off your mortgage. If the balance on your mortgage were $100,000, the difference would amount to $4,000 per year initially. Obviously a strategy like this would appeal more to an aggressive investor than a conservative investor. The key difference between the two options is that you are guaranteed to save the 7 percent interest by paying off the mortgage. Your return from investing in the stock market is not guaranteed.

Let's look at an example of a conservative investor who is deciding whether it makes sense to pay off his house with an inheritance he just received, or if he should invest the money. Again, the principle to be followed is that paying off your mortgage is the equivalent of making an investment offering the same guaranteed rate of return as the interest rate being charged on the loan. Since the interest savings is guaranteed, paying off a mortgage must be considered the equivalent of a very conservative investment. Let's assume that this individual, if he does not pay off his mortgage, would only feel comfortable investing in certificates of deposit or shorter-term Treasury bonds. For the sake of our illustration, let's assume that the interest rate on the home mortgage is 7.5 percent, Treasury bonds yield 5.7 percent, and CD's are offering a yield of 5.3 percent. This situation is a no-brainer. Paying off the loan will offer the greatest return on this person's money.

Let's look at another example of the same conservative investor with the same 7.5% mortgage. This time, though, let's assume that he obtained his mortgage when inflation and interest rates were low. He now finds himself in an inflationary environment where five-year Treasury notes are yielding 12 percent. He could take the $100,000 principal, purchase Treasury notes with it, and make an additional 4.5 percent in interest each year over the interest rate on his mortgage. This would make a lot of sense.

It has become very fashionable in financial planning circles, especially Christian financial planning circles, to make a blanket recommendation that everybody should liquidate their mortgage as quickly as possible. Normally, when this recommendation is made, the adviser will demonstrate the amount of interest that can be saved on the mortgage by paying it off early. The interest savings is real, but what must also be considered in making this decision is the *opportunity cost* of the money used to eliminate the mortgage. Money used to pay off the mortgage cannot be used for other productive investments. So, while it is true that paying off a mortgage early may indeed save you $100,000 in interest, it may also prevent you from *earning* $150,000 by investing the same money at a higher return than your mortgage interest rate.

Another difference between a house and other items on which you might carry debt is that a house is generally an appreciating asset, whereas cars and other items tend to depreciate in value over time. Because of this, you will normally build equity in a house, which is not necessarily true for these other items. It is not, therefore, always imprudent to carry debt on appreciating items.

Only you can make the decision about whether paying off your mortgage early is appropriate for your situation. You must weigh the financial factors and risks involved with investing the money against the emotional satisfaction and security of owning your home debt-free.

Husbands, I encourage you to be sensitive to your wives in this matter. Though this is not true in all situations, women, as a general rule, tend to be more security conscious than men, and men tend to be more aggressive investors than women. As a result, women often want to liquidate the mortgage early, while men commonly want to use the same funds for investment purposes. Spouses should discuss this subject openly and reach a decision that takes into consideration both persons' feelings and attitudes.

HOW TO PAY OFF YOUR MORTGAGE

Let's say that you have made the decision to pay off your mortgage early. How do you accomplish this? Generally, advisers recommend that you dispose of your mortgage early by making an additional principal payment each month along with your regular house payment. Another frequently suggested method is to pay half your mortgage payment every two weeks, resulting in an extra house payment each year. I do not recommend either method.

Assume that you make an extra principal payment each month on your mortgage. Eventually, you reduce the loan balance by $30,000 more than you would have by making normal monthly payments. Then, unexpectedly, your company downsizes. You lose your job, and you find yourself unable to make your mortgage payment for a few months. No problem, you think, since you have paid an extra $30,000 on your mortgage balance. The mortgage company will be understanding and allow you to skip a few payments. Right?

Unfortunately, that is not the way it works. Paying extra on your mortgage does not buy you the right to skip any payments during financially difficult times. The lender expects each payment to be made in a timely fashion. If you begin skipping payments, the lender has the right to foreclose on your home and sell it at whatever price it can procure in order to recover its money. Your extra mortgage payments have only afforded your lender the luxury of selling your house for a cheaper price to get all its money back. The lender appreciates that you were kind enough to build up the extra equity in your home.

Let me offer a better solution. If you decide to pay your house off early, make an extra principal payment each month, but make these payments to a liquid investment account, such as a mutual fund, not to the mortgage company. Continue making these additional payments to your investment account until the balance in this account equals the balance of your mortgage. Then pay off the mortgage in its entirety.

By abolishing your home loan in this manner, you will have liquid funds with which to make house payments for an extended period of time before the loan is fully paid, if that becomes necessary. If you instead pay the mortgage down gradually, the extra money will be illiquid and unavailable for making monthly payments during an emergency. In the above example, had you kept the extra $30,000 liquid, you would not have lost your home during your period of unemployment.

Another advantage of this technique is that it allows you to earn stock market returns on your money instead of merely saving mortgage interest expenses. Assuming that the stock market continues earning historical rates of return, which are substantially higher than mortgage rates, this would allow you to liquidate your mortgage even faster. The obvious assumption behind the successful use of this technique, of course, is that you do not dip into your accumulated funds for anything other than an emergency.

There is nothing wrong with paying your mortgage off early. Just do it in such a way that increases *your* security, not the *lender's* security.

## CHAPTER 7

STEWARDSHIP—GOD'S PLAN FOR PROMOTION

PARABLE OF THE TALENTS

In Matthew 25:14–29, Jesus gives us the parable of the talents. Within this parable are some of the most important biblical principles regarding prosperity and abundance in the entire Bible. These principles cover not only the wise management of our assets but they also give insight into how to increase our income, find favor with others, and achieve our total financial potential!

Matthew 25:14–29

14 "For it is just like a man about to go on a journey, who called his own slaves, and entrusted his possessions to them.

15 "And to one he gave five talents, to another, two, and to another, one, each according to his own ability; and he went on his journey.

16 "Immediately the one who had received the five talents went and traded with them, and gained five more talents.

17 "In the same manner the one who had received the two talents gained two more.

18 "But he who received the one talent went away and dug in the ground, and hid his master's money.

19 "Now after a long time the master of those slaves came and settled accounts with them.

20 "And the one who had received the five talents came up and brought five more talents, saying, 'Master, you entrusted five talents to me; see, I have gained five more talents.'

21 "His master said to him, 'Well done, good and faithful slave; you were faithful with a few things, I will put you in charge of many things, enter into the joy of your master.'

22 "The one also who had received the two talents came up and said, 'Master, you entrusted to me two talents; see, I have gained two more talents.'

23 "His master said to him, 'Well done, good and faithful slave, you were faithful with a few things, I will put you in charge of many things; enter into the joy of your master.'

24 "And the one also who had received the one talent came up and said, 'Master, I knew you to be a hard man, reaping where you did not sow, and gathering where you scattered no seed.

25 " 'And I was afraid, and went away and hid your talent in the ground; see, you have what is yours.'

26 "But his master answered and said to him, 'You wicked, lazy slave, you knew that I reap where I did not sow, and gather where I scattered no seed.

27 " 'Then you ought to have put my money in the bank, and on my arrival I would have received my money back with interest.

28 " 'Therefore take away the talent from him, and give it to the one who has the ten talents.'

29 "For to everyone who has shall more be given, and he shall have an abundance; but from the one who does not have, even what he does have shall be taken away."

WHAT STEWARDSHIP MEANS

Let's take a look at this parable verse by verse to ferret out the principles that Jesus is teaching us.

14a *"For it is just like a man about to go on a journey, who called his own slaves, . . ."* The word "like" indicates that the story Jesus is about to tell is analogous to a real life situation. Jesus was approaching the time that He would be crucified, raised from the dead, and ascend into heaven. Thus, in the symbolism of this parable, He was the man about to go on a journey. Those of us who have made a commitment to obey Him and His Word are His bondservants, or slaves.

14b *". . . and entrusted his possessions to them."* Herein we find the cornerstone principle of stewardship: *God owns everything!* We are merely stewards, or managers, of God's possessions. So many times we look at what we have and think that it belongs to us. The reality is that *everything we have belongs to God.* This is a critical concept to understand.

If something belongs to us, then we have the right to use it properly or to misuse it. We have the right to treat it in any manner that we please. It's *ours.* We can do with it what we want and nobody has the right to tell us otherwise.

If something belongs to another person, however, then we have no right to misuse it. The owner has the right to dictate how it will be treated. Furthermore, if we are employed by that person to use his or her resources to do a job, then we have an obligation to treat the person's possessions with respect. We must see to it that they are used to accomplish the job we have been hired to perform. Properly carrying out our job will further the good of our employer.

In our modern culture, we don't really have a good understanding of what stewardship means. Probably the best picture of stewardship the Bible gives us is found in the story of Joseph. As you remember, Joseph was sold by his brothers to Midianite traders who carried him to Egypt. There he was sold to a man named Potiphar, the captain of Pharaoh's bodyguard. As Joseph was faithful to fulfill the responsibilities given to him, God promoted him in Potiphar's service. He eventually reached the point where Potiphar placed him in charge of his entire household. He directed each of the other slaves in the jobs that they were to perform; he bought and sold for Potiphar; he managed Potiphar's money. Potiphar prospered because of Joseph's wisdom and diligence in handling his master's business. The Bible says that ". . . from the time he made him overseer in his house, and over all that he owned, the Lord blessed the Egyptian's house on account of Joseph; thus the Lord's blessing was upon all that he owned, in the house and in the field. So he left everything he owned in Joseph's charge; . . ." (Genesis 39:5, 6a).

The Egyptian still owned all the assets. Joseph's responsibility was to use Potiphar's assets to run Potiphar's household for Potiphar's good. To be a steward means to be a manager of someone else's assets for their good. I once heard Ron Blue, a respected financial planner in Atlanta, put it this way, "The owner has all the rights. The steward has only responsibilities."

God owns everything that we have. When we gave God our lives, we gave Him all of our possessions as well. Now, we are simply managers of God's possessions. We are to manage His possessions in the way that He wants them managed, for the good of His household. This principle of stewardship applies to more than just money. It applies to everything that has been placed in our charge, including our family, our time, and our ministry. We are but stewards over all of it.

I recently counseled with a couple who were having some serious marriage problems. The wife told me that she was committed to divorcing her husband. Though they had several areas that needed to be addressed, a major problem was how they communicated. They habitually spoke sharply to each other and continually tore one another down with their words. I explained to the husband that God gave him his wife for a purpose and wanted to develop certain qualities in her through their relationship. Apparently, God felt that he was ideally qualified for the job; otherwise, He would have given her to someone else. The husband had a responsibility, a *stewardship,* to help his wife become everything she was capable of being. He had no right to insult her because she didn't belong to him. She belonged to God, and he was misusing God's property. He was abusing his stewardship.

When we understand that everything we possess belongs to God and not to us, then we understand that we don't have the right to handle our possessions however we wish. We have a responsibility to handle them as God instructs. When we begin to act as though we are the owners of our possessions, our attitude is wrong, and we need to change it.

Paul tells us in I Corinthians 4:2 that the primary requirement of a steward is that he be found trustworthy. God is looking for people to whom He can entrust His possessions and know that they will be faithful in their use and management of them. Perhaps we need to look at wealthy Christians no longer as people who *own* many possessions, but rather as people to whom God has *entrusted* many possessions.

DEVELOPING ABILITY

15 *"And to one he gave five talents, to another, two, and to another, one, each according to his own ability; and he went on his journey."*

Many times we talk about the talents in this parable in terms of abilities, like the ability to sing or play the piano. While the principles in this parable may be properly applied to one's abilities, the fact is that Jesus was not referring to abilities in this story. A talent was a measure of money, as a dollar or a deutschemark is a measure of money today. The master in the parable was giving his servants varying levels of money.

When I first read this parable many years ago, it puzzled me that the master did not treat his servants equally. It did not seem fair to me that he gave more money, more material goods, to one servant than to another. If the master in this parable symbolizes the Lord, and he does, then that means God gives more material goods to some of His servants than to others. It appeared to me that the master was playing favorites. Yet, the Bible says that God is not a respecter of persons.

Then one day I heard a teacher explain why the master did what he did, and the verse suddenly made perfect sense to me. The Bible says that he gave to each one *"according to his own ability."* In other words, *the master gave his money to each of his servants based on their level of ability to handle that money in a responsible manner.* He was not playing favorites. He was not even really making choices among the servants. They had made those choices for him based on the level of ability that each of them had taken the time to develop. The master was just making a wise business decision. In any business endeavor, you promote those who are best qualified to do the job, and you give them the most responsibilities. That is all the master was doing. To do otherwise would have been foolish.

Sometimes we don't like to realize this truth, but God gives to His servants different levels of blessings and responsibilities, in various areas, based on the level of ability that *they* have developed in each of those areas. It is true that God *loves* every Christian the same amount. But, frankly, some Christians will make better use of the opportunities God gives them than will other Christians. God will honor the efforts of those who develop more ability in given areas than others, and He will bless them with a greater level of responsibility in those areas.

The good news is this: ability is something that *we* develop. We can take the initiative to increase our various skills and abilities and thereby position ourselves to receive promotion and greater levels of responsibility from God.

Many Christians are praying for abundance and believe that God will answer those prayers by causing them to win the lottery. They expect God to send Ed McMahon to their house during the Super Bowl to tell them they've won the big sweepstakes drawing. I am not saying that God will never send Ed McMahon to your house. However, Ed McMahon is not God's normal channel of prospering His people. Rather, God will generally prosper us through natural channels, such as our job, investments, and business opportunities, areas that require ability for us to do well in them. The greater our ability to exploit opportunities in these areas, the greater will be the rewards we derive from them.

We increase our skills and abilities in several ways, a key one being through furthering our education. Just by reading this book you are increasing your ability to manage money wisely. Furthering our education in a given area will increase our ability in that area. Many people will find that the answer to their prayer for abundance is to go back to school.

Another way that we can increase our ability is through experience. As we are faithful to apply our hands diligently in a given area, we learn from the experience itself, and our skills increase as a result. Sometimes an apprenticeship relationship will be the best avenue to achieve this experience. When I first started in the financial planning profession, I served a one-year apprenticeship with a veteran financial planner in Atlanta. I made no money during that period of time, but I received the education of a lifetime.

WE MUST USE WHAT WE KNOW

16 *"Immediately the one who had received the five talents went and traded with them, and gained five more talents. 17 In the same manner the one who had received the two talents gained two more."*

Each of these individuals applied his ability to the resources he had been given and caused his resources to increase. Applying our ability to our resources is one of the key principles of financial success. God is a God of increase. He created man to experience increase. He commanded Adam and Eve in the Garden of Eden to "be fruitful and multiply." He created everything living to reproduce, placing the seed for reproduction in the fruit itself. God wants us to take whatever resources He has given us and apply our ability to them to cause increase to take place.

What was different about these two stewards? It appears that they both acted in a similar manner, and they both doubled what the master had given to them. Yet, the story insinuates that there was something different about the first servant that distinguished him as having more ability than the second servant, because the master gave him more talents.

After studying this passage thoroughly, the only thing I can see that differentiated the two servants is that it says the first steward went *immediately* and traded with his money. It does not say this about the second steward. This implies the second steward may have required some additional time to prepare himself to take advantage of the opportunity that had been presented to him.

The first servant was already fully prepared for the task when the lord gave him the money, which is probably why he received the most talents. Perhaps the master had seen this steward studying about the financial markets and how they worked. Maybe he had conversed with the merchants and moneylenders to learn about commerce. Possibly the steward had even developed a written plan on how he could double an investment within a reasonable period of time. He had developed the knowledge on how to invest properly—all he needed was the seed capital! The master saw this servant's preparation and understood that he was the most qualified to handle the money.

I believe in the biblical principles of faith. According to Mark 11:24, one principle of faith is to believe that we have received the answer to our prayer before we see the answer with our eyes, i.e., before the answer physically manifests. James tells us that faith without works is dead. True faith will produce actions. In other words, if we really believe something, we will *act* like it is reality.

KEY POINT

I am convinced that one reason God has not blessed more people with financial abundance is because they have no idea what they would do with it if they had it! They have prayed for financial blessing, but they have not begun preparing themselves to receive it. They are waiting to receive it *before* they study how to manage and invest money. Faith does not wait until it sees the answer to prayer before it acts. Faith acts, and then it sees the answer to prayer. If we really believe that God is going to answer our prayers for abundance, then we should act on our faith and begin studying how to manage and invest money now. Then, when the answer to our prayer comes, we will be able to go "immediately" and apply what we know to cause our resources to increase.

RISK TAKING

These two stewards invested in such a way that they doubled their money in a relatively short period of time. They did not do this by putting their money in CD's or bank savings accounts. Just the very wording of this section of the parable implies that they put their principal at risk because it says they *traded* with their money. This implies that they had developed a knowledge of the financial markets as they existed at that time and then used those markets to increase their assets.

Many Christians are afraid to take any risk with their money for fear of losing some of it. They feel that taking any actions that would create the opportunity for a loss to occur would be an irresponsible use of the resources the Lord has given them. Yet, taking a calculated risk is exactly what these two stewards did, for which they were commended by their lord as being good and faithful stewards.

The lazy slave was told that, at the very least, he should have placed his money in the bank and drawn interest on it. This option is presented as the lowest of the options, however, and as one that is appropriate for someone who has developed little or no financial ability. Some people say they don't know anything about the financial markets, and, therefore, bank accounts are fine investments for them. This parable implies that this is an acceptable temporary solution, but that a better plan of action is to develop some knowledge about the financial markets and then utilize them to increase our net worth.

I remember when I first invested in the stock market, right after I graduated from college. I was afraid I would lose money and that God would be very displeased with me as a result. I invested in a stock, and, sure enough, I lost money. I learned something very important, however, from that experience. I learned that, after you have done your homework, the best way to become truly knowledgeable about something is to start doing it, while putting only a little at risk. Make your mistakes, and then learn from them. God is not displeased with us when we make mistakes. I believe that what displeases God is when we don't try something new for fear of making mistakes! The level of risk you take and the amount you place at risk should directly correspond to your level of knowledge. The more expertise you develop in a given area, the more risk you can afford to take.

18 *"But he who received the one talent went away and dug in the ground, and hid his master's money."*

Now we see why this servant received only one talent. As a matter of fact, after seeing what he did, I'm surprised that he even got one talent. First of all, it is obvious that he had not developed any financial ability to speak of, because the lord gave him only one talent. As I said earlier, ability can be developed. Even though this servant had no ability when the master gave him his one talent, he could have done what the second servant did. He should have taken some time to study and learn how to handle his one talent responsibly. But he was too lazy to do that. He did not work to develop any additional ability, nor did he use any of the little ability that he already had. He did not even take his money to the bank to earn interest, but rather he buried his talent because he was too lazy to do anything else. He did not want to change and grow. Rather, he was quite content to just not lose what he had been given. He had no desire to create increase for his master. As a matter of fact, the whole idea of creating increase was a foreign thought to him. God is pleased when we create increase, not when we just prevent loss.

Here is the problem with this steward's thinking: he acted as though the talent belonged to him. The talent did not belong to him; it belonged to his master. Had it been his talent, he would have had the right to bury it in the ground. But it was his master's talent, and he had been entrusted with it by his master to handle it in a responsible manner and create increase with it. His failure to do so is why the master was so upset with him.

THE BLESSINGS OF FAITHFULNESS

19 *"Now after a long time the master of those slaves came and settled accounts with them."*

At some point in time the master returned from his journey (just as Jesus will one day return) and settled accounts with each of the servants. This lets us know that the time will come when we will give an account to God of how we handled what He entrusted to our care.

20 *"And the one who had received the five talents came up and brought five more talents, saying, 'Master, you entrusted five talents to me; see, I have gained five more talents.' 21 His master said to him, 'Well done, good and faithful slave; you were faithful with a few things, I will put you in charge of many things, enter into the joy of your master.' "*

The second steward went on to report that he, too, had doubled what the master had given him. The master's words to him were identical to those spoken to the first slave.

The master commended both servants for being faithful. This gives us an idea of what God considers to be faithfulness. What had they done? They had applied what they knew to the resources they possessed and created increase for their master. In other words, they *acted* on what they knew until they brought a task to completion. Their wise actions brought them financial success. For this the master added to them other blessings and responsibilities many times over what they were originally given.

Increase and abundance came three ways for these slaves. First, they were given certain resources to begin with, based on the level of ability that they had developed. We can help ourselves in this regard simply by increasing our level of ability. Second, they created increase with what they had been given. This alone created a certain level of prosperity and abundance. They now had twice that with which they started. Both of these steps were really up to them. They made the decision to develop ability, and they made the decision to work with and develop what they had been given.

The third step was promotion from God as a reward for their faithfulness. God added blessings and higher levels of responsibility to them. The principle here is that the level of their reward was in direct proportion to their level of responsibility and faithfulness, but multiplied many times over.

The story beginning in Luke 19:12 brings out this point even more clearly. Here, Jesus is telling a parable similar to the parable of the talents. However, in this story, the master gave one mina (another measure of money) to ten different servants. The first servant multiplied his mina tenfold (wouldn't you like to know how he did that!). His reward was to rule over ten cities. The next servant multiplied his mina fivefold. His reward was to rule over five cities. The level of their reward corresponded directly to their level of faithfulness and the level of increase that they created, but was multiplied many times over. It is in this third step that true blessing and prosperity are experienced.

Stated another way, it is simply a fact that some Christians will work harder than other Christians to be more productive with what they have been given by God. God will reward these Christians with greater levels of abundance and responsibility.

All enterprises, including businesses, churches, ministries, and our personal financial affairs, operate according to certain principles of success. Those who operate in those principles the most diligently will experience the highest levels of success.

There's a story about an older farmer who lived in a small town. He was known for being a hard worker, and he had built the most fruitful and productive farm in his area. One day the new pastor at his church paid a surprise visit to the farmer. The pastor commented, "Jake, this sure is a beautiful farm. God has really blessed you." The old farmer responded, "He sure has, preacher. But you should have seen this land when the Lord had it by Himself. It wasn't anything but weeds."

The old farmer had learned a very valuable lesson. God desires to team with us to accomplish His will. Success comes as we work hard and act diligently, and then God blesses what we put our hands to. One wise person said the key to success is to pray as if everything depended on God and work as if everything depended on us. God's blessing is on all Christians. *What makes the difference is what we do with it!*

The faithful stewards were prepared to take advantage of opportunity when it came along. As we are faithful to apply ourselves to the opportunities that God gives us, we learn what we need to know to properly handle the next level of responsibility to which God wants to promote us. It was in working faithfully with a few things that one steward learned what he needed to know in order to be in charge of many things. It was in studying how to turn one mina into ten minas that another steward earned the right to invest that first mina. The lessons he learned from faithfully executing his investment plan gave him the experience he needed to faithfully rule over ten cities. It was in running Potiphar's household that Joseph learned the management principles that qualified him to rule over all of Egypt.

BEING PRODUCTIVE, THE SOURCE OF JOY

Notice also the words of the master to the stewards after he rewarded their faithfulness with greater blessings. He told them to "enter into the joy" of their master. A significant problem among Christians today is a lack of joy, as well as an absence of a sense of personal fulfillment. The servants in this parable entered into joy as a result of experiencing growth and increase in life. *To have true joy involves experiencing growth in life.* I personally believe that many people suffer from depression because they are stagnant and not developing personally.

From the time I was a young boy, I have always been a very ambitious and energetic person. Being goal-oriented and full of visions of what I wanted to accomplish in life, my aggressive attitude helped me achieve many of my goals as I was growing up. When I was fifteen years old, I placed second in the Georgia Teenage Bodybuilding Championships. I was an all-state trumpet player for five consecutive years in junior high and high school. Having started college when I was sixteen, I graduated from the Georgia Institute of Technology with a 4.0 GPA at the age of twenty. I fully expected to climb the corporate ladder and move quickly into management once I began my career.

When I graduated from college, everything changed for me. I found myself in a secure, but dead-end, job at a major corporation. Through a series of incidents and circumstances, I lost all hope of being rapidly promoted and hastily climbing the corporate ladder.

Early in my career at this company, I had the opportunity to meet with the director of accounting. He explained to me that my first promotion would come automatically after two years of working for the company. There was no way to accelerate the timing of that promotion, and I would have to do a very poor job to delay it. My second promotion would come automatically after another two years. Once again, there was no way to accelerate it, and only exceptionally poor performance would slow it down.

After that meeting, I made my mind up that I would work extra hard to see if I could achieve an early promotion. For the next eighteen months I gave that job my best effort, and, sure enough, my department manager requested my promotion six months ahead of schedule. I was elated. Then came the first of what would prove to be several disappointments in my career at that company. His request for my promotion was turned down for one reason: I hadn't worked there for two years. I quickly realized that for the next several years of my career, any extra effort on my part would be of virtually no benefit to me.

I cannot tell you what that realization did to my level of motivation.

Always before I had been able to get ahead and improve my lot in life by working hard and applying myself. Now I was being told that my extra effort would not be rewarded for years to come. It is very difficult to perform at your highest level when you know that it will be several years until your diligence begins to make a difference in your career. I watched people around me sloughing off and not working hard, knowing they would get essentially the same raises I would get and receive promotions at the same time I would receive them. Needless to say, this was very disconcerting.

After a period of years I realized that I had lost my vision and my goals in life. I was depressed and had put on fifteen pounds of excess weight. I tried to cover up my depression with lots of activity, but I couldn't escape that empty feeling in the pit of my stomach that served as a constant reminder to me I was going nowhere. I had no purpose in life and no real reason for waking up in the morning. Today would be just like yesterday, next week would be just like last week, and next year would be just like last year, so why try?

During that period of my life, I experienced depression first hand. Being stagnant in life was the reason for it. Only taking the time to seek God and allowing Him to restore my vision for life lifted me out of my depressed state. Fulfilling that vision necessitated a career change. It required other changes as well, many of them between my ears. I began setting new goals in life, and I saw myself growing and making progress toward those goals. The depression left me. God filled me with hope, and, more important than anything, He gave back to me the ability to dream.

Many times in the Body of Christ we talk about growing spiritually, and we stress the importance of this aspect of our lives. However, we need to begin emphasizing personal growth as well. God wants us not only to

KEY POINT

I am convinced, based on the above parable and my own personal experience, that people must have a sense of purpose in order to experience true godly joy. Not only must they have a sense of purpose, but they must also see themselves moving toward the fulfillment of that purpose for their joy to be complete.

grow as Christians but He also wants us to experience the joy of seeing ourselves grow as people.

GOD IS NOT A HARD MAN

24 *" 'And the one also who had received the one talent came up and said, 'Master, I knew you to be a hard man, reaping where you did not sow, and gathering where you scattered no seed.' "*

This verse reveals one of the lazy steward's biggest problems: he had an incorrect view of the master. This is the same problem many people have with God. They perceive God as a hard person, a mean taskmaster. This is not the view that the Bible gives us of God.

I John 4:8 tells us that "God is love." Hebrews 4, beginning in verse 15, states, "For we do not have a high priest who cannot sympathize with our weaknesses, but one who has been tempted in all things as we are, yet without sin. 16 Let us therefore draw near with confidence to the throne of grace, that we may receive mercy and may find grace to help in time of need." Jesus is not one who cannot sympathize with our weaknesses. Because He walked on the earth and was tempted in the flesh as we are, He is understanding and merciful to us when we fall and make mistakes.

Verse 16 in the passage above refers to God's throne as the throne of grace, not the throne of judgment. For the world, it will one day be the throne of judgment. For Christians, it is the throne of grace. It is where we go when we need help and mercy. Too often we approach God with the attitude that He is looking only at our faults. We must approach God with the understanding that through Jesus we *have been* forgiven for *all* of our sins. Jesus has already paid the price for all of our shortcomings. Any anger that God had toward man was taken out on Jesus at the cross. We can rest securely in the fact that God is a loving Father and that He *loves us.* That is the good news of the gospel.

What does God's mercy mean for us in practical terms? It means that we should not be afraid to take risks and fail! Observe what the Bible says in the following verses:

Psalm 37:23   The steps of a man are established by the Lord; and He delights in His way.

24   When he falls, he shall not be hurled headlong; because the Lord is the One who holds his hand.

Proverbs 24:16   For a righteous man falls seven times, and rises again, but the wicked stumble in time of calamity.

God does not expect the righteous to never stumble. He is not shocked and doesn't fall off His throne when you and I don't perform as well as we should. The Bible tells us that, instead of judging us and scolding us for the mistakes that we make, God is the One who holds our hand when we fall. He helps us to learn from our mistakes, picks us up, dusts off our britches, and tells us to try it again and to keep trying until we get it right. God is a good God!

OVERCOMING THE FEAR OF FAILURE!

25   " 'And I was afraid, and went away and hid your talent in the ground; see, you have what is yours.' "

Here is this steward's second problem. Because he had an incorrect view of his master, he acted in fear instead of with boldness.

KEY POINT

Fear will paralyze us and keep us from acting on what we know!

There are two key fears that keep Christians from acting on the knowledge they have to create, increase, and experience personal growth. The first fear involves being afraid of God, as we have discussed earlier. The second fear is the fear of failure.

Many times when we think of attempting something that we have never done before, the first thought that comes to our mind is "What if I fail?" The fear of failure has held people back from realizing their potential more than anything else of which I am aware. Why are we afraid of failing? Even more than being concerned about God's reaction to our failure, I believe we are concerned about what other people will think. We are afraid of being ridiculed. We are afraid of others chiding us for thinking we are so special that we could do something out of the ordinary.

If we are to ever begin achieving our potential as human beings, and especially as the people of God, we must learn to rise above the opinions of others. We must understand that criticism goes along with trying to break out of the mold and rise above the norm. Accept up front that, if you try to excel at anything, you will be ridiculed, especially if you fail. However, I can tell you from experience that just having the opportunity to succeed is worth that price.

I do not know of one person who has experienced success who has not also had some failures along the way, sometimes major failures. Failure can be painful, but even more important than the failure itself is the way you deal with it. Failure doesn't need to be the end of the line; it can be just the next step on the road to success. Many times you learn from the mistakes you make the very things that you must know to succeed the next time you try.

Starting my investment firm and leaving the security of my corporate job was one of the most difficult things I have ever done. Since I had always been very security conscious, God had to perform a major work in my heart for me to take this step of faith. Actually, for me, it was not a step of faith—it was a huge leap of faith! The biggest battles I fought had nothing to do with the business itself. Instead, they were battles fought in my mind. But I knew God was leading me in my venture, and I knew that God had promised His blessing upon whatever I put my hands to. An unbeliever doesn't have that promise. Only believers have that promise! That should give Christians great confidence when they step out and take risks!

I met with several failures along the way. I almost went out of business twice during the early years. I discovered many personal weaknesses that needed to be dealt with in order to continue moving forward. Aside from the rewards of the business itself, just the personal growth that I experienced by starting my own business was worth the venture. I became a new person over time, and I learned much about the faithfulness of God.

I also learned something else. I learned that I would rather try and fail than never try. Anybody can *not* try. Not trying is nothing special. Not trying takes no faith; it takes no character. It is not that only a small percentage of people are capable of great success. Virtually everybody, certainly every Christian, has the capability to achieve great success in life. It is that only a small percentage of the population ever takes that first step to achieve success. As Winston Churchill, famous British war leader, said, "Great people are, by and large, normal people who just did something that others did not do."

I used to have a fear that haunted me. Until I made the decision to at least give myself an opportunity to achieve something in life better than what I was experiencing, this fear tormented me. The fear was that someday when I was an old man, and it was too late in my life to even attempt achieving my dreams, I would look back over a life of mediocrity and ask myself, "Why didn't I at least try?" I was afraid I would then realize the fears that seemed overwhelming earlier in life were lies, phantoms, not real, and I would regret that I never faced them. When I reach that day of looking back over my life, I want to have the peace in my heart of knowing that I gave life my best shot, that I went after it aggressively and gave it everything I had. To think that I would give that up because of someone else's opinion of me is reprehensible.

Are you afraid that if you step out and try something out of the ordinary you will experience failure? Let me set your mind at ease. You will experience failure! You will probably fail several times at several things. Then you can join the legions who at least stepped up to the plate, even though they struck out. But there is no law that says you only get to bat one time. Only by stepping up to the plate and taking the chance that you will strike out will you ever get on base. Some will make it to second, and a few will even hit a home run. Just having the opportunity to score is worth taking the chance of striking out!

Yes, if you try to rise above the crowd and succeed at anything, you will have failures. But you will also have successes that you would never have otherwise experienced, you will learn things that you would never have otherwise known, and, most important, you will feel good about yourself for trying! Remember, the only people who never fail are those who never try.

THE RESULTS OF LAZINESS

26 *"But his master answered and said to him, 'You wicked, lazy slave, you knew that I reap where I did not sow, and gather where I scattered no seed.*

27 *" 'Then you ought to have put my money in the bank, and on my arrival I would have received my money back with interest.*

28 *" 'Therefore take away the talent from him, and give it to the one who has the ten talents.' "*

This illustrates a principle taught in John 15:2 where Jesus said "Every branch in Me that does not bear fruit, He takes away." I do not believe this verse is saying that God sends people to Hell just because they do not bear fruit. But I do believe that God will remove unfaithful stewards from positions of responsibility and give those responsibilities to others who have proven themselves to be faithful.

29 *"For to everyone who has shall more be given, and he shall have an abundance; but from the one who does not have, even what he does have shall be taken away."*

Verse 29 contains a major success principle. In context, this verse is telling us that those who experience abundance are those who apply what they know to the resources they have in order to create growth. God will not only give possessions and responsibilities to faithful stewards, but He will add to them the blessings and responsibilities of those stewards who were not faithful.

INCREASING YOUR NET WORTH

## CHAPTER 8

WHAT IS ABUNDANCE?

As we begin discussing the systematic accumulation of wealth, we must address the question, "How much wealth is appropriate for my situation?" In other words, at what point does one become greedy?

If I asked a dozen people to define financial abundance, I would likely get a dozen different answers, all of which might be correct. I believe we run into problems when we try to judge others by *our* standard of abundance. In particular, what many try to do is to set the level of financial success others should achieve by their own standard of what is correct. In their opinion, attaining wealth beyond a certain level is worldly. *No matter how hard you try to define it, the notion of financial abundance is subjective.*

Let me illustrate this truth with an example. One popular definition of abundance is "having enough to meet your needs plus some extra for giving to others." But how much is enough to meet your needs? Again, this is very subjective. I *need* a higher level of income than some because I have four children to support, while others may only have two children. My wife and I moved into a larger house after our third child was born because, as a five-person family, we needed more space than we did as a four-person family. Our third child necessitated the purchase of a van, a more expensive vehicle than the car we drove when we had only two children. But it was my wife's and my *choice* to have four children. We didn't *need* four children. In other words, we made certain choices that increased the level of our needs. Does that mean a married couple with only two children deserve a lesser income because they made a choice that resulted in a lower level of needs? That hardly seems fair.

I think we have to realize that since we are only human, and our minds were trained for many years by a fallen nature before we began renewing them to God's word, our standards fall far short of God's standards. It is hard enough to determine God's will for *our* lives. Let's not waste time try-ing to determine what is an "appropriate" level of financial abundance for everyone else.

Since abundance is a subjective matter, it is impossible to define it in concrete terms. What represents wealth to one person may represent lack to another. So, we have to conclude first that abundance is relative, and God deals with each person as a unique individual. Allow God to minister to you what plenty means in your life.

Second, we also must understand that how we view prosperity de-pends on our perspective. How we view things, how we think about things, is shaped by standards we have been taught and by our past experiences. As our perspective changes, so does our standard of affluence. Because of our biases, which we all have, we often try to judge God's will using our viewpoint, not His. What is God's perspective like? In Revelation 21, be-ginning in verse 18, John describes the heavenly Jerusalem by saying, "And the material of the wall was jasper; and the city was pure gold, like clear glass. 19 The foundation stones of the city wall were adorned with every kind of precious stone . . . 21 And the twelve gates were twelve pearls; each one of the gates was a single pearl. And the street of the city was pure gold, like transparent glass."

I believe it is obvious that God has a whole different mind-set than we have when He thinks of abundance. We must remember that God is a **big thinker,** much bigger than we are. It is difficult for us to even begin to con-ceive and judge God's will by our low level of thinking. But we do not have to remain as we are now. As we grow, God will change how we think, not only about money but about life! Remember this: God does not have lim-its; we do. Do not be bound by artificial limits of your own creation. Al-low God to set you free in your thinking and to change your perspective.

HOW MUCH IS TOO MUCH?

So, how high a level of financial abundance does God want us to achieve? I believe the Bible teaches that God will carry a person as far as he or she dares to go, subject to certain conditions. In other words, it is not our level of wealth with which God is concerned, but rather *it is our attitude about our wealth that concerns God.*

The fact is that there are certain temptations that go along with material possessions. Ignoring the reality of these temptations has caused many a Christian to shipwreck in their faith. Because of these temptations, many Christians have decided that the godly thing to do is to shun wealth and, therefore, remove the temptations from their lives.

I disagree with this approach. There are temptations that go along with success in any area of life. Should we, then, run from the temptations that come with success by running from success itself? Nonsense! Rather, we need to understand the nature of the temptations and then abide by God's word to handle them in a godly fashion when they surface. The Bible tells us to not be ignorant of the devil's schemes.

Financial success is no different from success in any other area of life. Temptations abound with the achievement of financial abundance. One such temptation is to place material possessions upon the throne of our lives. But, rather than shun the attainment of abundance, let's endeavor to overcome our flesh and grow in our faith. As we face and overcome these temptations, we not only mature in our faith and character but we also give God a higher level of resources with which to accomplish His will through us.

So, what are some of the guidelines we should follow in determining how much money is too much for us? Following are what I consider to be the most important standards for our lives regarding "how much is too much."

STANDARD #1: HAS OUR SPIRITUAL GROWTH KEPT PACE WITH OUR FINANCIAL GROWTH?

Numerous people come to know the Lord when they are in the pits of life. Their marriages are often on the rocks, their family life is in shambles, and they are broke financially. After becoming Christians, they begin to study God's word and learn His principles for successful living. Their marriages are healed. Their families are put back together. As a result of following God's principles of financial stewardship, they begin to grow and prosper financially.

At that point, a strange phenomenon often occurs. Because they are no longer desperate, they begin to feel that they are capable of controlling their own lives once again and no longer need God. They begin to ignore the God who saved them from the pits of life and, once again, chart their own course. I have seen this happen more times than I care to think about.

Sometimes, as these people begin to prosper financially, they become obsessed with the pursuit of wealth. It is not that these people directly deny God; they simply do not have time for Him anymore. They are working too many hours to spend time studying His word or praying. They are so tired from their endeavors that they stop attending church. From that point forward their life experiences a downward spiral of their own making. On more than one occasion, I have seen couples involved in this scenario end up divorced.

KEY POINT

If our spiritual growth does not keep pace with our financial growth, prosperity can ruin us. Obsession with wealth and the trappings that go with it can replace the hunger for God in our lives. When this occurs, we are setting ourselves up for ultimate failure.

I believe there are three questions that we can ask ourselves to determine if our level of wealth has exceeded our level of maturity:

a. **Have we maintained a giving heart?**—Notice I did not ask if we have continued to give. Sometimes giving can become part of our routine, and we do it without thinking about it. We give out of religious duty, or a sense of guilt or obligation. The question is not, "Have we maintained a certain level of giving?" Rather, the question is, "What is the condition of our heart with regard to the money we do give?" Do we look forward to the opportunity to be a blessing to others? Or do we give only a minimal amount that we feel meets our obligations? Do we give cheerfully, or grudgingly?

Our willingness or unwillingness to give away what we have is a measure of the degree to which our assets have a hold on our hearts (witness the rich young ruler compared to the widow who gave her last two coins). Like a safety valve, giving lets off pressure that could build into selfishness, which in turn could grow into idolatry! It is always easier to give away something that belongs to someone else than it is to give away our own possessions. When we understand that everything we have belongs to God, then we can give with joy!

I Corinthians 13:3 states, "And if I give all my possessions to feed the poor, and if I deliver my body to be burned, but do not have love, it profits me nothing." It is not the gift itself, or even the level of the gift, that pleases God. It is the attitude of the heart with which the gift is given that pleases God.

b. Have we let the pursuit of wealth cause other key areas of our lives to suffer?

I Timothy 6:3–11   If anyone advocates a different doctrine, and does not agree with sound words, those of our Lord Jesus Christ, and with the doctrine conforming to godliness,

4   he is conceited and understands nothing; but he has a morbid interest in controversial questions and disputes about words, out of which arise envy, strife, abusive language, evil suspicions,

5   and constant friction between men of depraved mind and deprived of the truth, who suppose that godliness is a means of gain.

6   But godliness actually is a means of great gain, when accompanied by contentment.

7   For we have brought nothing into the world, so we cannot take anything out of it either.

8   And if we have food and covering, with these we shall be content.

9   But those who want to get rich fall into temptation and a snare and many foolish and harmful desires which plunge men into ruin and destruction.

10   For the love of money is a root of all sorts of evil, and some by longing for it have wandered away from the faith, and pierced themselves with many a pang.

11   But flee from these things, you man of God; and pursue righteousness, godliness, faith, love, perseverance and gentleness.

At the time the apostle Paul penned these words to Timothy, Timothy had been established as the head elder of the church in Ephesus. Some estimates place the size of this church body at 50,000 people. Undoubtedly, Timothy was facing tests and temptations to which he was not accustomed. Paul, therefore, wrote to Timothy to encourage him to remain pure in his ministry and not to be drawn away by concerns about material possessions.

In verse 5, Paul refers to ungodly men who serve God because they think that godliness is a means of gain. Paul may be referring to one of two groups of people here. First, he may be speaking of charlatans who preach the gospel with the intention of taking up big offerings and enriching themselves. He may also be referring to people who serve God, not because they love Him, but because they know that following His principles will result in their prosperity. While living according to God's principles will produce fruit, this is obviously not the proper motivation for serving Him.

Then, in verse 6, Paul states that godliness, i.e., loving God and obeying His word, really is a means of gain, but only when accompanied by *contentment.* Contentment means that we have the joy of the Lord and maintain His lordship over our lives in spite of our circumstances. *Contentment does not imply that we lack desire to improve our lot in life.* It does mean, however, that our *commitment to* and our *love for* Jesus are not dependent on our circumstances.

I have known people who were Christians indeed, but they lacked a zeal in their love for God. They seemed to be consumed with improving their financial situation. A common attitude among these people was that they believed they would serve God more earnestly once they attained a certain stature in life. There was no contentment in their hearts.

When we require more money to have joy and to serve God with our whole hearts, our attitude is wrong. As a matter of fact, if we require anything outside of our relationship with God to have joy and to serve Him wholeheartedly, our attitude is wrong. Many times Christians seek to fill the emptiness in their lives with things that are temporal and unfulfilling. Isaiah puts it this way: "Why do you spend money for what is not bread, and your wages for what does not satisfy? Listen carefully to Me, and eat what is good, and delight yourself in abundance" (Isaiah 55:2).

I remember when, as a teenager, I first experienced the call of God on my life to teach God's word. I watched men standing behind the pulpit in front of large crowds and thought to myself how fulfilling that must be. Even though I was called to teach, God knew that I was too spiritually immature to be placed in front of a group of people. It was not until I realized that only a relationship with Jesus would satisfy me, not speaking in front of large crowds, that God began to open doors for me to minister publicly. Today I can truthfully tell you that as much as I enjoy teaching, I do not need it to be fulfilled. I would be just as happy if I never taught again in front of people, because my contentment is in the Lord.

This is the attitude God is addressing in I Timothy 6:6. When our eyes are solely on Jesus and we are serving God with our whole hearts in our current circumstances, God can trust us with blessings and promotion. *When we are discontent and are looking to material things to fulfill us, we are vulnerable to falling away from the Lord as we obtain a greater level of financial abundance.*

Verse 9 is a passage often used to preach against trying to improve your lot in life. When taken out of context, it sounds as though any desire or attempt to increase your financial position is sinful, and those with such desires will certainly turn away from God at some point. This verse is an excellent example of why it is important to read scripture in the context in which it is written. The next verse clarifies for us that Paul is referring specifically to those people who love money and place getting rich as a higher priority in their lives than serving God. Verse 10 begins with the word "For," tying what is said in the remainder of that verse to what was discussed in verse 9. In other words, "those who want to get rich" in verse 9 are the same people referred to in verse 10 as those who love money. Paul is saying that those who love money and act on their ungodly lust for riches experience harmful desires that eventually lead to their own destruction.

How can we tell if we are guilty of "loving money" and have established an ungodly priority structure in our lives? I believe that if our hunger for God diminishes because of energies spent on making money, then our priorities are wrong. Do not misunderstand me. You may well go through *seasons* in your life where the furtherance of your career does not permit you the time to engage in church and ministry activities to the extent that you would like. Such seasons occur and are natural, but they are also *temporary.* During such times, your hunger for God should not diminish, and your private time with God should not falter. However, if you reach the point where your hunger for God has lessened and your private time with God is suffering, both in terms of quality and quantity, then it is time to reexamine your priorities and determine if they are out of order.

Generally, seasons, as discussed above, are associated with specific projects in our lives that have time frames within which they will be accomplished. These "projects" may include such things as furthering your education or the startup time involved in a new business. If circumstances which are throwing your life out of balance seem to have no end in sight, what was intended to be a *season* may have become a *lifestyle.* If that has occurred, you must determine if the new lifestyle reflects your priorities. If not, a change in circumstances may be appropriate.

In verse 11, Paul concludes this particular discourse by admonishing Timothy to flee wrong attitudes and the love of money and to continue pursuing the things of God as the highest priority in his life.

c. Have we maintained a pure heart toward God?

Proverbs 30:7 Two things I asked of Thee, Do not refuse me before I die:

8   Keep deception and lies far from me, Give me neither poverty nor riches;

9   Lest I be full and deny Thee and say, "Who is the Lord?" Or lest I be in want and steal, And profane the name of my God.

Reading this passage of scripture used to bother me until I understood what the writer was saying. It bothered me, not because it said something that I did not like, but because it appeared to contradict other scriptures. Once I understood the message the writer was trying to convey, however, I saw that there was no such contradiction.

The writer makes two requests from God in this passage. The first request is that God keeps deception and lies from him. The second request is that God gives him neither *poverty* nor *riches.*

It was in this second request that I felt there was a possible inconsistency with other scriptures. One of the things that God did for several individuals in the Bible, once they committed their lives to Him, was to make them rich. Examples include such renowned men of faith as Abraham and King David. This writer requests specifically, however, that God not give him riches. This troubled me until I read on and saw how the writer defined riches. What he actually requests is that he never obtains so much wealth that it causes him to deny God.

The writer is acknowledging that there is a level of wealth in each of our lives that is beyond our ability to handle in a responsible manner, a level that would cause us to believe that we are self-sufficient and to deny God. He prays never to attain to this level of wealth.

Now, let me ask you a question. Is this level of abundance that would cause one to deny God the same for every individual? Of course not. As I said earlier, we run into real problems when we judge others by our standards. One size does not fit all.

A friend named Ron was telling me once of an acquaintance of his who had a very high annual income, well into six digits. This friend had purchased a $40,000 car with accompanying monthly payments of $800. Ron commented on how worldly his friend was. He said that his friend should have bought a smaller car that had only $400 payments and then given the other $400 per month to charity.

My comment to Ron was that his friend's payments were smaller as a percentage of total income than most people's car payments. In actuality, his "worldly" friend was acting in a more fiscally responsible manner than most people, probably including Ron. My point is that we can know within ourselves if we have achieved a level of material prosperity that has caused us to deny God. I don't think we can determine what this level of wealth is for others, though.

Not only will this level of wealth that causes one to deny God differ between individuals, but also it will increase for you as you mature spiritually. I know that I can responsibly handle a much higher level of finances today than when I first was born again. Ten years from now I will have matured even more spiritually, and I will then be able to faithfully manage even greater levels of financial abundance than I am capable of handling today.

> **KEY POINT**
>
> **The more we mature spiritually, the more wealth we can handle in a responsible and godly manner.**

CAN THE WEALTHY MAINTAIN A PURE HEART?

Is it possible to be affluent, then, and still maintain a proper attitude toward money and God? The answer is unequivocally yes. But nobody said it would be easy.

In Matthew 6, Jesus tells us that where our treasure is, there will our heart be also. He then tells us to lay up for ourselves treasures in heaven instead of spending all of our energies storing up riches here on earth. How can a wealthy person do this? Note the following passage of scripture in I Timothy 6:

17 Instruct those who are rich in this present world not to be conceited or to fix their hope on the uncertainty of riches, but on God, who richly supplies us with all things to enjoy.

18 Instruct them to do good, to be rich in good works, to be generous and ready to share,

19 storing up for themselves the treasure of a good foundation for the future, so that they may take hold of that which is life indeed.

In these verses, Paul tells Timothy to instruct wealthy people to be generous and to use their wealth to accomplish God's works. He says that by so doing, they will be laying up for themselves treasures in heaven. This shows that it is possible to be rich on earth and, yet, have a right heart toward God and a godly attitude toward money.

Matthew 6:33, a verse with which most of us are familiar, says it best: "But seek first the kingdom of God and His righteousness, and all these things shall be added unto you." In this verse we find an interesting dichotomy. God wants to bless us with material possessions. But more than that, He wants us to seek first His kingdom, for this is the way of ultimate success and personal fulfillment. Only when God's kingdom is our first priority can He trust us with material blessings.

How can we tell if money has too high a priority in our lives? The key is: what dominates our thought life? Money, or God? Understand that a love for money is not the sole domain of the rich. Many poor people lust after money as well. The problem is not dependent on how much wealth one actually possesses. Indeed, financial difficulties are often the source of an unnatural focus on one's financial affairs. It is difficult to concentrate on other activities when you are behind on your bills and struggling to make regular debt payments.

While developing a financial plan will require a certain amount of effort and focus in the short-term, one of the major long-term benefits of such a plan is to alleviate your mind of financial concerns. When you have a strategy in place to fix your money problems, your mind is free to focus on other areas, increasing your enjoyment of life and productivity as a person.

STANDARD #2: GOD WANTS US TO HAVE ENOUGH WEALTH TO FULFILL THE DREAMS HE HAS GIVEN US.

Psalm 37:4 states, "Delight yourself in the Lord; and He will give you the desires of your heart." As you mature spiritually and learn to find delight in God and His will for your life, God will give you dreams and desires. You will discover that these desires are part of His will for your life. God is a big thinker, and He wants His people to be big dreamers, so do not be surprised if the dreams God places in your heart are bigger than you think you can accomplish. They are! You will have to have God working with you to achieve these dreams. However, nothing gets accomplished unless somebody first has the vision for it.

Joseph had a dream given to him by God. It was a prophetic dream, through which God told him that one day he would be a ruler. Without a dream there is no purpose in life. A dream, an understanding of where God is bringing you, is key to enduring times of testing. If you have a dream, you know that the ultimate outcome of trying circumstances will be one of victory.

Christians should be bigger dreamers than anyone else in the world! God is the Creator of the universe. He is the One who holds the oceans in the palm of His hand and who knows the end from the beginning. The Holy Spirit is the very life of God. When His life comes inside a person, it should so energize that person and fill him with hope that he can hardly contain it! As you yield your life to God, He will place dreams on the inside of you. As you grow in your relationship with God, the dreams will get bigger. Understand that many of these visions will take a certain level of finances to achieve. God may use others to underwrite some of these, but some you will likely finance. God wants to bless you with the level of finances required to fulfill these dreams!

STANDARD #3: GOD WILL BLESS US FINANCIALLY TO THE EXTENT WE ARE WILLING TO PAY THE PRICE.

Some Christians have a problem with this statement. They think it is sinful to even talk of paying a price to achieve financial success. The fact is *a price must be paid to achieve success in any area of life.* Success does not come cheaply. Parents pay a price to raise godly children. Pastors pay a price to raise a solid church of strong believers who are impacting their community. The astronauts paid a price to walk on the moon. Jesus Himself paid a heavy price to save us. Yet, somehow, many Christians think that financial victory will come without a price.

We must understand that finances are only one area in which God desires that we thrive. The same principles that result in financial success apply to other areas of life as well. It is no more worldly to apply God's principles and succeed in the area of finances than it is to do so in any other area.

The tenth chapter of Proverbs, verse 4, states: "Poor is he who works with a negligent hand, but the hand of the diligent makes rich." *The level of financial blessing we walk in is directly related to our level of diligence.* Many times Christians fail at a task because of a lack of diligence and then blame their failure on God or the devil. "God apparently had other plans for me" and "The devil fouled up my plans" are statements we often hear when someone has not pushed a project through to completion. Don't get me wrong. I do believe that the devil will resist us anytime we step out to achieve something. In fact, he will resist *all* of our efforts to succeed at anything worthwhile. There are also times when we take a step in the wrong direction, and God creates circumstances that take us on another path. But this path will still lead to success. However, in the majority of cases, we either succeed or fail because we are diligent about doing the right things or we are not. We must learn to accept responsibility for our actions and the results they bring.

When I first began my financial planning practice, I worked between sixty-five and seventy hours a week. I kept this schedule for more than five years. During the first year, I worked in an apprenticeship program with a Certified Financial Planner practitioner while maintaining my full-time position as a financial analyst at a Fortune 500 company. I awoke every day at 4 A.M. and studied an hour and a half for my Certified Financial Planner exams. I would then exercise for about a half-hour, shower, dress, and leave for my full-time job. In the late afternoon I would leave this job and drive over to the financial planner's office, grabbing a hamburger and a Coke at McDonald's on the way. Many nights I would work there until 9 P.M. or later and then go home, only to do it again the next day.

After my year's apprenticeship was over, I started my own firm, Kays Financial Advisory Corporation. My schedule remained the same, except at night I would go to my own office instead of the other financial planner's office. Two and a half years passed before I was able to leave my position as a financial analyst and work full-time in my own business. However, God had given me a dream, and it burned inside me, compelling me to pay the price I was paying to achieve it. Once I was able to dedicate myself to financial planning on a full-time basis, the composition of my activities changed, but sixty-five- to seventy-hour weeks were still the norm for another two and a half years.

Was it worth the price I paid to start my own firm and become a financial adviser? Absolutely! Could I have succeeded with a lesser effort? Realistically, I don't think so. Many times I was tempted to quit and say that I had missed God's will in choosing this new career path. Had my wife not been as patient and understanding as she was during those years, I never would have made it. But *God's blessing* upon *my efforts* proved to be a winning combination.

Any endeavor at which you desire to succeed will require that a price be paid. Normally, God's blessings do not come in the form of a faith check in the mail. They do not come from sources unknown. Most often God's blessings will come, as Deuteronomy 28 tells us, by God blessing *what we put our hands to*. God will give us a business idea, an invention, a new way of doing something, or some other creative idea. Maybe God will show us a new service that would be a blessing to many people. Perhaps He will show us how to do something faster, easier, or more efficiently than it is currently being done. Maybe our current level of income is sufficient, and we just need to be more diligent to properly utilize the resources we already have. In whatever form it comes, financial abundance is usually a result of God blessing our faithful and diligent efforts. Our level of faithfulness and diligence will then determine the level of success we experience.

One word of caution: as much as I believe in hard work to achieve our goals, it is important to understand the potential to carry this concept too far. In our efforts to pursue our dreams, it is easy to lose touch with the balance God wants us to have in our lives. A person who achieves financial success at the expense of his family or health has paid a price that God never intended for him to pay. How can we determine if we have become out of balance in seeking success?

First, I cannot overemphasize the importance of being in agreement with your spouse concerning your goals and the cost of achieving them. When I decided I wanted to pursue financial planning as a career, my wife and I had an open and frank discussion of what would be involved. We prayed together and counted the cost as best we could. As much as I wanted to go after this new endeavor, I would not have pursued the career change without her full assent. *Determine together if the cost is reasonable in light of the likely reward.*

One factor in our decision for me to change careers when I did was that we had no children at the time. It made sense to make such a move before we started our family so that I could be home more after we had children.

Second, establish accountability with another Christian whom you respect. Allow him or her to help you maintain your sense of objectivity. Sometimes when you are very focused on an activity or goal, your perspective can become warped and it is easy to lose sight of what is really important in your life. The point of view of an objective outsider can often help you keep your priorities straight. Remain open to that person's counsel.

Also pay attention to your health. Physical signs of stress and strain can often serve as a warning that we are pushing too hard. Success is great, but only if we are physically able to enjoy its benefits.

There are several areas of our lives where diligence is required. Three of the main areas that affect us financially are:

1. OUR JOBS—Whether we are a business owner or an employee, our jobs are most often the primary vehicle that God uses to bless us financially. Even though we know that God's blessing resides upon us in our career endeavors, we need to work at our jobs as though our promotion depended on our efforts alone. We must be the best employees we are capable of being. It sounds old-fashioned, but hard work pays substantial dividends. Sometimes, this may involve working extra hours. Remember that there is no biblical commandment stating, "Thou shalt only work forty hours per week and no more."

2. OUR EDUCATION—Along with working hard at our jobs, we must be as knowledgeable and well prepared to do our jobs as possible. Many people can advance their careers and increase their income by furthering their education.

I have a friend named Chris for whom I have a lot of respect. Chris was heavily involved in drugs as a teenager before coming to know the Lord. Once he became a Christian, he worked various odd jobs, but none were of the type at which he could build a promising career. Unless Chris made some dramatic changes, he realized he was destined to work low-paying jobs for the rest of his life. His wife would always have to work, and they would be limited financially to having one or, at the most, two children.

Chris made a decision that he wanted more out of life than what he was experiencing. The only way he could see changing his circumstances was to attend college and obtain a degree. He and his wife told us that doing so would require a five-year commitment and asked our opinion of their decision. We remarked that five years would come and go rather quickly. They would be much better off with Chris's having a college education at the end of that time period, with a world of opportunities open to him, than they would be remaining in their current circumstances.

There was a price to be paid if Chris and his wife were to ever experience a higher level of financial blessing. Together, they made the decision that Chris should go for it. He worked full-time and went to school part-time for most of the five years. I have done this myself and can tell you from experience what an arduous task it is. I respect anyone who does it. But at the end of five years, Chris had his degree in hand.

Upon graduation, Chris landed a job with a major textile corporation. Because he has been diligent in applying himself, first to his education, and now to his job, he has been promoted three times within his first two years of employment. Chris has a brilliant future with unlimited potential ahead of him.

God promises to bless what we put our hands to. However, *we* have to make the decision to put our hands to something. We also decide how diligently we will apply ourselves to the tasks at hand. Furthering our education can be invaluable in increasing our worth in the marketplace. I am not saying that a college education is the only way to succeed financially, but for some people it is a necessity. Others own their own business or have other special circumstances that render a degree unnecessary. Chris was not in such a situation.

Once you are working in the field you desire, your educational process does not stop. A multitude of options are available from that point forward for continuing your education. Some may find it profitable to pursue advanced degrees. Others may want to pursue some of the many continuing education courses offered in almost every field imaginable.

My wife and I home-school our children. As you might guess, I am a big believer in self-education. Especially with recent advancements in computer technology, resources for home- and self-education are greater than ever before. This avenue of education may be the most appropriate for many.

However you decide to further your education and expertise, do whatever is necessary to stay on the cutting edge of your field.

3. OUR ADHERENCE TO GOD'S PRIORITIES AND PRINCIPLES—Spiritual growth and maturity do not come automatically. The greatest failure of most Christians is the failure to grow spiritually once they have committed their lives to Christ. Just as growth in any other area of life requires discipline and diligence, so does spiritual growth.

We face many situations in life where we must make a decision as to whether we will obey God's word or compromise. We must consistently choose God's way if we are to mature. There is no other path to learning God's principles than to study His word regularly.

In the book of Joshua, chapter 1, God told Joshua that he was to meditate on His words day and night and to never let them depart from his mouth. Meditating day and night implies a level of commitment somewhat greater than listening to a sermon once a week! Why was Joshua to commit himself to studying God's word like this? God went on to say that this would cause him to have good success wherever he went.

Fortunately, today, we have many tools available to help us study God's word and keep it at the forefront of our minds. I personally believe that cassette tapes were invented for Christians. You can listen to them while driving in your car, turning your automobile into a university on wheels. The average adult spends 300 to 400 hours per year driving in his or her car. Listening to teaching tapes during this time is the equivalent of attending six to eight college courses per year. In addition to Bible teaching tapes, educational tapes and courses are available on almost any topic you can imagine. Motivational tapes can serve as a source of inspiration as well as education.

Bible software can make Bible study more efficient and productive. There is a multitude of powerful and inexpensive Bible software programs available on the market. In addition, concordances, reference books, and commentaries are all available on disk to make one's Bible study more meaningful. There is no excuse for not studying God's word on a regular basis and learning His principles of success.

## CHAPTER 9

SAVING FOR EDUCATION AND RETIREMENT

Once you have established a budget, two of the key decisions you must make involve how much money you will save from each paycheck for retirement and your children's education.

Saving and budgeting are somewhat of a chicken and egg situation: you can't complete a budget until you know how much you want to save, but you do not know what is a reasonable savings figure until you have prepared a budget and determined how much discretionary income you have. To solve this dilemma, I recommend that you prepare a preliminary budget first, just to get an idea of what your cash flow situation looks like. Then compute your savings requirements. You may need to adjust your budget to accommodate your newly discovered savings needs, or you may have to adjust your savings goals because of budget constraints.

THE IMPACT OF INFLATION

One thing you must keep in mind when computing your savings requirements for retirement and your children's education is the impact that inflation will have on your plans. Because of inflation, things will cost more in the future than they do today. Education expenses, in particular, have risen rapidly for several years. If the school of choice for your children costs $5,000/year presently, then that cost will rise by some inflation factor each year until your children graduate. This must be factored into your needs computations.

In figuring the impact of inflation, Table 9-1 will be very helpful to us. This chart shows what $1.00 invested today would be worth over various

HOW MUCH DO YOU NEED TO SAVE?

$1.00 INITIAL INVESTMENT
COMPOUNDED ANNUAL RATE OF RETURN

TABLE 9-1

# YEARS	4%	5%	6%	7%	8%	9%	10%	11%	12%	13%	14%	15%
1	1.04	1.05	1.06	1.07	1.08	1.09	1.10	1.11	1.12	1.13	1.14	1.15
2	1.08	1.10	1.12	1.14	1.17	1.19	1.21	1.23	1.25	1.28	1.30	1.32
3	1.12	1.16	1.19	1.23	1.26	1.30	1.33	1.37	1.40	1.44	1.48	1.52
4	1.17	1.22	1.26	1.31	1.36	1.41	1.46	1.52	1.57	1.63	1.69	1.75
5	1.22	1.28	1.34	1.40	1.47	1.54	1.61	1.69	1.76	1.84	1.93	2.01
6	1.27	1.34	1.42	1.50	1.59	1.68	1.77	1.87	1.97	2.08	2.19	2.31
7	1.32	1.41	1.50	1.61	1.71	1.83	1.95	2.08	2.21	2.35	2.50	2.66
8	1.37	1.48	1.59	1.72	1.85	1.99	2.14	2.30	2.48	2.66	2.85	3.06
9	1.42	1.55	1.69	1.84	2.00	2.17	2.36	2.56	2.77	3.00	3.25	3.52
10	1.48	1.63	1.79	1.97	2.16	2.37	2.59	2.84	3.11	3.39	3.71	4.05
11	1.54	1.71	1.90	2.10	2.33	2.58	2.85	3.15	3.48	3.84	4.23	4.65
12	1.60	1.80	2.01	2.25	2.52	2.81	3.14	3.50	3.90	4.33	4.82	5.35
13	1.67	1.89	2.13	2.41	2.72	3.07	3.45	3.88	4.36	4.90	5.49	6.15
14	1.73	1.98	2.26	2.58	2.94	3.34	3.80	4.31	4.89	5.53	6.26	7.08
15	1.80	2.08	2.40	2.76	3.17	3.64	4.18	4.78	5.47	6.25	7.14	8.14
16	1.87	2.18	2.54	2.95	3.43	3.97	4.59	5.31	6.13	7.07	8.14	9.36
17	1.95	2.29	2.69	3.16	3.70	4.33	5.05	5.90	6.87	7.99	9.28	10.76
18	2.03	2.41	2.85	3.38	4.00	4.72	5.56	6.54	7.69	9.02	10.58	12.38
19	2.11	2.53	3.03	3.62	4.32	5.14	6.12	7.26	8.61	10.20	12.06	14.23
20	2.19	2.65	3.21	3.87	4.66	5.60	6.73	8.06	9.65	11.52	13.74	16.37
21	2.28	2.79	3.40	4.14	5.03	6.11	7.40	8.95	10.80	13.02	15.67	18.82
22	2.37	2.93	3.60	4.43	5.44	6.66	8.14	9.93	12.10	14.71	17.86	21.64
23	2.46	3.07	3.82	4.74	5.87	7.26	8.95	11.03	13.55	16.63	20.36	24.89

# YEARS	4%	5%	6%	7%	8%	9%	10%	11%	12%	13%	14%	15%
24	2.56	3.23	4.05	5.07	6.34	7.91	9.85	12.24	15.18	18.79	23.21	28.63
25	2.67	3.39	4.29	5.43	6.85	8.62	10.83	13.59	17.00	21.23	26.46	32.92
26	2.77	3.56	4.55	5.81	7.40	9.40	11.92	15.08	19.04	23.99	30.17	37.86
27	2.88	3.73	4.82	6.21	7.99	10.25	13.11	16.74	21.32	27.11	34.39	43.54
28	3.00	3.92	5.11	6.65	8.63	11.17	14.42	18.58	23.88	30.63	39.20	50.07
29	3.12	4.12	5.42	7.11	9.32	12.17	15.86	20.62	26.75	34.62	44.69	57.58
30	3.24	4.32	5.74	7.61	10.06	13.27	17.45	22.89	29.96	39.12	50.95	66.21
31	3.37	4.54	6.09	8.15	10.87	14.46	19.19	25.41	33.56	44.20	58.08	76.14
32	3.51	4.76	6.45	8.72	11.74	15.76	21.11	28.21	37.58	49.95	66.21	87.57
33	3.65	5.00	6.84	9.33	12.68	17.18	23.23	31.31	42.09	56.44	75.48	100.70
34	3.79	5.25	7.25	9.98	13.69	18.73	25.55	34.75	47.14	63.78	86.05	115.80
35	3.95	5.52	7.69	10.68	14.79	20.41	28.10	38.57	52.80	72.07	98.10	133.18
36	4.10	5.79	8.15	11.42	15.97	22.25	30.91	42.82	59.14	81.44	111.83	153.15
37	4.27	6.08	8.64	12.22	17.25	24.25	34.00	47.53	66.23	92.02	127.49	176.12
38	4.44	6.39	9.15	13.08	18.63	26.44	37.40	52.76	74.18	103.99	145.34	202.54
39	4.62	6.70	9.70	13.99	20.12	28.82	41.14	58.56	83.08	117.51	165.69	232.92
40	4.80	7.04	10.29	14.97	21.72	31.41	45.26	65.00	93.05	132.78	188.88	267.86

This chart shows what a $1.00 investment would grow to over various periods of time at various rates of interest.

periods of time at numerous rates of return. This same concept can be used to determine the impact of inflation as well. For example, the table shows us that $1.00 invested at a 10 percent rate of return will be worth $2.59 in ten years. Likewise, an item that costs $1.00 today will cost $2.59 in ten years if inflation averages 10 percent per year.

EDUCATION NEEDS ANALYSIS

Let's again turn to Tom and Mary Sue's situation to help us learn how to compute the level of savings required for our children's education.

Tom and Mary Sue have two sons, ages two and five. Let's assume that each child goes to college for four years, beginning at age eighteen. That means they have thirteen years left to save for their oldest boy's (Thomas's) education, and sixteen years to save for their youngest child's (Billy's) education. In their goals, they stated that they wanted to be able to provide $5,000 per year for four years for each child's college expenses.

First, let's figure out how much a college education will cost for Thomas (the entire analysis is presented in Exhibit 9-1). We must make some assumptions to do so, which will undoubtedly need to be adjusted as time goes by. An imperfect savings plan, however, is better than no savings plan. To compute projected education expenses for Thomas, let's assume the following parameters apply:

EXHIBIT 9-1

CHILD'S NAME: THOMAS

EDUCATION NEEDS ANALYSIS WORKSHEET

1. Years until college:	13	
2. Annual expenses (today's dollars):	$ 5,000	
3. Anticipated inflation rate:	7	%
4. Inflation multiplication factor (Table 9-1):	2.41	
5. Annual education expense (#2 x #4):	$ 12,050	
6. Total savings required (#5 x 4):	$ 48,200	
7. Anticipated annual investment return:	12	%
8. Investment return factor (Table 9-2):	31.39	
9. Annual savings required (#6 ÷ #8):	$ 1,535	
10. Monthly savings required (#9 ÷ 12):	$ 128	

Child: Thomas

Years until college: 13

Annual expense in today's dollars: $5,000

Anticipated inflation rate: 7 percent.

Table 9-1 tells us an item that costs $1.00 today will cost $2.41 in thirteen years at an average inflation rate of 7 percent. Multiplying today's annual education expenses of $5,000 by a factor of 2.41 reveals that Tom and Mary Sue must plan for Thomas's first-year education costs to be $12,050. Multiplying that first year's cost times four discloses that Tom and Mary Sue need to save $48,200 over a thirteen-year period in order to pay for Thomas's education expenses.

What about Billy's education? His situation appears as follows (the entire analysis is presented in Exhibit 9-2):

Child: Billy

Years until college: 16

Annual expense in today's dollars: $5,000

Anticipated inflation rate: 7 percent

EXHIBIT 9-2

EDUCATION NEEDS ANALYSIS WORKSHEET

CHILD'S NAME: BILLY

1. Years until college:	16
2. Annual expenses (today's dollars):	$ 5,000
3. Anticipated inflation rate:	7 %
4. Inflation multiplication factor (Table 9-1):	2.95
5. Annual education expense (#2 x #4):	$ 14,750
6. Total savings required (#5 x 4):	$ 59,000
7. Anticipated annual investment return:	12 %
8. Investment return factor (Table 9-2):	47.88
9. Annual savings required (#6 ÷ #8):	$ 1,232
10. Monthly savings required (#9 ÷ 12):	$ 103

Table 9-1 tells us that the factor for computing the effect of inflation on a dollar over a sixteen-year period at 7 percent inflation is 2.95. The first year of Billy's education will cost $14,750. Multiplying this figure by four reveals that Tom and Mary Sue must accumulate $59,000 over the next sixteen years to provide for Billy's education costs.

The next question that must be answered concerns how much money must be set aside for each child on an annual basis to reach these goals. Table 9-2 will help us here. This table shows us the value of $1.00 invested on an annual basis for various time periods at numerous rates of return. Based on the above data for the two children, we arrive at the following:

CHILD	THOMAS	BILLY
Savings required:	$48,000	$59,000
Years of saving:	13	16
Anticipated annual investment return:	12%	12%
Investment factor:	31.39	47.88
Annual savings required:	$1,535	$1,232
Total annual savings required:	$2,767	
Total monthly savings required:	$231	

We assume in our example that Tom and Mary Sue, since they have stated they are fairly aggressive investors, achieve a 12 percent annual rate of return on their invested savings. We come up with the investment factor by finding the intersection of the column showing the annual rate of return and the row showing the number of years that are available until the savings goal must be reached. We divide the required savings amount by the investment factor to arrive at the required annual savings. Dividing the required annual savings figure by twelve yields the amount of money that Tom and Mary Sue must set aside each month to meet their educational expense goals.

From looking at Tom and Mary Sue's budget in chapter 4, we immediately realize that they do not have this amount of money available for investing in order to meet their children's educational needs. This confirms their need to liquidate debt in order to free up cash flow for investment purposes.

RETIREMENT/FINANCIAL INDEPENDENCE ANALYSIS

Tom and Mary Sue's other primary long-term savings objective is to accumulate enough money for them to be able to retire at Tom's age fifty-five. They anticipate that at some point they will be able to invest 10 percent of their income for this purpose. Let's see if this will be adequate to meet their objective. Their entire retirement needs analysis is illustrated in Exhibit 9-3.

First of all, we must determine the level of income that Tom and Mary Sue will require during their retirement years in order to maintain their current lifestyle. A rule of thumb is that people will need approximately 60 to 70 percent of their working income to support their lifestyle during their retirement years. Many expenses that are incurred during your working years will either disappear or be reduced during retirement.

For instance, one assumption is that your house is paid off prior to retirement. Retirees generally have lower clothing expenses than when they were working. They normally consume less gasoline since they are not driving to work each day. They are using savings to generate income, so there is no need to save money out of their cash flow. I could go on, but you get the idea. Determine for yourself how much of your working income you will need during retirement to maintain your desired lifestyle.

Tom and Mary Sue have decided to plan for a retirement income goal of 70 percent of their current income. Assuming their house would be paid for at the time, they feel that this amount would allow them to enjoy a desired lifestyle during their retirement years. Since Tom and Mary Sue currently have a combined annual salary of $55,000, they need to plan for a retirement income of $38,500.

We cannot stop there, however. Remember our old nemesis, inflation? The effects of inflation must be accounted for, or the Smiths will come up woefully short in their retirement planning. To compute the impact of inflation on their retirement income needs, we must go back to Table 9-1. Let's assume that inflation averages 4 percent annually for the foreseeable future. Tom and Mary Sue want to retire in twenty years. If we look at the intersection of the column under 4 percent and the row for twenty years,

TABLE 9-2

HOW MUCH DO YOU NEED TO SAVE?

$1.00 ANNUAL INVESTMENT
COMPOUNDED ANNUAL RATE OF RETURN

# YEARS	4%	5%	6%	7%	8%	9%	10%	11%	12%	13%	14%	15%
1	1.04	1.05	1.06	1.07	1.08	1.09	1.10	1.11	1.12	1.13	1.14	1.15
2	2.12	2.15	2.18	2.21	2.25	2.28	2.31	2.34	2.37	2.41	2.44	2.47
3	3.25	3.31	3.37	3.44	3.51	3.57	3.64	3.71	3.78	3.85	3.92	3.99
4	4.42	4.53	4.64	4.75	4.87	4.98	5.11	5.23	5.35	5.48	5.61	5.74
5	5.63	5.80	5.98	6.15	6.34	6.52	6.72	6.91	7.12	7.32	7.54	7.75
6	6.90	7.14	7.39	7.65	7.92	8.20	8.49	8.78	9.09	9.40	9.73	10.07
7	8.21	8.55	8.90	9.26	9.64	10.03	10.44	10.86	11.30	11.76	12.23	12.73
8	9.58	10.03	10.49	10.98	11.49	12.02	12.58	13.16	13.78	14.42	15.09	15.79
9	11.01	11.58	12.18	12.82	13.49	14.19	14.94	15.72	16.55	17.42	18.34	19.30
10	12.49	13.21	13.97	14.78	15.65	16.56	17.53	18.56	19.65	20.81	22.04	23.35
11	14.03	14.92	15.87	16.89	17.98	19.14	20.38	21.71	23.13	24.65	26.27	28.00
12	15.63	16.71	17.88	19.14	20.50	21.95	23.52	25.21	27.03	28.98	31.09	33.35
13	17.29	18.60	20.02	21.55	23.21	25.02	26.97	29.09	31.39	33.88	36.58	39.50
14	19.02	20.58	22.28	24.13	26.15	28.36	30.77	33.41	36.28	39.42	42.84	46.58
15	20.82	22.66	24.67	26.89	29.32	32.00	34.95	38.19	41.75	45.67	49.98	54.72
16	22.70	24.84	27.21	29.84	32.75	35.97	39.54	43.50	47.88	52.74	58.12	64.08
17	24.65	27.13	29.91	33.00	36.45	40.30	44.60	49.40	54.75	60.73	67.39	74.84
18	26.67	29.54	32.76	36.38	40.45	45.02	50.16	55.94	62.44	69.75	77.97	87.21
19	28.78	32.07	35.79	40.00	44.76	50.16	56.27	63.20	71.05	79.95	90.02	101.44
20	30.97	34.72	38.99	43.87	49.42	55.76	63.00	71.27	80.70	91.47	103.77	117.81
21	33.25	37.51	42.39	48.01	54.46	61.87	70.40	80.21	91.50	104.49	119.44	136.63
22	35.62	40.43	46.00	52.44	59.89	68.53	78.54	90.15	103.60	119.20	137.30	158.28
23	38.08	43.50	49.82	57.18	65.76	75.79	87.50	101.17	117.16	135.83	157.66	183.17

# YEARS	4%	5%	6%	7%	8%	9%	10%	11%	12%	13%	14%	15%
24	40.65	46.73	53.86	62.25	72.11	83.70	97.35	113.41	132.33	154.62	180.87	211.79
25	43.31	50.11	58.16	67.68	78.95	92.32	108.18	127.00	149.33	175.85	207.33	244.71
26	46.08	53.67	62.71	73.48	86.35	101.72	120.10	142.08	168.37	199.84	237.50	282.57
27	48.97	57.40	67.53	79.70	94.34	111.97	133.21	158.82	189.70	226.95	271.89	326.10
28	51.97	61.32	72.64	86.35	102.97	123.14	147.63	177.40	213.58	257.58	311.09	376.17
29	55.08	65.44	78.06	93.46	112.28	135.31	163.49	198.02	240.33	292.20	355.79	433.75
30	58.33	69.76	83.80	101.07	122.35	148.58	180.94	220.91	270.29	331.32	406.74	499.96
31	61.70	74.30	89.89	109.22	133.21	163.04	200.14	246.32	303.85	375.52	464.82	576.10
32	65.21	79.06	96.34	117.93	144.95	178.80	221.25	274.53	341.43	425.46	531.04	663.67
33	68.86	84.07	103.18	127.26	157.63	195.98	244.48	305.84	383.52	481.90	606.52	764.37
34	72.65	89.32	110.43	137.24	171.32	214.71	270.02	340.59	430.66	545.68	692.57	880.17
35	76.60	94.84	118.12	147.91	186.10	235.12	298.13	379.16	483.46	617.75	790.67	1013.35
36	80.70	100.63	126.27	159.34	202.07	257.38	329.04	421.98	542.60	699.19	902.51	1166.50
37	84.97	106.71	134.90	171.56	219.32	281.63	363.04	469.51	608.83	791.21	1030.00	1342.62
38	89.41	113.10	144.06	184.64	237.94	308.07	400.45	522.27	683.01	895.20	1175.34	1545.17
39	94.03	119.80	153.76	198.64	258.06	336.88	441.59	580.83	766.09	1012.70	1341.03	1778.09
40	98.83	126.84	164.05	213.61	279.78	368.29	486.85	645.83	859.14	1145.49	1529.91	2045.95

This chart shows what a $1.00 investment each year would grow to over various periods of time at various rates of interest.

EXHIBIT 9-3

RETIREMENT NEEDS
ANALYSIS WORKSHEET

Name: Tom and Mary Sue Smith
Retirement income goal: $ 38,500
Anticipated inflation rate: 4 %
Number years until retirement: 20
Inflation multiplication factor (Table 9-1): 2.19
Inflation adjusted income goal: $ 84,315

REDUCTIONS TO INCOME NEED

1. Projected Social Security retirement benefits	$	0
2. Projected pension benefits	$	0
3. Projected other income	$	0
4. Total reductions to income need	$	0
5. Total inflation adjusted income need	$	84,315
6. Projected savings required (#5 ÷ .06)	$	1,405,250

CURRENT ASSET VALUE PROJECTIONS

1. Total current investable	$	78,705
2. Years until retirement		20
3. Expected average annual rate of return		12%
4. Investment multiplication factor (Table 9-1)		9.65
5. Value at retirement	$	759,503

PROJECTED SHORTFALL

1. Total amount needed at retirement	$	1,405,250
2. Projected value of current assets	$	759,503
3. Shortfall	$	645,747

ANNUAL INVESTMENT REQUIREMENTS

1. Total savings required	$	645,747
2. Years until retirement		20
3. Expected average annual rate of return		12%
4. Investment multiplication factor (Table 9-2)		80.7
5. Required annual investment	$	8,002
6. Required monthly investment	$	667

we find the appropriate factor to use is 2.19. In other words, we must multiply the Smiths desired retirement income by 2.19 to see how much income they will really need twenty years from now. The answer is $84,315. Sound a little intimidating? Now you can see why planning in advance is so important. Remember, when accumulating assets, time is one of your biggest allies!

The next question to be answered is, "How much money must I save by retirement age in order to generate my required income?" There are many different opinions on how this number should be computed. I will show you what makes sense to me.

One of the major concerns of retirees is running out of money before they die. Technology is advancing rapidly and medical discoveries are being made at an ever-increasing pace. As a result, I personally believe that average life spans, which have jumped dramatically during the last century, will continue to increase at an accelerated rate over the next several decades. I feel it is a mistake, especially for younger people, to plan for your investments to generate income only for a time period based on today's life expectancies.

Another major concern is maintaining your purchasing power during your retirement years. If your income does not grow during your retirement years, then inflation will gradually erode your purchasing power, and you will feel poorer each year even though your income has remained stable.

To solve both of these problems, let's do the following. The stock market has generated an average annual rate of return of 11 percent since 1925.[4] Let's assume that you want your assets invested a little more conservatively during your retirement years, and, as a result, your investments return approximately 9 percent annually. Let's then assume that you withdraw 6 percent of this 9 percent each year to provide needed income and that you reinvest the remaining 3 percent. This does two things: it allows your investment balance to grow by an average of 3 percent each year, and your income from your investments will also grow by an average of 3 percent annually. This gives you a hedge against inflation, allowing you to maintain your purchasing power during your retirement years, and it keeps you from outliving your income.

How does all this apply to the Smiths' case? We have determined that they will need an annual income of $84,315 once they reach Tom's desired retirement age of fifty-five. This figure would be offset by any income that is available from other sources, such as Social Security and pensions. However, Tom's employer offers only a defined contribution retirement plan, and, therefore, he cannot depend on pension income being available at retirement. Since Mary Sue works only part-time, it is not likely that she will accrue pension benefits either. Tom and Mary Sue have also determined that they would rather not plan on Social Security being available to help meet their retirement income needs. If it is available, great! They just do not want to be dependent on it in order to reach their objectives.

How much, then, do the Smiths need to accumulate in order to generate their desired level of retirement income? Divide the required annual income, $84,315, by 6 percent, and the result, $1,405,250, is the answer to our question. In other words, in order to meet the Smiths' retirement income objective, they must save $1,405,250 over the next twenty years.

The next question to be answered concerns how much Tom and Mary Sue must save each year over the next twenty years in order to reach this retirement savings objective. We will need both Table 9-1 and Table 9-2 to answer this question. We must first take into account the assets that Tom and Mary Sue have already accumulated. These assets will continue to grow until retirement. From the asset schedule the Smiths completed, we know that they have total investable assets of $78,705. The following analysis shows us what these assets will be worth at Tom's retirement age, based on the assumptions made, and the shortfall that will need to be made up by future investments:

Total investable assets:	**$78,705**
Years until retirement:	**20**
Expected average annual rate of return:	**12%**
Investment factor (Table 9-1):	**9.65**
Value at retirement:	**$759,503**
Amount needed at retirement:	**$1,405,250**
Shortfall:	**$645,747**

So, Tom and Mary Sue's current investable assets will grow to $759,503 by Tom's age fifty-five, leaving a shortfall in assets of $645,747. Note that this assumes the Smiths experience an average 12 percent annual return from their investments. This will require that some of their current assets be repositioned into higher returning investments. If they experience an average annual return of less than 12 percent, then their shortfall will be greater.

How much will Tom and Mary Sue need to invest each year in order to accumulate an additional $645,747 by their desired retirement age? Observe the following:

Savings required:	**$645,747**
Years until retirement:	**20**
Expected average annual rate of return:	**12%**
Investment factor (Table 9-2):	**80.7**
Annual investment amount required:	**$8,002**
Monthly investment amount required:	**$667**

We find then that Tom and Mary Sue will need to invest $667 each month in order to accumulate the additional assets needed to generate their desired level of retirement income.

When we look at the Smiths' cash flow analysis, we realize that they simply do not have enough income to reach all of their savings objectives. As you go through this analysis for your own situation, you may very well come to the same conclusion. How should this be handled? There are several alternatives to choose from at this point.

First, accelerating the liquidation of their debts will help generate additional cash flow needed for investment purposes. While this will benefit

EDUCATION NEEDS
ANALYSIS WORKSHEET

CHILD'S NAME: _____

1. Years until college:	_____
2. Annual expenses (today's dollars):	$ _____
3. Anticipated inflation rate:	_____ %
4. Inflation multiplication factor (Table 9-1):	_____
5. Annual education expense (#2 x #4):	$ _____
6. Total savings required (#5 x 4):	$ _____
7. Anticipated annual investment return:	_____ %
8. Investment return factor (Table 9-2):	_____
9. Annual savings required (#6 ÷ #8):	$ _____
10. Monthly savings required (#9 ÷ 12):	$ _____

RETIREMENT NEEDS ANALYSIS WORKSHEET

Name: _____

Retirement income goal: $ _____

Anticipated inflation rate: __ %

Number years until retirement: ___

Inflation multiplication factor (Table 9-1): ____

Inflation adjusted income goal: $ _____

REDUCTIONS TO INCOME NEED

1. Projected Social Security retirement benefits	$
2. Projected pension benefits	$
3. Projected other income	$
4. Total reductions to income need	$
5. Total inflation adjusted income need	$
6. Projected savings required (#5 ÷ .06)	$

CURRENT ASSET VALUE PROJECTIONS

1. Total current investable	$
2. Years until retirement	
3. Expected average annual rate of return	%
4. Investment multiplication factor (Table 9-1)	
5. Value at retirement	$

PROJECTED SHORTFALL

1. Total amount needed at retirement	$
2. Projected value of current assets	$
3. Shortfall	$

ANNUAL INVESTMENT REQUIREMENTS

1. Total savings required	$
2. Years until retirement	
3. Expected average annual rate of return	%
4. Investment multiplication factor (Table 9-2)	
5. Required annual investment	$
6. Required monthly investment	$

the Smiths down the road, it does not help them now. But it does show that getting out of debt needs to be a high priority for them.

Second, the Smiths could take steps to produce extra income in order to liquidate their debts faster and to then invest more. This can be accomplished in numerous ways, but any of them will require a sacrifice for the Smiths that they may or may not be willing to make.

Third, the Smiths could try to cut their expenses further to generate additional cash flow. Again, this may be possible, but there is a limit to how much a family can reduce their expenses. This, too, may not be a realistic option. As much as I believe in financial discipline, I also believe that life is to be enjoyed. Living on a bare bones budget can be tough on a family, especially if there are better options available.

A fourth option, and probably the appropriate one, is for the Smiths to adjust their goals. Maybe Tom and Mary Sue could consider working until his age sixty instead of retiring at his age fifty-five. Perhaps they can provide only $4,000/year for their children's education instead of $5,000.

Tom and Mary Sue have some important decisions to make at this point in their plan, but now they have the information they need to make those decisions. By taking the time to plan, they have taken control of their finances. They can make deliberate decisions in advance of situations instead of making decisions by default in the midst of problems.

## CHAPTER 10

INVESTMENTS AND THE ACCUMULATION OF WEALTH

"This stock has gone from ten to twelve dollars in the last few days," the broker said excitedly. "We believe it's going to go on up to fifteen within the next couple of weeks. You need to buy it now if you're going to take advantage of this one. This opportunity won't last long."

Unfortunately, the only way you learn some lessons is by making mistakes; no, make that by doing something stupid and then looking back over the experience when you're trying to figure out what happened. I *knew better* than to do what I was about to do. But the broker on the other end of the line, a gentleman I had never met, sounded so convincing. And after all, he did work for a major brokerage firm with a large research department. *And, and, and . . .*

"Okay," I said. "Go ahead and buy a hundred shares of it."

I had just graduated from college and started my first real job. I had some book knowledge about investing, but no real world experience. Even my book knowledge was very limited. Some would say I was wet behind the ears. Actually, I wasn't just wet; *I was soaked.* The broker with whom I was dealing could tell it, too. I was easy prey for his polished sales techniques.

"Great, Mr. Kays. I think you'll be real happy you did this."

Right. Kind of like I was real happy when I was a little boy and jumped in the pool before I knew how to swim.

One of my next conversations with the broker went like this:

"Gee, Mr. Kays. That last investment sure didn't do what we thought it would. But we've got another company here that we like a whole lot more. Let's dump that bad boy and get into this new company. It's just moved from twelve to fifteen dollars, and we think it has the potential to go all the way to twenty-five before it slows down."

After a few episodes like this, during which I lost more money than I made, I realized that this broker's research tools consisted of the newspaper's stock page, a dartboard, and an abundant supply of darts. Even a mule learns to stop certain activities after getting hit in the head enough times. Eventually I dissolved my relationship with this broker and set about to learn from the whole experience.

Are all financial advisers dishonest? Of course not. But you need to be aware of certain investment principles and have a little knowledge of how the real world works to protect yourself from those who are unscrupulous.

As you begin the process of accumulating wealth, the investments you choose will have a lasting impact on the rate at which your money grows and the level of wealth you actually achieve. For years, the investment strategy for most Americans was to save money and place it in either a bank savings account or a certificate of deposit. This strategy is flawed for several reasons. These instruments are fine for short-term savings, but they are not suitable for building your net worth. In this section, I will lay out for you the basic principles of investing your money for the long-term accumulation of wealth.

INFLATION AND TAXES

As you accumulate funds and invest, you will discover that there are two main obstacles that must be overcome: *inflation* and *taxes*. Even at the relatively tame rates we have experienced over the last several years, inflation still erodes your purchasing power over time, reducing the worth of your investments and income.

It is interesting to me how our perspective has changed. In the early 1970s, President Nixon instituted the now famous wage/price freeze. To explain why such a drastic measure was needed, the president gave a speech on television in which he painted a vivid picture of the economic menace inflation had become. Today, when I ask people at seminars to guess what the inflation rate was at the time of Nixon's speech, most respond with a figure somewhere in the double digits. Actually, the inflation rate, as measured by the Consumer Price Index (CPI-U), was 4.4 percent that year.[5] In the early 1970s, that was considered horrendous; today, over twenty-five years later, it is considered tame.

Taxes are the second issue that must be dealt with in the process of accumulating wealth. The government taxes interest earned on bonds, CD's, and other interest-bearing investments, as well as dividends earned on stock investments. The government also taxes the gain you realize when you sell an investment for a price greater than that at which you bought it. Depending on your tax bracket, taxes can reduce the real return on your investments by one-third or more.

The rate of return you achieve after taxes and inflation are considered is called your *real rate of return.* Money you receive after taxes and inflation is what you can take to the store to buy groceries.

The chart in Exhibit 10-1 shows the actual rate of return required to generate a 0 percent real rate of return, a level that would allow the purchasing power of one's assets to remain steady after taxes and inflation. The line across the top of the chart depicts various inflation rates; the column running down the left hand side shows the various federal income tax rates (state income taxes are not considered).

Choose the row showing your income tax bracket and pick the col-

EXHIBIT 10-1 ACTUAL RATE OF RETURN NEEDED
TO ACHIEVE A 0% REAL RATE OF RETURN

INCOME TAX RATE	INFLATION RATE						
	3%	4%	5%	6%	7%	8%	9%
39.6%	5.0	6.6	8.3	9.9	11.6	13.2	14.9
36%	4.7	6.3	7.8	9.4	10.9	12.5	14.1
31%	4.3	5.8	7.2	8.7	10.1	11.6	13.0
28%	4.2	5.6	6.9	8.3	9.7	11.1	12.5
15%	3.5	4.7	5.9	7.1	8.2	9.4	10.6

The number at the intersection of the inflation rate and the tax bracket shows the rate of return an investor must achieve to overcome the dual effect of income taxes and inflation, i.e., to achieve a 0% real return. For example, if inflation averages 5%, an investor in the 36% tax bracket must earn a 7.8% annual rate of return just to break even in real terms.

umn representing what you think inflation will average over the next several years. Even though inflation is cyclical in nature, I recommend using a figure close to 4 percent for long-term planning purposes. The box at the intersection of the row and column you have chosen tells you the rate of return you must obtain on your investments just to break even in real terms.

If we assume, for example, that you are in the 28 percent marginal tax bracket and you experience an average 4 percent rate of inflation over the next several years, then your investments must return 5.6 percent annually just to maintain their purchasing power. At this rate of return, all of the gain you experience is lost to taxes and inflation. This is why it is not smart to put all of your investment money into a bank savings account or CD, both of which pay an interest rate that is only slightly higher than inflation. If you are going to beat the inflation and tax trap, you must take the time to design a strategy that maximizes the use of your investment dollars.

Money earning a low rate of interest is inefficient money that is not working as hard for you as it should be. You must reallocate inefficient money so that all your money is working as hard as possible to maximize your net worth over time.

Exhibit 10-2 demonstrates the impact that inflation alone will have on your savings and income over a period of years. Let's assume once again that inflation averages 4 percent for the long term. At that rate, your money will be worth half its current value in seventeen years. If you are retiring at that time and plan on needing a certain level of income to maintain your current standard of living, double the amount of income you think you will need. Remember also, inflation doesn't stop when you retire. Many people who retire today may be retired for thirty or more years. Inflation will continue during that entire time period and must be planned for, or the results could be devastating to your financial well-being.

WHY DO WE HAVE INFLATION?

Our inflation problems began in earnest in the late 1960s when President Johnson tried to finance the Vietnam war and simultaneously expand our social system. There is only one way to accomplish such a strategy: print

EXHIBIT 10-2

EFFECTS OF INFLATION

YEAR	INFLATION RATE						
	3%	4%	5%	6%	7%	8%	9%
1	$0.97	$0.96	$0.95	$0.94	$0.93	$0.92	$0.91
2	$0.94	$0.92	$0.90	$0.88	$0.86	$0.85	$0.83
3	$0.91	$0.88	$0.86	$0.83	$0.80	$0.78	$0.75
4	$0.89	$0.85	$0.81	$0.78	$0.75	$0.72	$0.69
5	$0.86	$0.82	$0.77	$0.73	$0.70	$0.66	$0.62
6	$0.83	$0.78	$0.74	$0.69	$0.65	$0.61	$0.57
7	$0.81	$0.75	$0.70	$0.65	$0.60	$0.56	$0.52
8	$0.78	$0.73	$0.66	$0.61	$0.56	$0.51	$0.47
9	$0.76	$0.69	$0.63	$0.57	$0.52	$0.47	$0.43
10	$0.74	$0.66	$0.60	$0.54	$0.48	$0.43	$0.39
11	$0.72	$0.64	$0.57	$0.51	$0.45	$0.40	$0.35
12	$0.69	$0.61	$0.54	$0.48	$0.42	$0.37	$0.32
13	$0.67	$0.59	$0.51	$0.45	$0.39	$0.34	$0.29
14	$0.65	$0.56	$0.49	$0.42	$0.36	$0.31	$0.27
15	$0.63	$0.54	$0.46	$0.40	$0.34	$0.29	$0.24
16	$0.61	$0.42	$0.44	$0.37	$0.31	$0.26	$0.22
17	$0.60	$0.50	$0.42	$0.35	$0.29	$0.24	$0.20
18	$0.58	$0.48	$0.40	$0.33	$0.27	$0.22	$0.18
19	$0.56	$0.46	$0.38	$0.31	$0.25	$0.21	$0.17
20	$0.54	$0.44	$0.36	$0.29	$0.23	$0.19	$0.15
21	$0.53	$0.42	$0.34	$0.27	$0.22	$0.17	$0.14
22	$0.51	$0.41	$0.32	$0.26	$0.20	$0.16	$0.13
23	$0.50	$0.39	$0.31	$0.24	$0.19	$0.15	$0.11
24	$0.48	$0.38	$0.29	$0.23	$0.18	$0.14	$0.10
25	$0.47	$0.36	$0.28	$0.21	$0.16	$0.12	$0.09
26	$0.45	$0.35	$0.26	$0.20	$0.15	$0.11	$0.09
27	$0.44	$0.33	$0.25	$0.19	$0.14	$0.11	$0.08
28	$0.43	$0.32	$0.24	$0.18	$0.13	$0.10	$0.07
29	$0.41	$0.31	$0.23	$0.17	$0.12	$0.09	$0.06
30	$0.40	$0.29	$0.21	$0.16	$0.11	$0.08	$0.06

This chart reflects the purchasing power of a dollar after a number of years at various inflation rates.

money. By definition, inflation occurs when the money supply increases faster than the amount of goods produced by the economy. The seeds for inflation had been planted.

Then, in the early seventies, we were hit with the Arab oil embargo. Oil prices shot through the roof, causing inflation to do likewise, since oil represented a large portion of our Gross Domestic Product. A tighter monetary policy on the part of the Federal Reserve Board could have lessened the inflationary impact of the oil shock. Instead, the Fed chose the path of loose money, further exacerbating the inflation problem.

A second oil shock followed in the late seventies. This time oil prices soared above forty dollars a barrel. Not until Paul Volcker became chairman of the Federal Reserve Board and changed the central bank's monetary policy did inflation start to retreat.

Sadly, many people retired in the late 1960s who had no clue of what was about to happen to inflation. They thought that their retirement income would be sufficient for the rest of their lives, having never experienced sustained high inflation. Twenty years later, many of them were living on about one third of the purchasing power on which they retired.

TIME AND COMPOUNDING

When you start investing, one of your best friends is time. I do not preach a gospel of getting rich overnight. Rather, *I teach a philosophy that involves systematically accumulating wealth over an extended period of time.* The younger you can start saving and investing, the better off you are. One of the best gifts that parents can give their children is the knowledge of how to invest money. It is critical for parents to convey to their children the importance of starting an investment program as soon as they begin earning a steady income.

Exhibit 10-3 illustrates this point. Let's say that a young man named Stephen graduated from college and decided to invest $1,000 per year, beginning at age twenty-two. He had a steady job and few responsibilities. Being a responsible young man, he invested this money in a mutual fund that averaged a 12 percent annual rate of return, and he used an Individual Retirement Account (IRA) as the investment account in order to allow his money to grow on a tax-deferred basis (more on IRA's later).

After seven years, Stephen was unable to invest any more money. He had married, and he and his wife were starting a family. They had also recently moved into their first house. It seemed that, on their limited income, their expenses were too high to allow further investing.

Another twenty-two-year-old named Donnie graduated at the same time as Stephen. However, Donnie's parents had never impressed on him the importance of saving and investing at an early age. He spent his money as he desired during those first seven years after graduating from college and never saved a penny of it. Finally, after seven years, a caring friend gave him a copy of a wonderful book called *Achieving Your Financial Potential,* and he realized the need to start setting money aside in a long-term investment account. He tried to make up for not investing during those first seven years by investing $1,000 each year thereafter. He, too, used a mutual fund that averaged a 12 percent annual return and set up an IRA in order to defer taxes on the gains he realized.

Did you know that at age sixty-five, after investing $1,000 per year for thirty-seven years, Donnie would still have failed to catch up with Stephen, who only invested for seven years? Donnie invested a total of $37,000. Stephen invested a total of only $7,000.

What was the difference? Did Stephen receive a higher rate of return? No. They both averaged the same rate of return. The only difference between the two was that Stephen began investing at age twenty-two and Donnie began investing at age twenty-nine. Seven years of compounding made all the difference. Just from investing $1,000 per year for seven years, starting at age twenty-two, Stephen accumulated over $748,000 by age sixty-five. Think of that! He had accumulated almost three quarters of a million dollars at age sixty-five just because he had the foresight to invest a total of $7,000 in his early twenties! Yes, time is one of our greatest allies in investing.

What is the moral of this story? That only people who begin investing in their early twenties will accumulate a sizable amount of money? *No!* The moral of this story is to start saving and investing whatever amount you can *now!* Even if it does not seem like a lot of money, a little bit invested consistently can grow into large amounts, given an adequate rate of return and enough time.

EXHIBIT 10-3

THE POWER
OF COMPOUNDING

	STEPHEN		DONNIE	
AGE	SAVINGS	VALUE	SAVINGS	VALUE
22	$ 1,000	$ 1,120	$ 0	$ 0
23	$ 1,000	$ 2.374	$ 0	$ 0
24	$ 1,000	$ 3,779	$ 0	$ 0
25	$ 1,000	$ 5,353	$ 0	$ 0
26	$ 1,000	$ 7,115	$ 0	$ 0
27	$ 1,000	$ 9,089	$ 0	$ 0
28	$ 1,000	$ 11,300	$ 0	$ 0
29	$ 0	$ 12,656	$ 1,000	$ 1,120
30	$ 0	$ 14,174	$ 1,000	$ 2,374
31	$ 0	$ 15,875	$ 1,000	$ 3,779
32	$ 0	$ 17,780	$ 1,000	$ 5,353
33	$ 0	$ 19,914	$ 1,000	$ 7,115
34	$ 0	$ 22,304	$ 1,000	$ 9,089
35	$ 0	$ 24,980	$ 1,000	$ 11,300
36	$ 0	$ 27,978	$ 1,000	$ 13,776
37	$ 0	$ 31,335	$ 1,000	$ 16,549
38	$ 0	$ 35,095	$ 1,000	$ 19,655
39	$ 0	$ 39,307	$ 1,000	$ 23,133
40	$ 0	$ 44,023	$ 1,000	$ 27,029
41	$ 0	$ 49,306	$ 1,000	$ 31,393
42	$ 0	$ 55,223	$ 1,000	$ 36,280
43	$ 0	$ 61,850	$ 1,000	$ 41,753
44	$ 0	$ 69,272	$ 1,000	$ 47,884
45	$ 0	$ 77,584	$ 1,000	$ 54,750
46	$ 0	$ 86,894	$ 1,000	$ 62,440
47	$ 0	$ 97,322	$ 1,000	$ 71,052
48	$ 0	$ 109,000	$ 1,000	$ 80,699
49	$ 0	$ 122,080	$ 1,000	$ 91,503
50	$ 0	$ 136,730	$ 1,000	$ 103,603
51	$ 0	$ 153,137	$ 1,000	$ 117,155
52	$ 0	$ 171,514	$ 1,000	$ 132,334
53	$ 0	$ 192,096	$ 1,000	$ 149,334
54	$ 0	$ 215,147	$ 1,000	$ 168,374
55	$ 0	$ 240,965	$ 1,000	$ 189,699
56	$ 0	$ 269,880	$ 1,000	$ 213,583
57	$ 0	$ 302,266	$ 1,000	$ 240,333
58	$ 0	$ 338,538	$ 1,000	$ 270,293
59	$ 0	$ 379,162	$ 1,000	$ 303,848
60	$ 0	$ 424,662	$ 1,000	$ 341,429
61	$ 0	$ 475,621	$ 1,000	$ 383,521
62	$ 0	$ 532,696	$ 1,000	$ 430,663
63	$ 0	$ 596,619	$ 1,000	$ 483,463
64	$ 0	$ 668,214	$ 1,000	$ 542,599
65	$ 0	$ 748,399	$ 1,000	$ 608,831

Illustration assumes 12% annual rate of return and that taxes on the gains experienced are deferred.

A SAFE WAY TO LOSE MONEY

Sometimes when I recommend an investment to clients, they will ask me "Is it guaranteed?" Some people feel that they are just gambling with their money unless an investment guarantees the value of their principal. They don't want to take any risks with their hard-earned dollars. Unfortunately, what these people do not realize is that there are more risks involved with investments than just that of losing principal. *Purchasing power* risk, the risk that your principal will be worth less in the future than it is today because of inflation, is just as real a risk and must be planned for as well. What is the difference between losing 10 percent of your principal in a poor performing investment and losing 10 percent of your principal's purchasing power through inflation? None. *Nada.* There is no difference between the two.

A SAFE WAY TO LOSE MONEY		
$ 50,000.00	→	Invested in Account that Pays 6% Interest
+ $ 3,000.00	→	Interest Earned
- $ 990.00	→	Income Taxes (33%) Paid
$ 2,010.00	→	Interest After Taxes
- $ 2,500.00	→	Loss of Purchasing Power Due to Inflation (5%)
- $ 490.00	→	Real Loss After Taxes and Inflation

Assumes a 33% tax bracket and 5% inflation

The above illustration demonstrates a critical concept that I call "a safe way to lose money." Many times when people invest in an instrument that guarantees their principal and pays them a set rate of interest, what is really being guaranteed is that their money will lose purchasing power at a steady rate.

Let's assume for this example that Jane placed $50,000 of her savings into a certificate of deposit yielding 6 percent interest. Jane is retired, and she needs the income from the CD to augment her pension and Social Security income. At 6 percent interest, Jane earns $3,000 on her principal that first year. That's not great, but at least Jane's principal is still intact, and she did not lose any money. Or did she?

Jane's money is not in an IRA, so the $3,000 she earned is fully taxable. Her combined state and federal income tax bracket is 33 percent, so she paid $990 in taxes, leaving her with after-tax earnings of $2,010. However, inflation averaged 5 percent during the year, so her $50,000 lost $2,500 in purchasing power, resulting in a *real loss* for the year of $490.

Jane actually lost money in terms of purchasing power, even assuming she reinvested the $3,000 she earned. But Jane didn't reinvest the $3,000; she had to spend it to make ends meet. So after one year of using a "guaranteed" investment, her net purchasing power declined almost 7 percent. How long do you think a retired person could maintain his or her lifestyle if their accumulated assets lost 7 percent of their purchasing power every year? Obviously not very long.

RISK/RETURN TRADE-OFF

One of the first and most basic principles of investing is what is known as the *risk/return trade-off*. This principle states that, in a free market economy, investments that have higher risk levels associated with them should offer higher expected rates of return than investments with lower risk levels. If you think about it for a moment, this trade-off makes intuitive sense.

Let's examine the case of two investments, A and B, which both offer an expected 8 percent rate of return. Investment A has a risk level of 5 (based on some fictitious measure of risk), and investment B has a higher risk level of 7. Since they both offer the same rate of return, which investment would you choose? The rational investor would choose investment A, the investment with the lower risk level. If they are to attract investors, the sponsors of investment B must increase the expected rate of return of their investment over that of investment A. Only the expectation of achieving a higher rate of return would allow a prudent investor to justify assuming the higher risk level of investment B.

Let's look at another scenario. Assume once again that we are comparing two investments, A and B. This time, however, both investments have identical risk levels of 5 (according to the same fictitious measure of risk), but A offers an expected rate of return of 8 percent, while B offers a 10 percent expected return. The rational investor would always choose investment B, the investment with the higher expected rate of return, over investment A, since both investments entail the same level of risk. So, we derive three principles regarding the risk/return trade-off:

- **You should try to maximize your return at whatever risk level you are investing.**
- **You should try to minimize your risk for any level of return you are trying to achieve.**
- **The higher the risk of an investment, the higher should be its expected rate of return.** *Therefore, to increase your rate of return, you must increase the risk level of the investments you are using.*

As a result of the risk/return trade-off, investments can be categorized by their risk/return characteristics. Because of this, building a portfolio is often compared to the erection of a physical structure. The whole building is supported by its foundation. The strength of the foundation determines the stability of the entire edifice. The shape of the building, the quality of its construction, and the materials from which it is made all determine the level of adversity it can withstand.

The construction of an investment portfolio is similar in principle. Exhibit 10-4 demonstrates this concept. Investments toward the bottom of the building carry a lower level of risk and offer a relatively low potential rate of return. These investments form the foundation of one's portfolio. Because they are safe, their value stands up well in tough economic times. As you proceed to higher levels of the building, the higher are the risk levels and return expectations of the investments. Those at the highest level are speculative and offer little stability, but they afford the opportunity for large, quick returns. The shape of your personal "portfolio building" will depend on the return you desire and the level of risk you are willing to assume.

The bottom level of the building includes such items as certificates of deposit, annuities, bank savings accounts, and Treasury bills. These investments are interest-bearing instruments that guarantee investors' principal.

The next level higher includes such investments as real estate investment trusts (REIT's), utilities stocks, utilities funds, bond mutual funds,

EXHIBIT 10-4 # PORTFOLIO BUILDING

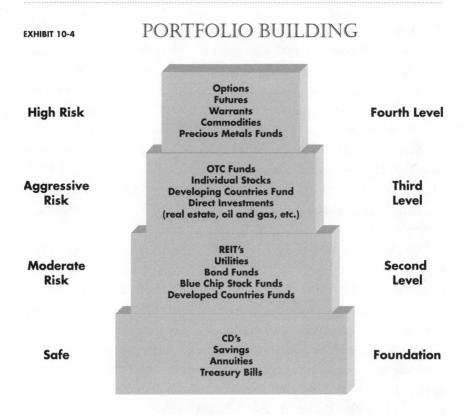

blue chip stock funds, and mutual funds that invest in developed foreign countries. Your principal is placed at risk with these investments and will fluctuate up and down in value. However, your principal will typically ex- perience less fluctuation in value than with investments that occupy higher levels of the building.

The third level includes investments such as over-the-counter stock mutual funds (OTC funds), individual stocks, and mutual funds that in- vest in the stocks of developing countries. Developing countries, also known as *emerging markets,* will often experience a faster economic growth rate than developed countries. Their stock markets will, therefore, sometimes experience more rapid appreciation in value than the markets of developed countries. However, their stock markets also carry a higher level of risk, due somewhat to the higher political risks of the governments involved.

Over-the-counter stocks are those that trade on the NASDAQ system. NASDAQ is a computerized network over which shares of stocks are traded. In contrast, an *exchange* is a physical location where stocks are traded. Generally, though there are some notable exceptions, smaller companies trade over-the-counter on NASDAQ, and larger companies trade on exchanges, such as the New York Stock Exchange (NYSE).

Successful smaller companies tend to grow faster than larger companies. They also usually pay a lower level of dividends, if they pay any at all. Most, if not all, of the excess cash they generate is reinvested in their own company instead of being paid out as dividends in order to finance their rapid growth.

Smaller companies also fail more often than larger, established companies, and they tend not to weather difficult economic times as well. This is what creates the higher-risk profile of this group of stocks.

Other investments included in the third level of the building are direct investments, such as real estate and oil and gas wells. Real estate investments may include residential rental houses, apartment complexes, strip shopping centers, and large regional malls, among other things. Direct investments were formerly marketed primarily as illiquid units of limited partnerships rather than as shares of stock. However, these types of investments are now frequently structured as units of trusts that trade on an exchange, giving them an element of liquidity that was formerly missing.

The top level includes those investments that entail the highest levels of risk, but which also offer the highest return potential. These investments would have to be considered speculative and include such things as options, futures, warrants, commodities, and precious metals mutual funds. If you're not sure what all of these investments are, don't worry. You are probably better off not knowing; some are not far from riverboat gambling. All of these investments can experience extreme fluctuations in value, and an investor can lose his entire investment in a short period of time with some of them. They are certainly not for the fainthearted or risk averse.

PRIMARY TYPES OF INVESTMENTS

If you are like most people, you get bombarded on a daily basis with newspaper ads, television commercials, radio ads, and telephone calls from investment salespeople who are all touting their latest and greatest financial product. Many of the investments advertised are legitimate and of a high quality. However, some of these products sound too good to be true, and they are.

Perhaps you have received one of those irritating phone calls from a salesperson touting a "hot" investment with a "potential" double-digit tax-free return. "The return is guaranteed and the investment is insured," he says. "Besides all that," the voice exclaims, "Mr. Famous Investor just put half a million dollars into it." The sales pitch goes on, "And by the way, Mr. Jones, we're the only company who has this product, and you better invest today, because it's selling so fast that we may not have any left tomorrow!" "Is it risky?" Mr. Jones asks. "Sure, it's got a little risk," the salesperson responds, "but we're guaranteeing it. And you know Mr. Famous Investor wouldn't be putting his money into it if he thought it was going to fail!"

Mr. Jones doesn't really understand the investment, but the potential double-digit rate of return sure sounds appealing. Especially if it's tax-free. And guaranteed. And insured. Besides, if Mr. Famous Investor just put a half million dollars into it, it must be good. So over the phone, having never met the financial salesperson and having no knowledge about the company he represents, Mr. Jones commits to sink (no pun intended) $5,000 into this wonderful new investment.

Unfortunately, this scene happens many times every day. In the majority of these cases, Mr. Jones ends up losing some or all of his money. Because Mr. Jones has never taken the time to learn the basics about investing or to develop a framework within which he will make investment decisions, he makes bad investment after bad investment and never seems to get ahead financially. There is no consistency in his investment program. He just invests in whatever sounds good whenever he has some extra money available.

The investment world can be very complicated. However, most people can consistently make very sound investment decisions without ever getting involved in the myriad complex financial products that Wall Street invents.

KEY POINT

The two primary keys to the long-term accumulation of wealth are saving and investing money on a regular basis, and consistently achieving an adequate rate of return on your invested assets.

TWO CATEGORIES OF INVESTMENTS

The investment world is really not as complicated as it may seem to a lay person. In fact, you can boil all investments down into basically two categories. Two. That's it. Virtually every investment will fall into one of these two categories or be a hybrid of the two. The two categories are *fixed return* and *variable return* investments.

A fixed return investment is one in which you are a *lender.* You lend money to an organization, such as a bank, a corporation, an insurance company, or even the government. In return for borrowing your money, the organization promises to pay you a certain rate of interest for a specified period of time. Interest payments are usually made on a monthly, quarterly, or annual basis. On the *maturity date,* the borrower repays the principal amount of the loan. The safety level of such an investment depends primarily on the creditworthiness of the organization to which you made the loan. Examples of fixed return investments include certificates of deposit and virtually any kind of bond, such as Treasury bonds, municipal bonds, and corporate bonds. For simplicity's sake, I will use bonds as the primary example of fixed return investments from this point forward.

With a variable return investment, you are not a lender, but rather you become an *owner.* Because you have taken on the risk of ownership, you do not receive a guaranteed rate of return on your investment. Instead, your rate of return will vary from year to year, depending on how well the asset performs in which you have taken an ownership position. Some years your return may be high, and some years it may be low. There may even be years when your return is negative. Examples of variable return investments would be stocks, real estate, precious metals, and oil and gas wells. Again, for the sake of simplicity, I will use stocks as the primary example of variable return investments.

THREE PRINCIPAL DIFFERENCES BETWEEN FIXED RETURN AND VARIABLE RETURN INVESTMENTS

Fixed return investments and variable return investments have different characteristics and, thus, serve different purposes in a portfolio. You must know the attributes of each type of investment and how they differ in order to know how much of each to include in your portfolio.

The first principle in this regard is that *short-term money belongs in fixed return investments.* By short-term money, I mean money that you will need to use within the next three to five years for expenditures of some sort. As I will demonstrate later, the stock market moves in cycles that are very closely related to our economy's business cycles. In general, these cycles last anywhere from three to seven years. So, if you need to pull your money out in three years to buy a car, make a down payment on a house, or for any other expenditure, there is too big a chance that you will be forced to sell your investments during a down cycle for a capital loss. Therefore, short-term money should be placed in fixed return investments of some sort, such as a money market fund, short-term CD's, or short-term bonds.

A second important distinction between fixed return and variable return investments is that with fixed return investments, *your principal is not at risk,* whereas, when you place money in a variable return investment, *your principal is at risk.* In other words, when you invest in bonds or CD's, the only thing that may vary over time is the amount of interest you earn. The value of your principal remains stable. With stocks, however, your principal value will actually fluctuate up and down, based on numerous factors that affect the value of the asset you acquired.

With bond investments, the return you will experience is certain, since your principal is stable and your interest rate is guaranteed. On January 1 of any given year, you can predict with perfect precision what your bond will earn by December 31, assuming it matures on or after that date. With stocks, however, your principal is at risk and your rate of return is not guaranteed. On January 1, you have no idea what your investment will be worth on December 31.

The one thing you must get used to if you invest in stocks is that the stock market goes up, and the stock market goes down. It is all a part of the cycles. As a matter of fact, the one thing I can almost guarantee people when they invest in stocks is that at some point they will lose money. In fact, if they stay invested long enough, they will lose money on a regular, periodic basis. Is that because they will make bad investments on a regular, periodic basis? No. It is due to the cycles that the market experiences.

Why then would someone willingly choose to invest in stocks when they could have a guaranteed return on their money and never experience a down market? Because of the third distinction between stocks and bonds! *Over long periods of time, the stock market has substantially outperformed the major fixed return investments.*

Since you have taken on an additional risk by investing in stocks, the risk of ownership, you would expect to have the potential to earn a higher average rate of return than with a fixed return investment. Otherwise, you would not assume the additional risk. Has this indeed proven to be the case? The answer is an emphatic yes! During the time period from 1925 to 1997, the average annual return for large company stocks was 11 percent.[6] This was more than double the 5.2 percent return offered by long-term government bonds during the same period.[7]

To summarize the above, then, fixed return investments offer safety of

KEY POINT

As a general rule, the longer an investor can keep his money invested, the more stock-oriented his portfolio should be, since the risk of losing principal is lessened by lengthening one's investment time horizon.

principal and certainty of return for the risk-averse investor. They are also appropriate vehicles for short-term savings. Variable return investments, on the other hand, are the most efficient way to accumulate assets over a long period of time for the investor who is willing to place his principal at risk.

## CHAPTER 11

FIXED RETURN INVESTMENTS FOR SAFETY AND INCOME

Though there are many types of fixed return investments, there are three key ones on which I want to focus: bonds, CD's, and annuities.

BONDS

Bonds are the classic fixed return investment. When you buy a bond, you are lending money to an organization. The borrowers may include, among others, the government, a corporation, or a bank. The borrower pays you a specific interest rate for a predetermined period of time and then returns your principal on the maturity date.

The value of a bond purchased on the open market is guaranteed only if you hold that bond until maturity. Many people are not aware of this fact, but between the time that you purchase a bond and its maturity date, the value of that bond fluctuates up and down on a daily basis. The force driving these changes in bond prices is fluctuating interest rates.

To illustrate this point, let's say that Pete goes to Uncle Sam to purchase a thirty-year Treasury bond, i.e., a bond issued by the Treasury of the United States that matures in thirty years. "Pete, I'd love to sell you a bond," Uncle Sam says. "We've got this debt we're trying to finance, and we need more patriotic people just like you to help us do it. Here's how the system works. You write me a check for some multiple of a thousand dollars [bonds sell in units of $1,000; this is called the bond's *par value*]. I will pay you six percent interest each year for the next thirty years [assume this is the going interest rate at the time Pete purchased his bond]. At the end of thirty years, I'll pay your principal back." Pete writes the Treasury a check for $1,000 and begins collecting his $60 interest every year (actually Treasury bonds pay half the annual interest twice a year).

Pete works with Marty. One day, about a year after Pete bought his bond, he and Marty are discussing investments at the office. When he tells Marty about the bond that he owns, Marty decides that he, too, wants to purchase a U.S. Treasury bond. The next day, Marty approaches Uncle Sam to make his investment. Uncle Sam says, "Marty, I'd love to sell you a bond. We've got this debt we're trying to finance, and we need more patriotic people just like you and Pete to help us out. You know the procedure. Just write me a check for some multiple of a thousand dollars, and we'll be in business." Just as Marty is signing his check for $1,000, Uncle Sam says, "Oh, by the way, I meant to tell you that over the last year since Pete bought his bond, interest rates have dropped a percentage point. I'm only paying five percent interest on new bonds instead of the six percent interest rate that Pete receives. So, your interest will total only fifty dollars each year."

Marty thinks for a minute about what Uncle Sam has just said. If he buys a new Treasury bond, he'll receive only $50 each year for his $1,000 investment. Pete's bond, on the other hand, is paying $60 interest each year. Perhaps Pete might be convinced to sell his bond to Marty, giving Marty a little extra interest over what a new bond would pay him. So Marty puts off his purchase with Uncle Sam.

Marty approaches Pete the next day at the office. "Pete," Marty says, "you remember that bond we were talking about yesterday, the one you bought a year ago from Uncle Sam? Do you think you might be interested in selling that bond to me?" Pete responds, "It's interesting you should ask. I *am* interested in selling that bond. Just write me a check for eleven hundred and fifty dollars, and it's yours!"

Is Pete trying to take advantage of his friend Marty, or is his bond really worth $1,150? His bond is really worth about $1,150. Let me explain. I'm sure you will agree with me that a bond paying $60 interest each year is worth more than a bond that pays $50 interest each year. Since new bonds are issued at $1,000 par value, Pete's bond, which pays a higher interest rate than new bonds being issued, has increased in value due to the

1 percent drop in market interest rates. This increase in value, called a capital gain, is in addition to the interest that he has received.

Here's how it works. If interest rates drop after you buy a bond, then your bond's value increases. Conversely, if interest rates go up while you are holding the bond, then the principal value of your bond drops. This movement in price is exaggerated the longer the time period until the bond matures. Longer-term bonds go up in value more than shorter-term bonds when interest rates drop, and they drop in value more than shorter-term bonds when interest rates go up.

What rate of return did Pete earn on his bond investment during the year he held it? Approximately 21 percent! How so? Since interest rates dropped a full percentage point during his holding period, his thirty-year Treasury bond increased in value about 15 percent. Pete still received the 6 percent interest payment from the government as well. Fifteen percent appreciation plus 6 percent interest yields a total return of 21 percent! Not bad for a stodgy old Treasury bond.

If you could predict the direction of interest rates, then, with perfect precision (which, by the way, nobody can do), you would buy long-term Treasury bonds when interest rates were high and coming down. This would give you capital appreciation in addition to the interest the bonds yielded. Then, when interest rates bottomed and began going back up, you would sell your long-term bonds to avoid a loss of principal as interest rates climbed. You would shift your money over to short-term bonds that matured in maybe six months or a year. Since you would hold these short-term bonds to maturity, you would experience no loss of capital from the rising interest rates. You would keep reinvesting your principal in these short-term bonds at higher interest rates each time they matured until rates peaked and started heading south again. At that point you would shift your money back into long-term bonds and replay the whole cycle.

Unfortunately, you can't predict the trends in interest rates perfectly, but at least now you understand how the bond market works.

So, you can really use bonds for two separate and distinct purposes. One, more suited for conservative investors, is to buy them and hold them until they mature. You do this if you are interested only in the steady income they generate and/or the safety of principal they offer. Since you are holding them until maturity, you do not care about fluctuations in interest rates. Your bonds will mature at full value.

The other use for bonds is more suited for aggressive investors. Here, you buy long-term bonds when interest rates are high, hoping that rates drop at some point after your purchase. If that happens, your bonds will experience capital appreciation in addition to the interest they pay, making them a legitimate growth investment.

BOND RATINGS

Since the safety of a bond investment depends upon the creditworthiness of the organization to whom you are lending money, it would be nice if there was some relatively easy way of knowing how creditworthy that organization is. That is the purpose of ratings firms. These companies do extensive research on corporations, municipalities, and even foreign countries, in order to determine how financially sound they are. Ratings are assigned to bonds based on the issuers' levels of financial strength. The lower the credit rating of a bond, the higher the interest rate it will have to pay in the open market in order to attract investors, due to the risk/return trade-off discussed earlier. It is important to companies and other bond issuers, therefore, to maintain a high credit rating in order to minimize the interest rate they must pay for money they borrow.

Below is an example of how two of the major ratings firms rate bonds for credit risk:

MOODY'S	STANDARD AND POOR'S[8]
Aaa	AAA
Aa	AA
A	A
Baa	BBB
Ba	BB
B	B
Etc.	Etc.

JUNK BONDS

Bonds with ratings above the line are considered to be investment grade. Ratings below the line imply that there is an element of speculation involved in the safety level of the bonds, i.e., the issuer is not strong enough financially for its bonds to be considered investment grade. This means there is a definite risk that the issuer may not be able to make the interest payments on its bonds or repay the principal on maturing bonds in a timely fashion. Because these lower rated bonds carry a higher level of risk, they must pay a somewhat higher interest rate in order to attract investors. These bonds are, therefore, also called *high-yield bonds,* or *junk bonds.*

Junk bond funds are mutual funds that invest in less-than-investment-grade bonds. Junk bond funds are considered lower-risk investments than individual junk bonds because the risk of default is spread across many bonds. Some junk bond funds will invest in only "higher-quality junk," that is, bonds near the top of the speculative ratings. I once heard a fund manager comment that the junk bonds in his portfolio were of such high quality that they spelled junk "j-u-n-q-u-e." Other junk bond fund managers will try to provide the highest yield possible on their funds, meaning that their portfolios are filled with lower-rated junk bonds. This strategy increases the yield of the fund, but it also increases the risk of default of the bonds in their portfolio.

CERTIFICATES OF DEPOSIT

Most people are familiar with Certificates of Deposits, so I will say very little about how they work. CD's are offered by banks and maintain the same level of safety as any other money on deposit at the bank. Bank accounts are insured by FDIC (Federal Deposit Insurance Corporation) up to $100,000. When you purchase a CD at a bank, it normally carries some type of early withdrawal penalty. CD's can be purchased for varying lengths of maturity, normally ranging from one month to five years. Longer-term certificates typically pay a higher interest rate than shorter-term certificates, as is also the case with bonds.

Many people are not aware that CD's can be purchased through brokerage firms as well as banks. Brokerage firms do not issue Certificates of

Deposit; they trade certificates on the open market that have been issued by banks. CD's that are acquired through a bank and do not trade on the open market maintain a constant principal value. CD's that trade on the open market behave more like bonds, with their principal value fluctuating up and down based on the trends in interest rates.

ANNUITIES

Annuities are issued by insurance companies, which are rated for safety just like bond issuers. As with bonds, the safety level of an annuity depends upon the creditworthiness of the insurance company issuing it. Even though annuities are fixed return investments like bonds, they are not traded on the open market, so their principal value does not fluctuate like that of bonds.

There are two basic kinds of annuities that would be considered fixed return investments: *fixed annuities* (also called deferred annuities) and *income annuities* (also called immediate annuities). Fixed annuities are typically used during the wealth accumulation phase of one's life; income annuities are most often used during the income distribution phase.

1. FIXED (OR DEFERRED) ANNUITIES—Think of a fixed annuity as being similar to a tax-deferred CD with a variable interest rate. Since annuities are issued by insurance companies, the FDIC does not insure them. They are protected only by the financial strength of the companies themselves, which is why you should purchase annuities from insurance companies with strong credit ratings.

The interest paid on an annuity is tax-deferred. *Tax-deferred* interest is different from *tax-free* interest. *Tax-deferred* means that you do not pay taxes on the interest you earn until you withdraw it from the investment account. This may not occur until you are very old. *Tax-free* means that you never pay tax on the interest earned. The interest paid by municipal bonds is tax-free (at least with regard to federal income taxes), whereas the interest paid by an annuity is tax-deferred.

Normally, the interest rate paid on a fixed annuity will vary over time. The frequency of rate changes will vary from company to company, but typically the interest rate is adjusted yearly. This may work in your favor or against you. If market interest rates increase while you are holding your annuity, the interest rate you are paid should also go up. However, if rates drop during your holding period, the interest you earn on your annuity will likely go down as well.

Insurance companies normally charge a surrender penalty on principal withdrawn from a fixed annuity during the first few years of a contract. Again, this will vary from annuity to annuity, but a typical structure is as follows:

YEAR	1	2	3	4	5	6	7	8 +
Penalty	7%	6%	5%	4%	3%	2%	1%	0%

This means if you withdraw principal during the first year of the annuity contract, the insurance company will charge you a 7 percent penalty on the amount of principal withdrawn. Each year that goes by, the penalty drops by a percentage point. Principal that stays on deposit at the insurance company for a full seven years can be withdrawn penalty-free.

KEY POINT

Be aware! Interest that is withdrawn from an annuity prior to age $59^1/_2$, with certain exceptions, is subject to a 10 percent tax penalty levied by our good friends in Washington. The government gives tax-deferred status to annuities because they want to encourage people to save for retirement. The government does not want you to use annuities as a way to avoid paying taxes on short-term investments that are not being used for retirement savings.

In my opinion, deferred annuities are a good way for very risk-averse investors to accumulate money.

2. INCOME (OR IMMEDIATE) ANNUITIES—Income annuities are designed to generate income as opposed to accumulate wealth. Think of an income annuity conceptually as a mortgage in reverse. When you make payments on your mortgage, each payment consists of interest and some principal.

At the end of your mortgage loan period, your principal balance has been reduced to $0.

Income annuities are similar, only opposite (sounds like something Yogi Berra would say). You deposit a lump sum into an income annuity. You then tell the insurance company over how many years you want the annuity to pay you a monthly stream of income, with each payment consisting of interest and some principal.

KEY POINT

Once an income annuity has matured, your principal balance is $0.

There are several methods by which an income annuity can pay income to you, called *settlement options*. The three main settlement options are:

a. **Payout within X years**—You can choose a set number of years over which the income annuity will self-liquidate. If, for instance, you choose a ten-year payout period, the insurance company will make 120 monthly payments to you, each payment consisting of interest and some principal. At the end of ten years, your balance in the annuity account is $0.

b. **Lifetime payout**—With the lifetime payout option, the insurance company guarantees that they will pay you monthly income for the rest of your life, however long that may be. How can they do this? Because their statisticians, known as actuaries, can predict with great accuracy the average life expectancy of the pool of people who have chosen this settlement option. If one person outlives their expected mortality age, the probability is that someone else will pass away earlier than anticipated.

A major problem with this option is that the insurance company does not commit to pay money to you or your heirs for a minimum period of time, but rather for only as long as you live. Remember that at the end of the payout period, the value of your annuity is $0. This means that if you deposited $100,000 with the insurance company today, chose the life income settlement option on an income annuity, and then died a month later, your heirs would receive nothing. The insurance company would keep the remaining balance of your $100,000.

In my opinion, this payment method is a gamble and a terrible choice for a settlement option. I believe there are much better income alternatives than this one.

c. **X years certain**—This is an improved version of the lifetime income option. With this option, the insurance company pays you a stream of income for the rest of your life, but they guarantee that they will make monthly payments to you and/or your heirs for at least X years. You decide how many years X is.

Let's assume that you have chosen the lifetime income option, ten years certain. If you die in five years, the insurance company will continue making payments to your heirs for another five years. On the other hand, if you live longer than ten years, the insurance company will continue paying you a monthly income for the remainder of your life.

This is a better alternative than the straight lifetime income payout option. As a general rule, however, I do not recommend income annuities as a way to draw income from your accumulated savings.

ANNUITY INCOME ALTERNATIVES

If you are a conservative investor and want to use annuities as a way to draw income during your retirement years, I recommend one of two approaches. First, use a regular fixed annuity and draw out the interest as it is earned. The interest will be fully taxable in the year in which it is withdrawn. Since there will generally be a 10 percent tax penalty on the income you withdraw if you are under age $59^{1}/_{2}$, you do not want to use this option until you have reached that age. While this option is okay, it is really not much different than investing in a CD. I would choose this option only if (a) the interest rate being paid on the annuity is significantly higher than that available on CD's, or (b) I had used a fixed annuity, which contained a large amount of tax-deferred interest, to accumulate assets. This interest would become taxable upon cashing in the annuity.

A second approach, and I think a better one, is called a *split annuity.*

Basically, this involves splitting your lump sum into two annuities, a fixed annuity and an income annuity with, say, a ten-year-payout period. You can vary the length of the payout period on the income annuity to whatever time period you desire. You must calculate how much of your lump sum would need to be placed in the fixed annuity so that, at current interest rates, it will grow back to your original total lump sum balance over the ten-year period. You place the remainder of the funds in the income annuity to generate monthly income over the ten-year period.

Over the ten-year period, the income annuity will pay you a steady stream of dependable income. The fixed annuity will grow back to approximately the same level as the lump sum with which you started. Initially, this doesn't appear to accomplish any more than what investing in a CD would do for you. Here's the difference: the majority of the income generated by the income annuity is a return of your own principal, which is, of course, tax-free. The interest that accumulates in the fixed annuity does so on a tax-deferred basis.

Using a split annuity, you will shelter from income taxes a high percent of the income generated during the payment period of the income annuity. The tax benefits are what make this technique attractive to conservative investors.

At the end of ten years you end up with a fixed annuity that has roughly the same balance as the lump sum with which you started ten years earlier. At that point, you begin drawing interest from it as it is earned, which is fully taxable. However, you have successfully sheltered a substantial portion of your income from taxes for several years, something you could not have accomplished with a CD.

Who eventually pays the taxes on the interest that has built up in the deferred annuity? Your heirs. They will pay the taxes from the balance in the annuity and keep what is left over. While this may bother some people, I am of the opinion that anything the heirs receive is a gift. Your objective is to maximize your retirement income, not the size of your heirs' inheritance.

## CHAPTER 12

USING MUTUAL FUNDS TO GROW YOUR ASSETS

Before I discuss variable return investments in general, and stocks in particular, I would like to talk with you about mutual funds as an investment vehicle. For most people, mutual funds are the best way to invest in the stock market. Why?

Let's suppose that you want to invest in stocks. You go out and buy shares of stock in one company. It may be a very good quality blue chip company. After you make your investment, some unexpected bad news comes out about the company, and the share price drops dramatically. You could lose a lot of money quickly under these circumstances. It is entirely possible that the company in which you invested could even go out of business. If that were to happen, you could actually lose all of your investment. This type of loss is *permanent,* not *cyclical.*

On the other hand, let's suppose that you owned stock in one hundred different companies, and one of them went out of business. This company's failure costs you only 1 percent of your portfolio instead of your whole investment. While this sounds good, there is one problem. To efficiently develop a stock portfolio of one hundred different quality companies may require an investment of several hundred thousand dollars, putting it beyond the reach of most people.

This is where mutual funds enter the picture. With a mutual fund, typically thousands of investors from across the country pool their funds together. Maybe none of them has several hundred thousand dollars individually, but corporately they may have millions, or even billions, of dollars available to invest. A fund manager will take this money and develop a diversified portfolio of stocks, often investing in over a hundred different companies. When you buy a share of the mutual fund, you automatically own a fraction of every share of stock in that fund. It is as though you have your own portfolio of 100 stocks (or however many are in the particular fund that you own). However, instead of needing a million dollars to develop this professionally managed portfolio, most mutual funds have minimum investment requirements of $500 to $2,500. What a deal!

THE NUTS AND BOLTS OF MUTUAL FUNDS

The advantages of mutual funds for the average investor are numerous. They include:

1. PROFESSIONAL MANAGEMENT—A full-time investment professional decides which stocks to buy, when to buy them, and when to sell them. This benefit alone justifies the use of mutual funds for the majority of investors. Most people have no clue how to even begin picking stocks. With a mutual fund, you have some of the top investment professionals in the country managing your portfolio for you. The typical fee received for managing a mutual fund is between .75 percent and 1.5 percent annually. This is a real bargain for what you get.

2. DIVERSIFICATION—When you invest in a mutual fund, you are instantly diversified among what is often 100 stocks or more. This diversification increases the safety and the predictability of your investment.

3. DOLLAR COST AVERAGING—This is a disciplined method of regular investing, which can only reasonably be achieved with mutual funds, not with individual stocks. It consists of investing a set amount on a consistent basis. In a fluctuating market, this technique will normally reduce the average cost of your investments below their average price. I will discuss this technique in more detail later.

4. PURCHASING OF PARTIAL SHARES—You cannot purchase partial shares of individual stocks. Mutual funds allow you to invest exact dollar amounts because you can purchase partial shares. For instance, if you want to invest

$500 in a mutual fund, and $500 buys you 59.86 shares, then you acquire 59.86 shares, and it will not cost you extra to make such a purchase. This is what makes mutual funds so well suited for dollar cost averaging.

5. AUTOMATIC REINVESTMENT OF DIVIDENDS AND CAPITAL GAINS—You can instruct mutual fund companies to automatically reinvest dividends and capital gains distributions at no cost when they are paid. This allows you to purchase more shares of the mutual fund with the income the fund generates, keeping all your money working for you all the time. This prevents idle money from accumulating. You will probably want to do this if you are still in the phase of your life where you are accumulating assets. Once you are drawing income from your investments, you may want the dividends and capital gains paid to you in cash.

6. AUTOMATIC BANK DRAFTS—One of my favorite features of mutual funds is that you can instruct them to automatically draft your bank account once a month for a preauthorized investment amount. This is convenient, and it makes your investing automatic. In some respects, it is similar to payroll deduction.

7. LIQUIDITY/GUARANTEED REDEMPTION OF SHARES—By law, mutual funds are required to buy your shares back from you at the closing market price on any business day in which you instruct them to do so. This means you do not have to be concerned about being unable to find a buyer for your shares, guaranteeing liquidity for your investment.

For the sake of our discussion, I have been referring primarily to stock mutual funds. However, you can invest in almost any financial market through the vehicle of mutual funds, including bonds, foreign stocks, and real estate investment trusts. There are even mutual funds now that sell stocks short and buy options.

PICK A FUND THAT MATCHES YOUR OBJECTIVES

Each fund has a stated objective, such as maximum growth or generating a high level of income. When picking a mutual fund, it is important to match a fund's objectives to your own investment goals. If a fund's objective is aggressive growth, and you want to maximize your income, then that fund is not an appropriate investment for you.

Normally you will find that funds emphasizing stability in value tend to pay higher dividends, and funds that are trying to maximize their total return tend to pay lower dividends. The reason for this is logical. Funds that emphasize low volatility are likely to be investing in older, more mature blue chip companies. These companies tend to fluctuate less in value and to pay a higher level of dividends. These funds may also be investing a portion of their assets in bonds, which also pay high dividends.

Funds that attempt to maximize their growth in value are likely to be investing in younger, smaller, more aggressive growth companies. These companies tend to pay a lower level of dividends than older, more established companies, if they pay any dividends at all. Instead of paying excess cash flow out to investors in the form of dividends, they are plowing this money back into the company to fuel its growth.

PROSPECTUS

How can you tell what a fund's objectives are? By reading its *prospectus*, a legal document that provides standard information about the fund. Securities laws require that investors be given a prospectus for any fund in which they invest. It is always a wise idea to read this document before investing in a fund, but it is especially critical if you are a novice investor or if you are choosing your own mutual funds rather than using a financial adviser.

Important information items provided by the prospectus include:

1. FUND OBJECTIVES—This section explains the objectives of the fund. This will let you know if the fund is trying to accomplish the same investment objective(s) you are.

2. INVESTMENT PARAMETERS—Each fund should have a clear-cut investment strategy that the manager will follow. This section of the prospectus reveals what the fund is allowed to invest in to execute that strategy. You may agree with the objectives of the fund, but not agree with how its manager is trying to achieve those objectives. For instance, the fund may have

an objective of aggressive growth, which happens to be your objective as well. However, you might read in the prospectus that the fund is allowed to invest up to 25 percent of its assets in commodities. If you do not want to invest in commodities as a way to achieve growth, then this would not be an appropriate fund for you.

3. FUND EXPENSES—This is one of the most important pieces of information in the prospectus. Securities laws require that mutual funds list in the prospectus all the expenses that the fund expects to incur in its operation. While most mutual fund salespeople are honest and forthright about the fund's expenses, some are not. The information with which they provide you can be confirmed or refuted by the prospectus. Since the prospectus is a legal document, it may reveal more details and provide more precise and accurate information than the person recommending the fund to you.

MUTUAL FUND EXPENSES

A fund may incur several types of expenses in its daily operation. Two of the main expenses you want to examine are the commission, or load, and the management fee.

LOAD VERSUS NO-LOAD FUNDS

Load is another word for commission. Loaded funds have a commission, which is generally used to compensate the financial adviser who sold you the fund, built into either their sales price or their operating expenses. No-load funds do not carry this expense since you deal directly with the fund itself and avoid the middleman. This allows you to save the commission.

LOADED FUNDS

When you look up the price for a mutual fund in the newspaper, you will see two prices listed, the NAV and the offering price. NAV stands for *net asset value.* This number is computed by adding up the value of each of the stocks within the fund, in order to determine the total worth of the fund, and then dividing this figure by the total number of the fund's outstanding shares. This is the actual value of a share of the fund. It is the value you would receive if you liquidated your shares. The *public offering price* (POP) is the net asset value plus any up-front commission charged for purchasing a share of the fund. So, you buy shares of a mutual fund at the public offering price, and you sell shares at the net asset value. For no-load funds and loaded funds which do not levy their commission up front, the public offering price equals the net asset value.

There are several ways in which the load may be charged. *Front-end loaded funds* are those that include the cost of the commission in the selling price of the fund itself. The commission is paid up front under this method. The commission amount will vary from fund to fund, but as a general rule it will average about 4.5 to 5 percent. It may be smaller for larger investment amounts, such as $100,000 and above.

Until the early 1980s, loaded funds controlled a large majority of the market share for mutual funds. Then, in the early eighties, no-load mutual funds started gaining in popularity and began to take over a greater percentage of the market. Loaded funds were forced to devise new commission structures in order to compete more effectively with no-load funds. One step they took was to reduce the average load from 8.5 percent to the current 4.5 to 5 percent range. They also developed various load structures in which the load was paid over time instead of up front. One of the most popular load schemes has been what is commonly referred to as "B" shares. Here, no commission is taken out of the funds at the time shares are purchased. However, if you sell shares of your investment within a predetermined period of time, typically the first five years, you will pay a surrender penalty according to a schedule similar to this one:

YEAR	1	2	3	4	5	6
Surrender Penalty	5%	4%	3%	2%	1%	0%

This means that if, within one year from your date of purchase, you sell any of your shares, the fund will charge you a 5 percent surrender penalty on the shares sold. Shares sold during the second year incur a 4 percent surrender penalty, etc. After holding your shares for a full five years, you may sell them at no surrender charge. However, do not make the mistake that many investors make and conclude that these funds become no-load funds after five years. They do not. Actually, you have paid the load over the five years.

How has this happened? "B" share funds charge the commission on an annual basis, instead of charging it up front, through what is known as a 12b-1 fee. This fee, named after the section of the securities laws that discusses it, is also frequently referred to as a marketing reimbursement expense. Through whom are these funds marketed? Brokers and commission-oriented financial planners. So, who gets reimbursed by these 12b-1 fees? The mutual funds are reimbursed for the commissions they have paid to the brokers and financial planners who sold the funds. In actuality, 12b-1 fees are usually another method of charging commissions.

Generally, when a broker sells a fund with a 12b-1 expense, the broker is still paid the bulk of his commission up front. He may also receive a small annual trail commission as well. The fund recoups its cost of commissions through the 12b-1 fee. Let's say that the broker is paid 5 percent up front for selling shares of the fund. It will take the fund five years to recover this cost if the 12b-1 fee is 1 percent annually, which is typical. The surrender penalty is put in place to ensure that the fund recovers its commission expenses in the event that you withdraw your money before the five years is up. Therefore, the fund is not any more a no-load fund after five years than a car is free after you have completed the payments on a five-year loan. After five years the car is paid for, as is the load on the mutual fund.

One other type of load structure charges annual commissions indefinitely. Typically, under this structure, a fund will impose a 1 percent surrender penalty during the first year of ownership after purchasing shares of the fund. After one year, the surrender penalty is waived. However, the 12b-1 fee continues indefinitely. Over a number of years, this can be the most expensive load structure of all. The selling broker generally makes a much smaller commission up front than under other load structures, but he or she receives a larger annual trail commission.

Unscrupulous Practices

As in any profession, there are honest mutual fund salespeople, and there are dishonest mutual fund salespeople. I am not in any way implying that there is anything immoral or unscrupulous involved in charging a load. *There is not.* Brokers are in the business of advising clients on what investments to make, and the commission is a perfectly legitimate way for them to get paid for the service they provide. Honest brokers will explain the load structure in a clear fashion so that their clients know what their services will cost. However, unscrupulous brokers will sometimes try to pretend that the load does not cost the client anything.

For example, a lady who worked for a large local bank came into my office about a year ago. She and her husband had done an excellent job of saving over the years, and together they had accumulated about $100,000. They had always invested in Certificates of Deposit since she worked for a bank. When their latest CD came due, they decided to invest the $100,000 in a mutual fund. The bank that she worked for had a brokerage subsidiary affiliated with it, so she decided to seek counsel from one of its brokers regarding appropriate mutual fund investments. After a brief discussion, she invested $100,000 in three loaded mutual funds.

I was curious if the broker had told her about the load included in the funds' expenses, so I asked her, "Did the adviser mention anything to you about the five percent commission these funds charge?"

"Why, no," she responded. "He didn't say anything at all about these funds charging a commission."

"Well, these funds carry a five percent commission," I said. "You paid the broker five thousand dollars to recommend these three funds to you."

"You're kidding," she said. "In fact, I asked him how much it would cost me to invest in these funds. He told me that it wouldn't cost me anything. He said the mutual fund reimbursed him for selling their shares."

While what the broker told her was technically true, the mutual fund *was* the entity that cut him the commission check, he had falsely implied that the commission would not cost her anything.

"Technically, the fund did write him the commission check," I told her. "But where do you think the fund got the money to pay him? From the money you invested. If you tried to sell your shares the next day, they would have been worth ninety-five thousand dollars. His advice cost you five thousand dollars."

For obvious reasons, she was upset to learn what had happened. Understand when you buy loaded mutual funds from a broker that you are paying him a commission for his advice. Before you engage a financial adviser, make sure you understand exactly what services will be rendered and what will be the cost to you for those services.

NO-LOAD FUNDS

No-load funds are just what they say they are. These are mutual funds that do not impose a commission for the purchase of their shares. You deal directly with the fund itself and cut out the role of the broker, thus eliminating the commission.

I am often asked, "How do no-load mutual funds stay in business if they do not charge a commission?" You must understand that the load is unrelated to how mutual funds stay in business. The load is how the broker stays in business.

All mutual funds, load and no-load, charge a fee to manage the portfolio of securities. The management fee will generally average between .75 to 1.5 percent annually, depending on the type of fund. Stock funds, for instance, generally charge a higher management fee than do bond funds. The commission charged by load funds is in addition to the management fee *and is unrelated to it.* Some have said that no-load funds charge a higher management fee than do their loaded counterparts, but I know of no evidence to support such a statement. Management fees appear to be consistent between the two.

The difference between the load and the management fee is an important distinction to understand. A prospective client once told me that he had asked his broker if the mutual funds being recommended to him were load or no-load funds. The broker responded that all mutual funds charge management fees. While the statement made by the broker was true, it was *unrelated* to the question posed by the client. The broker was trying to give his client the impression that management fees and loads are synonymous. They are not.

No-load funds have been around for decades, but they really began to gain in popularity in the 1980s. Consumers were becoming more educated with regard to investments, and many became convinced that they could do as good a job as a broker in picking quality mutual funds. If that is true, then it does not make sense to pay commissions for advice that is not needed.

Picking up on this trend, publications began to proliferate that encouraged investors to do their own fund picking and provided tools to help them do so. One company well known for providing investment research and commentary is Chicago-based Morningstar®, Inc.[9] Morningstar offers a comprehensive line of print, software, and Internet-based products for professional and individual investors. *Morningstar Mutual Funds,* its flagship publication, is available by subscription and in most libraries. It provides an excellent overview of individual mutual funds, rating each fund based on its performance and level of risk.

I must admit that I am a big fan of no-load mutual funds. I sold loaded funds for the first five years of my career. Then I changed how I conduct business and began offering a fee-based money management service that utilizes no-load mutual funds. I am convinced that if investors are willing to do some self-education and spend a few hours in the library, they can indeed do just as good a job picking mutual funds as brokers. All other things being equal, eliminating the load improves the performance of your investment. However, if you do not feel comfortable picking investments, or do not have the time to do the initial research, then there is nothing wrong with paying a load for professional advice.

ADVANTAGES OF NO-LOAD FUNDS

No-load funds, I feel, have certain inherent advantages over loaded funds. The first benefit is obvious: all other things being equal, no-load funds are less expensive than loaded funds. Remember the lady who bought the loaded funds at her bank's brokerage subsidiary? She paid $5,000 in commissions to invest $100,000 in mutual funds. That's a lot of money! I went on to ask her how long the broker spent with her to sell her the three mutual funds. She told me about thirty minutes. To put what had happened in perspective for her, I explained that she had just paid this man $10,000 an hour for his advice. Personally, I'd rather do an afternoon of research in the library.

The second advantage of no-load funds is that they offer more flexibility than loaded funds. Let me explain. Mutual funds are sold in families.

A family of funds may offer a few funds, or it may offer many different funds. As a general rule, however, it will offer only one fund of any particular type.

Let's say that you have done some research and decided you want to invest in an aggressive growth stock fund that utilizes primarily the securities of smaller companies (in the profession we refer to these stocks as *small cap stocks)* that trade over-the-counter. You perform further research and decide that the OTC fund offered by the XYZ family of funds is one of the best-managed OTC funds available. The fund is managed by John Q. Expert, a man respected as one of the top money managers in the country. Mr. Expert has managed XYZ's OTC fund for twenty years. During this time, he has amassed the best performance record of any living OTC fund manager. All things considered, you decide that this is the most appropriate fund for you, and you decide to invest your money in it. You realize that XYZ is a family of loaded funds, but, since this will likely be a long-term investment, you decide that paying the 5 percent up-front load XYZ charges is acceptable.

Two months after you make your investment in XYZ's OTC fund, Mr. Expert, the manager who built the fund's outstanding track record, leaves the mutual fund company to start his own private money management firm. The minimum account size his new firm will accept is $500,000. Your investment account is only $15,000. The person who takes over the management of XYZ's OTC fund is Susie Average, a manager who is not nearly as talented as John Q. Expert. Under Susie's leadership, the fund's performance starts to suffer. Now you are left with several choices, none of which is very appealing.

First, you could just leave your money in the fund and be satisfied with a lower than average rate of return. Obviously, this choice is not acceptable, as it could cost you a tremendous amount of money over a period of years.

Second, XYZ allows you to switch between funds in its family at no charge. Virtually all loaded funds give you this privilege. Here's the problem: XYZ offers only one true OTC fund. The ability to switch into another type of fund at no cost does not provide you with any benefit since you want to be invested in an OTC fund.

Third, you could do more research and move your money to another mutual fund family's OTC fund. This option, however, costs you a second 5 percent load. If you choose this option, you've paid a total of 10 percent in commissions after only two months, and there is no guarantee that the fund manager of this new fund will remain in his position for more than two months. The possibility exists that you could be faced with the same set of poor choices again in the near future.

What is a better alternative? Let's assume that the same thing happens as before, only this time you decide to deal with no-load funds instead of loaded funds. When the manager quits and you realize that the person replacing him will not be able to maintain the fund's excellent performance record, your available options are much more attractive. You are not limited to using just one family's funds in order to avoid paying a sales commission. Instead, you do some research, find another great performing OTC fund from another family of no-load funds, and switch your money to the new fund. Now, you are still invested in an OTC fund with an excellent performance record, and you are not two commissions in the hole. It did not cost you a sales charge to invest in the first fund, and it will not cost you a sales charge to switch to the new fund. I think you can see the additional flexibility that no-load funds offer by making available to you a much larger universe of funds should you need to adjust your portfolio.

BUYING LOADED MUTUAL FUNDS

Loaded mutual funds are generally purchased through brokers or financial planners who offer brokerage services on a commission basis. You can buy loaded funds directly from the fund family, but you will typically still pay the full commission. You do not save this money by dealing directly with the fund family, as is the case with no-load funds. Brokers and planners may work for large national brokerage firms or smaller independent broker/dealer firms. Let me offer you one word of caution. If the broker's firm offers its own family of mutual funds, its brokers are sometimes paid a higher commission to recommend that firm's mutual funds to their clients. The performance records of a brokerage house's mutual funds may not be as good as those of funds in another mutual fund family. Ask the broker directly if he is given a higher level of compensation for recommending his firm's in-house mutual funds. If he is, you have to question the objectivity of his recommendations. Consider going elsewhere if this occurs in order to get impartial advice. If the broker says he doesn't receive a higher commission level for recommending his own firm's funds, then ask him to justify his recommendations by comparing the performance of his company's funds to those offered by independent mutual fund companies.

BUYING NO-LOAD FUNDS

No-load funds can be acquired from a variety of sources. Many people purchase them directly from the fund families themselves. Most fund companies have an 800 number you can call to order a prospectus, as well as an application, for the fund in which you are interested.

DISCOUNT BROKERAGE FIRMS

In recent years, several national discount brokerage firms, such as Charles Schwab, Fidelity, and Jack White, have begun offering programs that allow you to purchase shares of no-load funds in an account established at their company. These brokerage firms typically offer hundreds of no-load mutual funds from the top fund families in the country. Why would an investor purchase no-load funds through a discount brokerage firm instead of acquiring them directly from their fund family? Convenience.

Let's say that you want to invest in mutual funds from three different families. This requires opening three different accounts and getting three sets of statements each month. You will also receive three sets of any other paperwork that may be involved. If you ever want to switch your money from one of these fund families to a different one, you must open another account at the new firm and then transfer your money from the first family to it. The transfer process usually includes filling out a transfer form at the new fund family, which they mail to the old one, or writing a letter to the old fund family requesting the transfer of your money to the new one. Then you wait while your old account is liquidated and the proceeds are mailed to the new fund family. The whole procedure, from start to finish, may take two to three weeks or longer.

If, instead, you invest in no-load funds through a discount brokerage firm, you need to establish only one account. You receive one consolidated statement at the end of the month, which shows your positions in all your investments. If you want to switch investments to a different family of funds, no problem. There is no need to fill out a new application and establish another account elsewhere. You simply pick up the phone and instruct the trader as to what changes you want made in your account. Generally, the fund out of which you are transferring will be sold at the end of the day, and the new fund will be purchased at the close of the next business day.

NO TRANSACTION FEE PROGRAMS

When you trade mutual funds through a discount brokerage firm, you may or may not be charged a transaction fee. Originally, when the discount brokerage firms first began offering these services, all trades incurred a transaction fee. Though it was typically less than the fee charged for trading individual securities, it was still there. This fee was avoided when you dealt directly with the fund families. In recent years, however, most large discount brokerage firms have begun offering the ability to trade many of their no-load funds at no cost, making this option even more appealing.

FEE-BASED INVESTMENT MANAGEMENT SERVICES

The third way you can acquire no-load funds is through a fee-based investment manager. A fee-based manager *manages* portfolios of investments for clients on an ongoing basis as opposed to selling investments. Instead of earning a commission from the investments he recommends, or from making transactions, he uses investments that pay them no commissions, such as no-load mutual funds. He may also use individual securities as well. Fee-based managers feel that receiving compensation only from their clients, and not from the investments they use, gives them a higher level of objectivity in the investment choices they make for clients. They are not tempted to make unnecessary transactions and "churn" clients' accounts since they do not get paid for making transactions.

Many advisers, especially those paid on a commission basis, tout the "buy and hold" philosophy of investing in mutual funds. This line of thought says that once you buy a mutual fund, plan on holding it for the long term and not making any switches. I personally believe, however, that various circumstances may arise that warrant a change in investments.

For example, perhaps a fund with historically high returns begins to seriously underperform other funds in its category due to a change in managers. This would justify switching into a better-managed fund. Maybe an investment category, such as bonds, becomes undervalued due to a false inflation scare and presents an unusually good buying opportunity. This would justify a switch from a less opportune investment. For whatever reasons, as we move through the different stages of an investment cycle, there will be times when making adjustments to your portfolio can be profitable.

Instead of using a buy-and-hold philosophy, fee-based money managers typically make periodic changes to portfolios that they deem to be appropriate. This ongoing management gives the adviser the opportunity to adjust the risk level of clients' portfolios as circumstances warrant. It also gives them the ability to take advantage of opportunities that arise.

A money manager normally charges a fee based on a percentage of the assets he or she manages. This gives managers the financial incentive to increase the value of their clients' assets, since doing so increases their revenue. In other words, it aligns the managers' incentive with their clients' objective of maximizing their return. If managers makes money for clients, their revenue increases; if managers loses money for clients, their revenue decreases.

Many years ago, professional fee-based money management was available on a wide scale for only the very wealthy. Now, however, individuals with as little as $50,000 (even less in some situations) can generally have access to a professional money manager. Investors with sizable accounts should seriously consider fee-based managers as an alternative to a typical brokerage arrangement.

## CHAPTER 13

VARIABLE RETURN INVESTMENTS—USING AMERICAN FREE ENTERPRISE TO ACHIEVE YOUR GOALS

A variable return investment is one in which you take an ownership position. Your rate of return is not guaranteed, as with a fixed return investment, but rather it depends on how well the asset you own performs. There are several examples of variable return investments:

1. Stocks
2. Real Estate
3. Precious Metals
4. Commodities
5. Cable Television Operating Systems
6. Oil and Gas Wells
7. Precious Gemstones
8. Miscellaneous Others

A detailed discussion of each of these investments is beyond the scope of this book. So, for our purposes, I will focus on stocks. Most people have been exposed to the stock market in some form or fashion, and it has been one of the most consistently profitable variable return investments over time. The stock market is also readily accessible to almost anybody.

As we move through this section, I am going to teach you several basic investment principles. Many of these principles apply to virtually all variable return investments, even though I am using the stock market specifically as our example.

INVESTMENT CYCLES

Let's begin this discussion by looking at Exhibit 13-1, titled "Investment Cycles." One of the cornerstone principles of investing in the stock market is that stock prices fluctuate in cycles. They go through periods when their value increases, and they go through periods when their value decreases. I have labeled the cycle shown in Exhibit 13-1 as the stock cycle. You see the ups and the downs, but the long-term trend has been upward at an average annual rate of approximately 11 percent.[10]

When stocks go up for an extended period of time, investors develop

EXHIBIT 13-1　　　　INVESTMENT CYCLES

PRICE

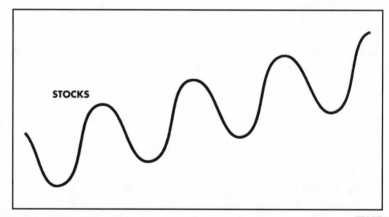

STOCKS

TIME

> **KEY POINT**
>
> It is absolutely essential that you understand and place faith in the cyclical nature of the stock market if you are to profit from it and feel comfortable with it. A failure to do so will cause you to misjudge the psychology of the market and to make bad decisions at critical times!

a euphoric attitude. They begin to feel that stocks will go up forever and never experience a down cycle. During these periods, the philosophy of "buy low and sell high" is replaced with "buy high and sell higher." People figure it doesn't matter what they pay for a stock; it will go up in value regardless of what they pay for it. All that matters, they think, is that they buy stocks, regardless of their prices.

When this euphoria occurs, a speculative bubble develops in the stock market. People begin to bid stock prices to unreasonably high levels. At some point investors realize their error and begin unloading their shares. The herd mentality takes over, the bubble bursts, and stock prices come tumbling down. If you understand the cyclical nature of the stock market, you know that when this euphoria develops, it is not the time to get excited and refinance your house to invest in stocks.

KEY POINT

There are actually two reasons you may lose money in the stock market. The first is because you made an investment that went bad. This occurrence is irrespective of cycles. While this can happen with mutual funds, the risk of this happening is much higher with individual securities. During your investment career, you may or may not experience this event. If you do, there is a definite possibility that the loss will be permanent.

The second reason for losing money is because of market cycles. There is no question as to whether or not you will experience this type of loss. You will! Even if you make perfect investment choices, you will still likely suffer periodic losses due to cycles. However, as opposed to a loss caused by making a bad investment, *cyclical losses are always temporary.* In this section, since I am discussing the stock market as a whole, I am referring specifically to cyclical losses.

Down cycles *always* follow up cycles in the stock market, and up cycles *always* follow down cycles. Understand that down cycles are just part of the ball game. Novices always wonder if they can lose money when they invest in the stock market. Let me set your mind at ease. Not only *can* you lose money if you invest in the stock market, but you *will* lose money at some time or other. In fact, if you remain invested long enough, you will lose money on a periodic basis. Does that mean you've made a mistake when you lose money in the stock market? Does it mean your aunt Tilda was right when she told you to put all your money in CD's? *No!* It just means that we're in the down part of the cycle, and it will eventually be followed by the next up cycle.

Remember how investors become euphoric during the up cycle of the market? They do just the opposite when a prolonged down market occurs. Their unbridled optimism is replaced with a deep pessimism, and fear sets in. They begin to feel that the market may drop indefinitely and eventually go to 0. Even if the investments they own are already priced below what they are actually worth, they reason that they should sell them anyway because they will undoubtedly drop further in value. As a result, they often sell their investments near the bottom of the price cycle. This is one of the worst mistakes that investors can make.

If you understand the cyclical nature of stocks, then you know that every down market is always, let me say that again, *always,* followed by an up market. It may not happen tomorrow, but it *will* happen. Therefore, when prices are depressed and the average investor would not touch the stock market with a ten-foot pole, that is your cue to buy more, if feasible, and increase your stock holdings. Share prices may stay depressed for a while, but if you buy stocks when their prices are cheap, you will eventually be rewarded for your wise actions.

INVESTING IN VALUE

It is interesting to me that people love to buy everything on sale except stocks. When prices have been reduced on an item, it is usually because there is a problem of some sort. If car prices are dramatically reduced, it is because cars are not selling well. The dealers lower their prices in order to move the inventory. People do not look at the low prices and then convince themselves not to buy cars because they fear the auto company is going out of business. No! They buy the car at the low price and then brag to their friends about the good deal they got. They tell their friends how smart they were for waiting until the cars went on sale before they bought one.

These same value shoppers will look at stocks when prices are depressed and convince themselves to not buy them because they fear the economy is going down the tubes. They wait until the economy is strong again (also cyclical) and then pay twice for a stock what they could have paid while prices were depressed. If investors would shop the stock market like they do the supermarket, most would fare much better.

Do your homework, but don't be afraid to buy stocks when prices are down. It may mean that the economy is having problems, but the economy will bounce back, and so will most stocks' prices when it does.

WHY SOME INVESTMENTS INCREASE IN VALUE WHEN OTHERS DECLINE

The next point to understand about variable return investments is that they do not all move in the same cycle. Some variable return investments even travel in opposite cycles from each other. When two investments travel in opposite cycles, this means the same economic forces that cause one investment to go up in value cause the other investment to go down in value. Two such investments are said to be *negatively correlated*. Remember this term and use it frequently in conversations with your friends. They will be very impressed with you.

In Exhibit 13-2, I have superimposed the gold cycle over the stock cycle. This illustration shows that the prices of stocks and gold move in opposite directions over the long term. Do they really? Yes. For example, if you go back to the 1970s, probably the one word that best describes the decade's economic conditions is the word "inflation." The 1970s were a decade of unusually high inflation. How well did gold perform during the seventies? Incredibly well! Gold prices began the decade at $35/ounce and peaked at over $800/ounce.

How did stocks perform during the same time period? Very badly! The Dow Jones Industrial Average peaked at over 1000 in 1968. In August of 1982, it dropped into the upper 700s, resulting in a net loss of over 20 percent during that fourteen-year period. Only the dividends paid kept the total return of the stock market positive during that time period.

Then came the 1980s. Paul Volcker had taken over as chairman of the Federal Reserve Board. He changed the monetary policy of our central

EXHIBIT 13-2

INVESTMENT CYCLES

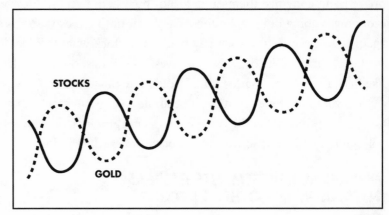

PRICE

STOCKS

GOLD

TIME

bank to fight inflation as opposed to constantly increasing the money supply in a vain effort to generate continual economic growth. Inflation came
down dramatically as a result of the new policy, and interest rates followed
closely behind.

How has gold performed during the 1980s and 1990s? Terribly! As of
this writing, gold has lost almost two thirds of its value from its cyclical
peak.

How have stocks performed during the same time period? Incredibly
well! Indeed, since 1982, stocks have experienced one of the biggest bull
markets of this century.

So, it appears that stocks and gold do indeed move in opposite cycles
from each other and are, thus, negatively correlated.

DIVERSIFICATION INCREASES SAFETY

Now look at Exhibit 13-3. I am not suggesting that you do what this exhibit illustrates, but catch the concept I am trying to communicate. If
you put half your money in stocks and half your money in gold at the
beginning of the time period illustrated, the dashed line in the middle
represents the average value of your account over time. You will notice
that this dotted line is much smoother than either of the lines repre-

EXHIBIT 13-3

INVESTMENT CYCLES

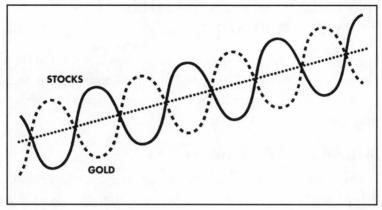

PRICE

STOCKS

GOLD

TIME

senting the stock cycle or the gold cycle. In other words, diversifying your funds between the two negatively correlated investments has reduced the volatility of your portfolio below that of either of the individual investments.

The volatility in the value of your investments, i.e. the magnitude of the ups and the downs, is a measure of the risk in your portfolio. If you reduce the volatility, then you reduce the risk of your portfolio. Therefore, it follows that the lower your risk tolerance, the more you should diversify your portfolio. The more aggressive your investment style is, the less you should diversify.

KEY POINT

The key to reducing the risk level of your investment portfolio is to diversify your funds among negatively correlated investments. You have probably heard the phrase "diversification reduces risk" a hundred times. While that is true, it is not the whole story. Diversifying among similarly correlated investments only slightly reduces your risk. The real key to reducing risk is to diversify between *negatively correlated* investments.

INVESTMENT STRATEGIES AND TECHNIQUES

There are a variety of investment strategies you may want to employ with regard to your stock investments. Most investors will likely find mutual funds to be the preferred vehicle for investing in stocks and executing these strategies.

DOLLAR COST AVERAGING

Dollar cost averaging (DCA) is one of my favorite investment techniques. It is especially effective for newer investors who are just getting started. The beauty of this investment technique is in its simplicity. Do not let its simplicity fool you, though. It is a very powerful technique for accumulating wealth.

DCA consists of investing a set amount of dollars each month into a mutual fund. Because you invest a set amount of money each time, when share prices are high, your dollars buy fewer shares. When share prices are low, your dollars buy more shares. Because of this phenomenon, over time in a fluctuating market, you develop a heavier weighting of lower-priced shares in your portfolio. In other words, you reduce the average *cost* of your shares below their average *price.*

Exhibit 13-4 illustrates this point. In this example we have two investors, A and B, who each decide to invest $500 per month into a stock mutual fund. They both use the same stock fund, but they invest in two different calendar years.

The year investor A used DCA, the stock market really did quite well, which was reflected in the share price of the mutual fund. The first month, the fund's shares were priced at $5.00 each. Investor A's $500 acquired 100 shares. The fund's price went up in February and March, dropped in April back to the original price of $5.00 per share, and then steadily climbed each month until the end of the year. When December's investment was made, the $500 purchased fifty shares at a price per share of $10.

The year investor B used DCA, the stock market did not perform nearly as well, once again reflected in the fund's share price. As in the case

EXHIBIT 13-4

DOLLAR COST AVERAGING

MONTH	INVESTOR A			INVESTOR B		
	AMOUNT INVESTED	SHARE PRICE	# SHARES PURCHASED	AMOUNT INVESTED	SHARE PRICE	# SHARES PURCHASED
January	$500	$5.00	100	$500	$5.00	100
February	$500	$6.00	83	$500	$4.00	125
March	$500	$7.00	71	$500	$2.00	250
April	$500	$5.00	100	$500	$3.00	167
May	$500	$6.00	83	$500	$2.00	250
June	$500	$6.50	77	$500	$1.50	333
July	$500	$7.00	71	$500	$2.00	250
August	$500	$7.50	67	$500	$3.00	167
September	$500	$8.00	63	$500	$3.00	167
October	$500	$8.50	59	$500	$2.00	250
November	$500	$9.00	56	$500	$3.50	143
December	$500	$10	50	$500	$5.00	100

	INVESTOR A	INVESTOR B
Amount Invested:	$6,000	$6,000
# Shares Purchased:	880	2,302
Ending Share Price:	$10	$5.00
Ending Value:	$8,800	$11,510
Average Cost Per Share:	$6.82	$2.61
Average Price Per Share:	$7.13	$3.00

Dollar cost averaging (DCA) involves investing an identical amount of money each month into a mutual fund. The steady investment amount purchases more shares at lower prices and fewer shares at higher prices, resulting in a heavier concentration of lower-priced shares. By maintaining this discipline, DCA forces investors to invest in down markets. While DCA does not assure a profit or protect against a loss in value during market declines, it does reduce the risk of investing a majority of one's money at a market top.

with investor A, the first month's $500 investment was made at $5.00 per share, allowing investor B to acquire 100 shares. Instead of going up as the year progressed, however, the market went through a severe correction, and the price of the mutual fund's shares plummeted. By March the share price was down to $2.00 and the $500 investment purchased 250 shares. In June the share price bottomed at $1.50. The stock market then started to recover, and, by the end of the year, the mutual fund finally reached its original share price of $5.00. This was a tough year. Investor B was patient, though, and kept investing his $500 faithfully on a monthly basis.

The amazing thing is that at the end of their one-year investment periods, Investor B accumulated significantly more money than investor A. Even though they both invested $6,000, Investor A's shares were worth $8,800, while investor B's shares were worth $11,510. While the market did not perform as well during the year that investor B was investing, his $500 monthly purchases bought a lot of shares at very low prices when the market was down. When the fund's share price finally recovered to its original value, those low-priced shares scored some very impressive gains.

KEY POINT

The power behind DCA is that it forces you to invest when the market is low. Psychologically, it is difficult to invest when there are problems in the economy and the stock market is performing poorly. Yet this is when share prices are depressed and bargains can be obtained. If you are dollar cost averaging, then you are committed to investing each month, regardless of how the market is performing. The key to success using DCA is to maintain your discipline regardless of what is happening in the economy and the stock market.

AUTOMATIC BANK DRAFTS

I highly recommend that you take advantage of automatic bank drafts to execute your dollar cost averaging strategy. With automatic bank drafts, you authorize the mutual fund to deduct a certain dollar amount each month from your bank account. This way, you do not have to write the monthly investment check. If you have to write the check, you will probably do it for about three or four months. Then, undoubtedly, some type of emergency will arise, requiring you to not make one month's investment. Other expenditures will begin to take priority over your investment program, and, before you know it, a year has gone by and you have not invested. If the bank is drafting your account automatically, it happens without you having to think about it. Frankly, once the automatic drafting is set up, you will probably not go to the trouble of canceling it. Five years from now, when you are looking at the balance that has accumulated in your account, you will be thankful you set up the bank drafts.

The fact that DCA forces you to invest when the market is low is an important concept. In 1987, I was using a mutual fund for clients that executed its bank drafts on a particular Tuesday each month. On October 19 of that year, known today as Black Monday, the Dow Jones Industrial Average plunged over 22 percent and the stock market experienced its worst one-day decline in history. The day after the crash just happened to be the Tuesday of that month in which this stock fund executed its bank drafts. I actually had a couple of clients call me and ask if there was any way to cancel the drafts for that day because of the market's dive!

Think of it. In one day these clients had the opportunity to acquire shares at a 22 percent discount. What would possess someone to try to avoid this type of buying opportunity and wait until share prices were higher before acquiring them? Yet, that is our natural tendency. Fortunately, it was too late to cancel the bank drafts for the next day, so the clients were forced to invest at what has turned out to be one of the best buying opportunities of all time! The stock market has increased in value over fivefold since the day of the crash, not counting the dividends that

KEY POINT

If you take only one piece of advice from this book, do this: start a dollar cost averaging program with a stock mutual fund immediately with whatever amount you can afford to invest on a monthly basis! Just getting started is more important at this point than the amount of the investment itself. Dollar cost averaging does not assure a profit or protect against a loss in value during market declines, but it does reduce the risk of investing a majority of one's money at a market top. It also helps lessen the pain of a down market by using it as an opportunity to purchase more shares at low prices.

have been paid. Automatic bank drafts and DCA forced people to do what they would not have done on their own.

WEIGHTED ASSET ALLOCATION

An aggressive long-term investor may want to utilize only the stock market and not diversify beyond that. However, less aggressive investors may want to add downside protection to their portfolios by diversifying their investments more broadly. Diversifying, especially among negatively correlated investments, reduces the overall risk level of one's portfolio.

When I put together an investment portfolio for a client, I divide investments into four broad categories: debt (bonds), equities (stocks), real estate, and tangible assets (see Exhibit 13-5). Tangible assets would include such things as precious metals (e.g. gold and platinum), precious gemstones, oil and gas wells, energy mutual funds, and other miscellaneous items. I place stocks and bonds into one broader category called *financial assets*. I place real estate and tangible assets into another category called *real assets*. If desired, investments can be made in all four of these categories via mutual funds. For many people, this will be the most practical way to invest.

I place stocks and bonds in the same category because they tend to move in similar long-term cycles. Their cycles will not line up perfectly, but they are close. Financial assets tend to perform well when the inflation rate is either declining or low and stable.

In the same manner, I place real estate and tangible assets together in their own category because their values, too, tend to move in similar cycles. Real assets tend to perform especially well when the inflation rate is either increasing or high and stable.

THE ROLE OF INFLATION IN THE INVESTMENT MARKETS

If one studies inflation statistics over the last few decades, you cannot help but notice a correlation between the rate of inflation and the performance of certain investment classes. Why would inflation impact the various investment markets?

By definition, inflation is an increase in the money supply relative to the amount of goods in circulation. Basic economics tells us that when the

EXHIBIT 13-5   # ALLOCATION OBJECTIVES

DEBT—BONDS			% ALLOCATION
1. Government Bonds	%	$	
2. Corporate Bonds	%	$	
3. Municipal Bonds	%	$	
4. Zero Coupon Bonds	%	$	
5. Bond Funds	%	$	
6. Certificates of Deposit	%	$	
7. Fixed Annuities	%	$	
EQUITIES—STOCKS			**% ALLOCATION**
1. Individual Stocks	%	$	
2. Domestic Stock Funds	%	$	
3. Foreign Stock Funds	%	$	
4. Variable Annuities	%	$	
REAL ESTATE			**% ALLOCATION**
1. Apartments	%	$	
2. Single Family Residences	%	$	
3. Offices	%	$	
4. Shopping Centers	%	$	
5. Health Care Facilities	%	$	
6. REIT's/REIT Funds	%	$	
7. Warehouses	%	$	
8. Self Storage	%	$	
TANGIBLE ASSETS			**% ALLOCATION**
1. Precious Metals/P.M. Funds	%	$	
2. Oil and Gas Wells	%	$	
3. Energy Funds	%	$	
4. Commodities	%	$	
5. Rare Coins	%	$	
6. Precious Gemstones	%	$	
		TOTALS:	**100%**

supply of an asset is stable, and demand for it rises, its price goes up. Because of their limited supply, real assets are directly impacted by inflation. An escalation in the money supply results in an expanded demand for hard assets, forcing their prices northward. Therefore, hard assets tend to be good inflation hedges and perform well during periods of high or rising inflation.

Inflation impacts stocks and bonds largely through its effect on interest rates. Bond investors demand a rate of return that exceeds their expectations of future inflation. Therefore, when inflation rises, so do interest rates. Higher interest rates have a direct mathematical correlation with lower bond prices, explained in chapter 11.

Elevated interest rates also have a strong, if less direct, influence on stock prices. When a company has to pay higher interest rates for borrowed money, its higher level of payments either reduces its profit margins or forces it to raise prices in order to maintain its margins. However, if it chooses the latter route, higher prices will likely result in a lower demand for its products. Either way, higher interest rates reduce a company's profitability.

Increased rates may also prevent companies from borrowing at all if they cannot invest the money at a higher return than the rate they are paying on the borrowed funds. The lack of liquidity may force such companies to slow, or even abandon, their plans for expansion. This action would result in fewer jobs being produced for the economy, resulting in slower economic growth. Slower economic growth implies a lessening in demand for companies' products, again reducing their profitability.

I could go on, but I think you can see how elevated interest rates depress the values of stocks and bonds. The driving force behind the level of rates is inflation. Since inflation has opposite effects on financial assets and real assets, one would expect that these two investment categories would be negatively correlated.

KEY POINT

Financial assets and real assets are negatively correlated!

We have already looked at the negative correlation between stocks and gold.

Let's look back over the last few decades to see whether history bears out this broader negative correlation between financial assets and hard assets. The 1970s were a time period of high and largely increasing inflation. What investments performed well during this decade? Hard assets. Gold, as discussed earlier, started the decade at $35/ounce and eventually reached over $800/ounce at the peak of its cycle. Real estate was the major go-go investment of the decade. In some instances, you could have made a bad real estate investment and still chalked up a profit because inflation would have bailed you out.

Stocks and bonds, on the other hand, performed miserably during this period of high inflation. As inflation skyrocketed, so did interest rates, forcing bond prices downward. High interest rates choked off economic activity, causing corporate profits to suffer and the stock market to languish. I remember one point when Fortune 500 quality companies had to pay over 20 percent interest rates on borrowed funds. Most companies cannot borrow at these rates profitably.

Then, in the 1980s, a different scenario unfolded. As the Federal Reserve Board instituted a tighter monetary policy, inflation gradually came down, and interest rates followed. Declining interest rates forced bond prices upward in one of the most spectacular bond rallies of this century. Lower interest rates sparked economic growth, corporate profits soared, and, in response, the stock market soared as well.

Real estate, however, entered into a painful recession during the latter part of the decade—a recession that lasted for about seven years. Gold began a decline that eventually cut its price by two-thirds!

The evidence clearly supports that financial assets and hard assets do indeed move in opposite cycles over long periods of time, establishing their negative correlation.

When developing a client's portfolio, I assign a set percentage of the portfolio to each broad category, i.e., financial assets and real assets. The percentage allocations depend largely on the trend and level of the inflation rate. If inflation is low, or high but trending downward, I assign a heavier allocation to financial assets (stocks and bonds). If inflation is high, or low but trending upward, I increase the allocation to real assets (real estate and tangible assets).

The specific investments that I recommend in each category depend largely on the risk tolerance of the investor. For instance, if the economic environment is conducive for financial assets, as it has been for several years, I normally assign a heavier allocation to stocks than bonds for aggressive investors. These same investors would want to emphasize longer-term bonds over shorter-term bonds, possibly even using very volatile and high-risk long-term zero coupon bonds at times. Normally, these investors would also have a significant portion of their portfolio invested in aggressive growth stocks rather than conservative stocks.

For conservative investors I would tend to use a higher percentage of bonds during the same time period. Shorter-term and intermediate-term bonds would likely be emphasized over longer-term bonds. Blue chip stocks, as opposed to the stocks of aggressive, smaller companies, would dominate the stock allocation.

During inflationary times I increase the emphasis on real estate and tangible assets. To fill this need, one may invest in the hard assets themselves or in stock funds that invest in hard asset–related companies, such as oil companies and gold mining companies. Limited partnerships in sound oil and gas investments would also be suitable, though I prefer the liquidity that royalty investment trusts and mutual funds offer.

The principles contained in this section on investing, properly applied, should give you a solid framework for making sound investment decisions.

LONG-TERM PERFORMANCE

Remember that wealth will not be amassed overnight. It will take a disciplined long-term approach to investments to lead to the accumulation of capital over a period of years. Will using the information presented in this section, properly applied, truly make a noticeable difference over time?

Exhibit 13-6 compares the difference in wealth a 4 percent *extra* annual return would make over a period of years. Assume Robert invested $10,000 at age thirty. If he achieved a 9 percent annualized rate of return on his money, by age forty his investments would be worth nearly $26,000, representing a gain of nearly $16,000. If, instead, he had managed to achieve an average annual return of 13 percent during this same time period, his investments would be worth over $38,000 at age forty, a gain of over $28,000. An additional 4 percent return per year resulted in almost twice the gain in earnings over a ten-year period.

This difference in earnings becomes even more dramatic over twenty

EXHIBIT 13-6

WEALTH ACCUMULATION PHASE

AGE	AMOUNT INVESTED	VALUE AT 9%	VALUE AT 13%
30	$10,000	$10,900	$11,300
31	0	11,881	12,769
32	0	12,950	14,429
33	0	14,116	16,305
34	0	15,386	18,424
35	0	16,771	20,820
36	0	18,280	23,526
37	0	19,926	26,584
38	0	21,719	30,040
39	0	23,674	33,946
40	0	25,804	38,359
41	0	28,127	43,345
42	0	30,658	48,980
43	0	33,417	55,348
44	0	36,425	62,543
45	0	39,702	70,673
46	0	43,276	79,861
47	0	47,171	90,243
48	0	51,417	101,974
49	0	56,044	115,231
50	0	61,088	130,211
51	0	66,586	147,138
52	0	72,579	166,266
53	0	79,111	187,881
54	0	86,231	212,305
55	0	93,992	239,905
56	0	102,451	271,093
57	0	111,671	306,335
58	0	121,722	346,158
59	0	132,667	391,159
60	0	144,618	442,010
61	0	157,633	499,471
62	0	171,820	564,402
63	0	187,284	637,774
64	0	204,140	720,685
65	0	222,512	814,374

years. At an average 9 percent return, Robert's balance amounts to $61,088 at age fifty, a gain of more than $51,000. At an annual average return of 13 percent, his balance at the same age is more than $130,000, a gain of more than $120,000. This illustration shows the dramatic difference in asset accumulation that a few extra percentage points in one's annual return can make over an extended period of time.

INVESTING FOR RETIREMENT

When people retire, they often have the mistaken assumption that they must invest all of their assets in instruments designed to generate income, such as bonds or the stocks of utilities companies. Retirees still need an element of growth in their portfolios, however, in order to provide them with a hedge against inflation. Retirees should be concerned with getting the best *total return* that they can achieve at a given risk level, rather than simply focusing on the amount of income their investments generate. Total return equals the dividends and interest earnings *plus* any capital gains experienced.

If a retiree's investments do not generate an adequate level of income, he or she can always sell some of the growth their investments have experienced to supplement their income. Financially, a retiree should care only about having an adequate amount of money to achieve his or her financial goals, i.e., spending, gifting, etc. It really does not matter if the money comes from realizing a capital gain or receiving a dividend. Focusing on total return rather than income opens up a wider universe of investments from which to choose. Some of these other investments may offer higher rates of return at a relatively conservative risk level.

Exhibit 13-7 shows the impact an extra annual return of 3.5 percent can make on a retiree's lifestyle. Assume Mary retires at age sixty. She rolls over her 401(k) balance of $100,000 to an IRA, from which she will need to draw income to supplement her pension. By focusing on income producing investments only, she realizes an annual return of 6 percent on her IRA account. Every year this account generates an income of $6,000, and her $100,000 principal stays intact.

While this may sound secure, the problem is that inflation is constantly eroding the purchasing power of both Mary's savings and her fixed

EXHIBIT 13-7 RETIREMENT INCOME PHASE

AGE	AMOUNT INVESTED	INCOME AT 6%[1]	VALUE AT 6%[1]	6% INCOME AT 9.5% RETURN[2]	VALUE AT 9.5%
60	$100,000	$6,000	$100,000	$16,000	$103,500[3]
61	0	6,000	100,000	$6,210	$107,123
62	0	6,000	100,000	$6,427	$110,872
63	0	6,000	100,000	$6,652	$114,752
64	0	6,000	100,000	$6,885	$118,769
65	0	6,000	100,000	$7,126	$122,926
66	0	6,000	100,000	$7,376	$127,228
67	0	6,000	100,000	$7,634	$131,681
68	0	6,000	100,000	$7,901	$136,290
69	0	6,000	100,000	$8,177	$141,060
70	0	6,000	100,000	$8,464	$145,997
71	0	6,000	100,000	$8,760	$151,107
72	0	6,000	100,000	$9,066	$156,396
73	0	6,000	100,000	$9,384	$161,869
74	0	6,000	100,000	$9,712	$167,535
75	0	6,000	100,000	$10,052	$173,399
76	0	6,000	100,000	$10,404	$179,468
77	0	6,000	100,000	$10,768	$185,749
78	0	6,000	100,000	$11,145	$192,250
79	0	6,000	100,000	$11,535	$198,979
80	0	6,000	100,000	$11,939	$205,943
81	0	6,000	100,000	$12,357	$213,151
82	0	6,000	100,000	$12,789	$220,611
83	0	6,000	100,000	$13,237	$228,333
84	0	6,000	100,000	$13,700	$236,324
85	0	6,000	100,000	$14,179	$244,596

[1] Assume investments average a 6% annual rate of return, all of which is withdrawn for income.
[2] The income level assumes that the investments average a 9.5% annual rate of return. At the end of each year, 6% of the account balance is withdrawn for income, leaving 3.5% to be reinvested each year. Note that the income (6% of the account balance) grows by 3.5% annually.
[3] Since 3.5% is reinvested in the account each year, the balance grows by 3.5% annually.

retirement income. At an average inflation rate of 5 percent, her purchasing power is cut in half after fourteen years. If Mary is your mother, I hope your house has an apartment downstairs because it will be difficult, if not impossible, for Mary to continue her lifestyle on half the purchasing power on which she retired.

If Mary could increase her average rate of return by a mere 3.5 percent per year, it could make a dramatic difference in her situation over a period of years. Let's say that Mary, by focusing on total return instead of on the income level her investments generated, experienced a 9.5 percent return on her investments. She continued to withdraw 6 percent of her principal balance every year for income, and she reinvested the remaining 3.5 percent of her return back into her principal balance in order to provide her with a hedge against inflation. Fourteen years later, Mary's annual income has increased from the initial $6,000 to $9,712. Not only has her income increased dramatically, but her principal balance has grown to $167,535, an increase of nearly 68 percent. Do you think this would make a difference in Mary's lifestyle over a period of years? You better believe it would!

What I am hoping you see from these illustrations is that you do not have to do wild and crazy things and try to "get rich quick" in order to make a substantial difference in your net worth over time. You simply need to consistently apply some sound, basic investment strategies to achieve a solid rate of return and give your assets an appropriate amount of time to grow.

SAVING TAXES

Taxes are simply other expenses that take away from your effective rate of return. If you can invest in such a way as to reduce your tax burden without reducing your return, you will be better off than if you pay taxes on every penny of investment gains that you earn.

Many investments that offer tax benefits carry a level of risk, or possess a lack of liquidity, that may make then unsuitable for you. However, there are vehicles, such as Individual Retirement Accounts (IRA's), that are not investments in and of themselves. Rather, they are tax-deferred

> **KEY POINT**
>
> **Never make an investment based on the tax benefits alone. Make sure that the investment is sound on its own merits, and let the tax benefits be icing on the cake.**

accounts into which you place investments. As long as the investments remain in these accounts, they continue to experience certain tax benefits.

Why does the government allow such tax-deferred vehicles when they reduce its revenue? Tax-deferred accounts encourage several behavior patterns that the government deems favorable. First, when individuals can invest money and avoid taxes on the investment gains for an extended period of time, it encourages them to save more money, resulting in a higher national savings rate. A higher national savings rate results in lower interest rates and, therefore, lower financing costs for the government. It also creates a larger pool of funds from which the borrowing needs of the private sector can be met. The other major reason the government allows tax-deferred savings accounts is because they encourage individuals to save for their retirement years. Government leaders recognize that as the baby boom generation reaches retirement age, Social Security retirement income benefits will have to be scaled back in some form or fashion. This will be easier for the electorate to swallow if they have done a better job of saving for their own retirement.

INDIVIDUAL RETIREMENT ACCOUNTS (IRA'S)

Traditional IRA's are accounts designed to help individuals save money specifically for their retirement years on a tax-deferred basis. Individuals are allowed to contribute 100 percent of their income, up to $2,000 per year, into an IRA. If an individual has a nonworking spouse, together they can invest 100 percent of their combined income up to $4,000 per year in their IRA's, but neither spouse can invest more than $2,000 in his or her individual account.

Many types of investments are permitted in IRA accounts. Banks have done such a good job of marketing their IRA's that many people think they are the only institutions at which you are allowed to establish IRA's. This is not true. As a matter of fact, I generally recommend establishing IRA's at a discount brokerage firm and using no-load mutual funds as the investments within your account.

Dividends, interest, and capital gains within an IRA are not taxed as they are earned. What would normally be taxed as investment income is not taxed until it is withdrawn from the IRA, which may not be for many, many years.

Contributions to an IRA may or may not be tax-deductible in the year in which they are made, depending upon the income level of the taxpayer and whether either spouse has a qualified tax-deferred savings plan available to that spouse through his or her employer. I will not get into the technical details of this rule, but some people can deduct all of their IRA contributions, some people can deduct part of their IRA contributions, and some people cannot deduct any of their IRA contributions. It wasn't always this complicated, but in 1986, Congress decided to *simplify* the tax code, and this was the result.

You must pay taxes on deductible IRA contributions when you withdraw them. Regardless of whether you deducted your contributions or not, you must pay taxes on your dividends, interest, and capital gains when they are withdrawn from your account. You will also incur an additional 10 percent tax penalty, courtesy of our good friends in Washington, on most withdrawals from an IRA made prior to age $59^{1}/_{2}$ (how in the world did they come up with this number?).

The government wants you to defer taxes in an IRA, but not indefinitely. Therefore, it makes you gradually withdraw money from your account on an annual basis beginning (are you ready for this?) by April 1 of the year after the year in which you turn age $70^{1}/_{2}$ (if this is tax simplification, I'd hate to see this thing when it was complicated!).

ROTH IRA

The Taxpayers Relief Act of 1997 made available a new type of nondeductible IRA, dubbed the Roth IRA. The Roth IRA differs from traditional IRA's in several key respects.

All contributions to a Roth IRA are made on a nondeductible basis. Investment gains accumulate tax-free within the account. But, unlike existing nondeductible IRA's, subject to certain conditions, individuals will have the ability to withdraw money from their accounts completely tax-free. Generally, to withdraw funds on a tax-free basis, the money must remain within the account for five tax years, beginning with the tax year in which a contribution was made. Tax-free withdrawals may be made under any of the following circumstances affecting the account holder:

- On or after attaining age $59^{1}/_{2}$;
- Upon death to their estate or a named beneficiary;
- Upon disability;
- For qualified first-home purchases.

Contributions to a Roth IRA, like those to a traditional IRA, are limited to $2,000 annually and are reduced by any amounts contributed to traditional IRA's. However, contributions can be made after age $70^{1}/_{2}$, and no distributions are required after attaining age $70^{1}/_{2}$.

An intriguing advantage to Roth IRA's lies in the area of nonqualified distributions. With traditional nondeductible IRA's, the IRS assumes that any nonqualified distributions consist first of investment gains, which are subject to taxation and the early withdrawal penalty. As of this writing, the IRS assumes any nonqualified distributions from a Roth IRA consist first of principal and are not subject to taxation or the early withdrawal penalty. This adds an element of liquidity to Roth IRA's that is missing from traditional nondeductible IRA's.

SAVINGS PLANS FOR THE SELF-EMPLOYED AND SMALL EMPLOYERS

Self-employed individuals and small employers are allowed to establish various types of tax-advantaged savings plans. The first of these plans is a simplified (there's that word again) employee pension plan (SEP). A SEP is similar to an IRA, but much higher contribution levels are allowed.

Another tax-deferred savings plan is the *SIMPLE IRA*. This type of account allows employees to make voluntary tax-deductible contributions to their account in addition to the contributions the employer makes.

Keogh plans are a third type of tax-advantaged savings plan. These plans are more expensive to administer than a SEP and are more complex, but they also make available more liberal contribution limits.

Rules governing these saving plans are very detailed and complex.

> **KEY POINT**
>
> **If a self-employed person has employees, and they make a contribution for themselves to a tax-advantaged savings plan, the law generally requires that they make contributions for their employees as well. Therefore, it is critical to learn all the requirments for employee contributions when establishing a tax-advantaged savings plan. I recommend that you consult with a tax adviser when setting up one of these plans.**

Consult with a professional tax adviser before setting up one of these plans to ensure that you comply with the applicable regulations.

SAVINGS PLANS FOR CORPORATE EMPLOYEES

Tax-advantaged savings plans for corporate employees fall into two categories: defined contribution plans and defined benefit plans.

Defined contribution plans are your standard corporate savings plans. The most popular of these is the 401(k) plan. Employee contributions to 401(k) plans are tax-deductible. Many times employers will match employee contributions up to a certain level. Assets within the plan grow tax-deferred until they are withdrawn. The deductible contributions and any investment income generated by the investments within the account are taxable only in the year in which they are withdrawn.

Generally, I recommend taking as full advantage of 401(k) plans as possible. First, contributions are fully tax-deductible, which is not the case with IRA contributions for many individuals. For most employees, this means that Uncle Sam is footing the bill for up to one third or more of their contributions. Second, there is a good probability that your employer

> **KEY POINT**
>
> **The IRS places limits on how much can be contributed to all tax-advantaged savings plans, both for corporate employees and for self-employed individuals. Be very aware of these contribution limits when you establish one of these plans. Penalties can be levied for contributions over the allowed limits.**

will match a portion of your contributions. While it is usually wise to contribute as much as you are allowed to these plans, if you do not invest at least the amount that your employer will match, you are leaving money on the table.

Most 401(k) plans have several investment vehicles available. In most situations, I recommend allocating a high percentage of your funds to stock accounts since, over the long term, they will likely generate the highest returns. Because contributions are being made by payroll deductions, you are using dollar cost averaging to build your assets.

Upon retirement, you can roll the taxable proceeds from your 401(k) plan into an IRA. Even though some companies allow you to keep your assets in their 401(k) plan after you retire, I think it is normally wise to roll your assets into an IRA anyway. IRA's give you similar tax-deferral benefits as a 401(k) plan, but they also generally offer more flexibility with regard to available investment options, especially if the IRA is established at a national discount brokerage firm. Many 401(k) plans offer very limited investment options, often as few as five to seven investment funds. An IRA account at a discount brokerage firm will typically offer you hundreds of investment options, including many of the top performing mutual funds in the country, as well as individual securities. I personally cannot see any benefits to deliberately limiting your investment options by keeping your money in a company 401(k) plan after you retire. A possible exception, however, is that tax considerations will cause some people to benefit from liquidating their 401(k) plan and taking the money directly rather than rolling the assets into an IRA. Check with your tax adviser before making decisions on how to handle your 401(k) plan when you leave your employer.

Defined benefit plans are your classic pension plans. With these plans, your employer defines what income benefits it will pay to retirees. These benefits are based on several factors, the primary ones normally being the retiree's age and years of service with the company. Typically, contributions to these plans are made totally by the employer.

Profit sharing plans give employers the opportunity to share profits of the business with employees in a tax-advantaged manner. Many employers feel that employees work harder if they have a financial stake in the

> **KEY POINT**
>
> In general, employers are starting to move away from defined benefit plans and are shifting to defined contribution plans. Defined contribution plans place a portion of the burden of saving for retirement on the employees, and they are less expensive for employers to maintain.

profits of the business. Therefore, they like the incentives that these plans provide for employees. Contributions, made by the employer, vary each year based on the level of profits experienced by the business.

SAVINGS PLANS FOR CHARITABLE, EDUCATION, AND HOSPITAL INSTITUTIONS

The primary tax-advantaged savings plan available for employees of most charitable, education, and hospital institutions are *403(b) plans*. These plans, also known as tax-sheltered annuities, are very similar to 401(k) plans. Generally, contributions are the sole responsibility of the employee, but contribution limits differ from those of 401(k) plans.

One problem with many 403(b) plans is that they often use only commissionable investments, which commonly carry long surrender penalty periods of five or more years. This reduces the flexibility of these plans and makes the investment choices less favorable than the no-load investments normally found within 401(k) plans.

Many discount brokerage firms offer 403(b) plans. Federal laws require that contributions be made to a 403(b) account via payroll deduction, meaning that your investment choices will be limited to those sponsors allowed by your employer. However, many employers' 403(b) plans allow the assets within the plan to be *transferred* to any 403(b) plan set up by the employee. If you are not satisfied with the investment choices offered by your employer, talk to your benefits department about adding a plan offered by a discount brokerage firm that would allow for investments into no-load mutual funds. If they do not show any interest in this idea, then you may want to check into the possibility of transferring the assets in your existing 403(b) plan into a 403(b) plan offered by a discount brokerage firm. Make sure you understand any surrender penalties that may apply before you initiate such a transfer.

Many charitable, educational, and hospital organizations also offer defined benefit pension plans. Often, both the employer and the employee contribute to the pension plan. As with pension plans offered by other corporations, these plans will pay a specific level of retirement income to retirees based on a formula that takes several factors into consideration. The most important of these factors are typically, once again, the retiree's age and years of service with the employer.

PROTECTING WHAT YOU HAVE

## CHAPTER 14

HOW MUCH INSURANCE DO YOU REALLY NEED?

Some Christians wonder whether carrying insurance shows a lack of faith in God and His promises for our provision. I believe that God will provide for all my needs, but that does not mean that I do not get a job or that I fail to take prudent steps to protect my family and our assets. As implied in the parable of the talents, God is pleased when we take action to wisely utilize the resources He has given us.

Insurance is a way to protect our assets and to care for our families. Deciding how much and what types of insurance to carry is an important part of an overall plan. Just like other financial products, all insurance is not created equal. To make wise insurance decisions, you must understand the scope and intent of the various options available to you.

THE CONCEPT OF RISK MANAGEMENT

Insurance is a key component of your *risk management* program. Expressed in investment terms, risk management involves taking a guaranteed minor loss (the relatively small premium you pay) in return for protection from an unpredictable and potentially devastating financial loss. It may seem unwise to pay premiums every month to protect you and your loved ones from something that will probably never happen, but you will be thankful you have it if you need it. As a wise steward, your objective in buying insurance is to carefully evaluate your needs so that you carry the appropriate amounts of the right types of insurance at affordable rates.

Catastrophic losses will strike only a small percentage of the population each year. It is impossible to accurately predict who will be affected and the costs they will incur. It is possible, however, to accurately predict the level of risk of a large group of people by using probability theory. The concept of insurance says that instead of each individual taking his own chances, as small as they may be, of incurring a large loss, we will pool our resources by paying premiums to an insurance company. This pool will be paid out to cover the losses of the few who do experience a catastrophe. Yes, insurance companies are in business to make a profit, as are all businesses, but they nevertheless supply a sort of "community protection" for those who need it.

Those who pay premiums but do not suffer a loss will be out the amount of their premiums. This is the "guaranteed loss" mentioned above. But those who do experience a loss will be saved from financial calamity by the joint contributions of the whole group.

To accurately predict the collective risk of a group, insurance companies employ statisticians called actuaries. Actuaries evaluate groups based on distinct factors such as age, gender, income level, and so on. They accumulate accurate statistics on how many people in each category experience financial loss each year due to covered circumstances, such as illnesses for health insurers, accidents for casualty insurers, or deaths for life insurers. They also monitor the average costs of those losses.

Based on all of these precise calculations, the actuaries then develop risk pools of individuals, and premium rates are established for each category according to its corresponding risk level. Those individuals who fall into higher risk categories pay higher premiums. For example, teenagers, as a group, pay higher auto insurance premiums because they have the worst track record for accidents. By the same token, women, on average, pay lower life insurance premiums than men because they have longer life expectancies.

Because the whole system is based on statistical averages, it may seem unfair to have to pay premiums even though you may never suffer a loss. To many, insurance is a "necessary evil," but a more constructive perspective is that you are investing a relatively small amount to protect the assets that you have worked so hard to earn. Let's look at how we can minimize the amount that we spend on insurance while maximizing our coverage for every dollar spent.

REDUCING INSURANCE COSTS

Insurance companies insure policyholders for a variety of unfortunate events. These events can be of a catastrophic nature, or they can be very minor. Very minor events occur with much greater frequency than catastrophic events. In your own life, think of how many times your car has sustained a nick or a ding relative to the number of major auto accidents in which you have been involved. If policyholders filed claims for every little covered cost they incurred, the insurance company would sustain exorbitantly high overhead expenses to process them all. Paying for all those minor claims would be very expensive as well. This would boost the cost of insurance to prohibitively high levels.

To help remedy this situation, the insurance company makes a deal with policyholders. If you, the policyholder, will assume the responsibility for the cost of those little incidents and only use the insurance company to reimburse you for the costs of significant claims, then it will reward you with lower premiums.

DEDUCTIBLES

The prudent use of deductibles is one way you can reduce your insurance premiums. The deductible is a set amount that individuals pay for damages before the insurance company pays anything. If you have a $250 deductible on your auto policy, then you pay the first $250 for needed repairs, and the insurance company pays only the repair costs above that level. Increasing your deductibles is one way that you can insure yourself for minor expenses and only use the insurance company for larger claims. Raising your deductible, therefore, reduces your premiums.

There are trade-offs involved. Raising your deductible on a policy will not reduce your premium as much as you have raised your deductible. Normally, if you have a very low deductible, upping it a little will reduce your insurance premiums significantly. However, once you have increased them to a certain level, raising them farther does not reduce your premium enough to justify the higher deductible.

As I discuss the various types of insurance, I will often suggest a level of deductibles that I believe to be optimal, based on my experience.

However, because the price structures of policies vary from company to company, my suggested levels should serve only as a starting point for your analysis. The optimum package for you will require a balance between premiums, deductibles, and levels of coverage. Many times you can significantly raise the level of coverage within a policy and incur only a slightly higher premium if you raise the deductible at the same time.

CO-INSURANCE

Some types of insurance, in particular health insurance, contain co-insurance provisions. Co-insurance means that once the deductible has been met for a claim, you share some portion of the remaining expenses with the insurance company. A common co-insurance split is 80/20, meaning that you pay 20 percent of the costs of the claim above the deductible, and the insurance company pays the other 80 percent of the costs.

Why is there co-insurance? To give policyholders some level of personal responsibility for the costs they incur. Take health insurance for example. If insurance companies paid 100 percent of our medical expenses, then people would go to the doctor for every little ache and pain they felt, driving the costs incurred by the insurance companies through the roof. Let's face it, some aches and pains are too minor to be worth a trip to the doctor. If insured individuals incur an out-of-pocket cost every time they go to the doctor, they are less likely to go to the doctor for minor ailments. They will instead visit their doctor only when they experience problems that actually require the attention of a physician.

TYPES OF INSURANCE COVERAGE

There are many different types of insurance coverage. Some are considered to be more standard than others. The fact is, you can probably find an insurance company willing to insure you for almost any esoteric calamity that could possibly occur. During the early 1990s recession, some insurance companies actually offered policies that paid employees their salaries if they were laid off from their jobs.

Some of the more standard types of insurance include the following categories:

1. PROPERTY AND CASUALTY (P&C) COVERAGE—Standard P&C coverage includes homeowners and auto insurance. It may also include coverage for boats and other similar items that expose you to liability or property damage risks. Also covered under this category is a little-known, but very important, type of insurance known as umbrella liability coverage.

2. ACCIDENT AND HEALTH COVERAGE—This type of coverage pays medical expenses associated with accidents or illnesses. Such expenses typically include hospital costs, doctors' fees, and various types of specialized care costs.

3. DISABILITY INCOME INSURANCE—Disability income insurance covers just what its name implies. Instead of covering expenses associated with an accident or an illness, as is the case with medical insurance, it covers the loss of income that such an event would cause, due to your inability to perform the functions of your job.

4. LIFE INSURANCE—When a breadwinner of a family dies, not only is it a tremendous emotional blow to the family but it is a major financial blow as well. Provisions need to be made to pay off any outstanding debts of the decedent and the surviving family, to cover the costs of future expenses, such as college education costs, and to provide income for the surviving family. Life insurance provides a lump sum of money that can be used to satisfy these needs.

A good way to get started in analyzing your risk management program is to complete an inventory of all your existing insurance policies. Most people do not know how much protection they carry in various areas, resulting in improper coverage amounts and the inefficient use of their premium dollars. Exhibit 14-1 shows Tom and Mary Sue's inventory. A blank form is provided at the end of the chapter for your personal use.

EXHIBIT 14-1

PAGE 1 OF 2 PAGES

INSURANCE INVENTORY

TOM AND MARY SUE SMITH

LIFE INSURANCE

INSURANCE COMPANY	POLICY NUMBER	INSURED PARTY[1]	OWNERSHIP CODE[2]	BENEFICIARY CODE[2]	FACE AMOUNT	TYPE POLICY	NET CASH VALUE	ANNUAL PREMIUM
Employer	111-1111	H	H	W	$ 250,000	Term	$	$ 94
Private	222-2222	H	H	W	$ 500,000	Term	$	$ 650
Private	333-3333	W	W	H	$ 50,000	Term	$	$ 82
					$		$	$
					$		$	$

DISABILITY INCOME INSURANCE

INSURANCE COMPANY	POLICY NUMBER	INSURED PARTY[1]	WAITING PERIOD	BENEFIT PERIOD	MONTHLY BENEFIT PAYMENTS	ANNUAL PREMIUM
Employer	XY147	H	6 months	65	$ 2,000	$ —
Private	PT298	H	6 months	65	$ 750	$ 400
					$	$
					$	$

HEALTH INSURANCE

INSURANCE COMPANY	POLICY NUMBER	TYPE[3]	BENEFIT AMOUNT	DEDUCTIBLE AMOUNT	ANNUAL PREMIUM
Employer	123-45-6789	M	$ 80/20	$ 250/person	$ 790
Private	D10011	D&V	$ 50/50	$ 100/person	$ 180
			$	$	$
			$	$	$

[1]H=Husband W=Wife CH=Child O=Other   [2]H=Husband W=Wife J=Joint O=Other   [3]M=Major Medical D=Dental V=Vision S=Supplemental

INSURANCE INVENTORY

TOM AND MARY SUE SMITH

HOMEOWNERS INSURANCE

PROPERTY LOCATION	INSURANCE COMPANY	POLICY NUMBER	DWELLING COVERAGE AMT.	LIABILITY COVERAGE AMT.	MEDICAL COVERAGE AMT.	DEDUCTIBLE AMOUNT	ANNUAL PREMIUM
123 Elm St.	XYZ Company	HO 555-555	$ 125,000	$ 100,000	$ 5,000	$ 250	$ 400
			$	$	$	$	$
			$	$	$	$	$

VEHICLE INSURANCE

VEHICLE	INSURANCE COMPANY	POLICY NUMBER	LIABILITY COVERAGE AMT.	MEDICAL COVERAGE AMT.	COMPREHENSIVE COV. DEDUCTIBLE	COLLISION COV. DEDUCTIBLE	MISCELLANEOUS COVERAGES[4]	ANNUAL PREMIUM
Ford	XYZ Co.	23 2333	$ 100/300/50	$ 5,000	$ 100	$ 250	T, R, U	$ 650
Honda	XYZ Co.	34 3444	$ 100/300/50	$ 5,000	$	$	T, U	$ 300
			$	$	$	$		$
			$	$	$	$		$
			$	$	$	$		$
			$	$	$	$		$

MISCELLANEOUS INSURANCE

TYPE OF INSURANCE	INSURANCE COMPANY	POLICY NUMBER	ITEM INSURED	AMOUNT OF COVERAGE	DEDUCTIBLE AMOUNT	ANNUAL PREMIUM
Umbrella	XYZ Company	UM 888 888	—	$ 1,000,000	$	$ 130
Personal Articles	XYZ Company	PA 999 999	Wedding Ring	$ 10,000	100	$ 40
				$	$	$
				$	$	$

[4]T=Towing R=Car Rental U=Uninsured Motorist

PROPERTY AND CASUALTY INSURANCE

As stated earlier, the three main areas included in the category of property and casualty insurance are homeowners insurance, auto insurance, and umbrella liability insurance.

HOMEOWNERS INSURANCE

Generally, homeowners insurance pays for sudden and accidental damages incurred in and around your home. If there is a snowstorm, and an overhanging branch from a tree falls through your roof, your homeowners insurance pays for the costs of the repair.

PROPERTY DAMAGE

One night my family and I came home to find several fire trucks parked on our street. One of our neighbors had gone shopping and accidentally left a burner of the stove turned on. A short in the electrical system caused a spark that started a fire in the kitchen. The fire then spread through the whole house. The bright flames and billowing smoke caught the attention of another neighbor, who called the fire department. Upon their arrival, the firefighters connected their hoses to the nearest hydrant, but it did not work. With great frustration, they found the next hydrant to be inoperative as well. Searching for a fire hydrant that actually pumped water cost the firefighters fifteen minutes of precious time, time that they did not have. The house burned to the ground.

What would a homeowners policy cover in such a situation? If the damage could be repaired, the insurance company would pay for the cost of the repairs over and above the deductible. In the case of our friends, the damage could not be repaired, so the insurance company paid to have the house rebuilt.

Most homeowners policies are written in such a way that the insurance company will pay the cost of having the damage repaired or the structure replaced. This is called *replacement cost coverage.* Older policies were not generally written this way, but rather covered the home up to a specific dollar amount. For instance, if you purchased a house that cost $50,000, you might have purchased an insurance policy that covered damage to the physical structure of the house up to a maximum of $50,000.

The problem with these policies became agonizingly apparent during the inflationary decade of the seventies. Homes increased in value very rapidly. Many insurance policies were not updated to keep their level of coverage current with the inflated values of houses. People would submit claims for damage that had occurred, only to find that the level of their coverage was significantly less than the cost of the damage. I only mention these types of policies because, even though they are considered antiquated, there are still people who have these older policies who have not updated their coverage for many years. It would be an excellent idea for these individuals to change their coverage to a replacement cost policy.

THE 80 PERCENT REPLACEMENT COST RULE

These older policies have an interesting and often overlooked feature, known as the 80 percent replacement cost rule. Let's say that Bill and Joan bought a house many years ago for $50,000. At that time, they purchased a homeowners policy that covered up to $50,000 of damage to the house. Due to appreciation, their house is now worth $125,000. One night, Joan is cooking shrimp flambé for dinner, and the kitchen catches on fire. After the damage is appraised, they find out that the cost to repair the kitchen will be $20,000. "No problem," Bill says. "We have $50,000 of insurance coverage. The insurance company will pay the full bill for the repairs." Is Bill correct? Unfortunately, no.

The 80 percent replacement cost rule says that for the insurance company to pick up the full tab for the damages, minus the deductible, the homeowner must carry coverage for at least 80 percent of the replacement cost of their home. If the coverage is less than this amount, the insurance company will pick up only a portion of the repair costs. The following formula is used to figure the percent of the damage claim the insurance company will pay for:

$$\frac{\textbf{Actual Coverage}}{\textbf{.8 x Replacement Cost}} = \textbf{Percentage of payment for damage claim}$$

In the case of Bill and Joan, 80 percent of the replacement cost of their home is $100,000. They should have updated their policy to provide at least this minimum level of coverage. Their $50,000 of coverage is half the required minimum amount, so the insurance company will only pay for half the cost of the repairs to the kitchen, or $10,000. Bill and Joan will have to pay the other $10,000 out of their own pocket.

If you have one of these older types of policies, make sure that your level of coverage keeps pace with the replacement value of your home. Better yet, upgrade your policy to a replacement cost coverage policy.

CONTENTS COVERAGE

Not only does homeowners insurance cover damage to your home, but it also covers damage to the contents of your home. Contents would include such things as furniture, jewelry, stereos, and clothing. These items may be insured for either their actual cash value or their replacement cost. The actual cash value is normally computed as the cost of the item minus depreciation. Obviously, this amount may fall well short of what it would cost to replace the item today. Considering the slight difference in premiums, replacement cost coverage is the better choice.

The amount of coverage the policy provides for contents is usually 50 to 80 percent of the coverage it provides for the dwelling. Be prepared, if you make a claim under this provision, to justify your loss by submitting a list of those items damaged or destroyed.

KEY POINT

Homeowners policies contain internal sublimits on the amount of protection provided for many of the items covered by this provision. For instance, the policy may provide $50,000 coverage for contents, but cover losses on jewelry only up to $1,500. Review your policy's sublimits to determine if you have significant exposure on any valuable items. If so, you may wish to acquire additional coverage on those items.

LIABILITY COVERAGE

The other type of coverage provided by your homeowners policy is liability protection. Why do you need liability protection?

Picture this: it is a beautiful winter morning. A steady snowfall the night before left eight inches of fresh snow on the ground. Whenever it snows, all the neighborhood kids gather at your house to sled because your driveway is the one that goes down at a forty-five-degree angle. You love kids, so you enjoy the sounds of screaming and laughter outside. All of a sudden, you hear a scream that is not accompanied by laughter. You rush outside to discover that one of your neighbor's children tried to "surf" down your driveway on his sled and fell, breaking his arm in two places. You call his parents, and the child is rushed to the nearest hospital to have his broken bone set and his arm put in a cast.

Days later, you are reflecting on the incident when you hear a knock at the door. It is someone from the sheriff's office. You are being sued because it was your yard in which the child was playing when he pulled his foolish stunt and broke his arm. Not only are you being sued by the child's parents for reimbursement of the medical expenses they incurred in treating the child's broken arm but you are also being sued for an additional $25,000 for negligence. Are you liable? Very possibly.

This is why you have liability coverage on your homeowners policy. This coverage will not only pay for the medical costs of treating the child's broken arm but, if you lose the court case regarding negligence, the insurance company will also pay the settlement costs, up to the limits of your policy.

Some homeowners policies are issued with liability limits of $25,000. Raising this level of coverage to $100,000 will probably cost an additional $10 to $15 per year. This is a small price to pay for the additional protection.

AUTOMOBILE INSURANCE

Your automobile insurance policy contains many different types of coverage, including:

Collision coverage—Collision protection covers you for the costs of repairs to your car in the event of an accident in which you are at fault, or if your vehicle is involved in a "hit and run" accident in which you are not at fault. Many policies are issued with $50 deductibles. This is too low a deductible in my opinion. Raising this deductible to $250 will reduce your premium.

If the insurance company determines that it will cost more than the value of your car to repair it, then it will *total* it. This means that it will set a fair market value for your car and then buy it from you for this amount instead of paying to have it repaired. Generally, you would rather have a car repaired than totaled, because it is unlikely that you will be able to purchase a quality replacement car for what the insurance company will pay you.

When the insurance company offers you a price for which it will purchase your totaled car, realize that this is just a first offer, *not a final offer*. **Do not accept their first offer on the spot!** Remember the slogan "everything is negotiable." Be prepared to negotiate with the insurance company for a higher amount. Agents will often have the authority to settle with you for a price higher than their first offer.

How do you negotiate for a higher price? Arm yourself with data on comparable vehicles selling for higher amounts! You can find numerous books that give current values for used cars of virtually every make and model. Look through the classified ads in your local newspaper for cars of the same make, model, and year as yours, or as close as possible, with comparable mileage. Many cities have tabloids that are filled with ads containing the above information about cars for sale. The point is, do your homework and be prepared to prove to the insurance company why your car is worth more than what it is offering.

Liability coverage Liability coverage for automobile insurance is very similar to the liability coverage for homeowners insurance. If you have an accident that is your fault, there are several expenses that may be incurred for which you could be held liable.

The property damage portion of your liability coverage pays for the expense of having the other party's car repaired. There are many more expensive luxury cars on the road today than there were a decade ago. As a result, property damage expenses can run very high. Therefore, I recommend property damage limits of $50,000.

The bodily injury section of the liability coverage pays for medical expenses incurred by the other parties involved. However, in our litigious society, you may get sued for a lot more than just the medical expenses resulting from the accident. You may get sued for lost income due to the accident, as well as pain and emotional suffering. Liability costs can run into the hundreds of thousands of dollars, or even higher. Raise this coverage to at least $100,000/$300,000. This means that the insurance company will pay liability claims of up to $100,000 per person injured, up to a maximum of $300,000 per accident. In a later discussion on umbrella liability insurance, I will explain why I chose these limits.

Some insurance companies provide only "single limit" liability coverage. In such instances I recommend that you set the coverage limit at a minimum of $300,000. This means that the insurance company would pay up to this amount for all bodily injury and property damage claims resulting from an accident in which you are at fault.

Comprehensive (other than collision, or OTC) coverage This protects you from expenses for physical damage sustained by your car for reasons other than a collision.

Let's say that you are driving down the highway at 55 mph. A tire of the eighteen-wheeler in front of you flicks a loose rock off the road into your windshield, cracking it. Comprehensive coverage would pay for the repair of your windshield. Another example of this type of claim is hail damage to your car.

KEY POINT

As your car ages and its value depreciates, you may reach a point where it no longer makes financial sense to carry comprehensive or collision coverage on your vehicle. For instance, assume the value of your vehicle is only $1,000, and your deductible for collision coverage is $250. The insurance company is on the hook for a mere $750. If your annual premium for this amount of coverage is $250, then your cost per dollar of insurance is much too high. It makes more sense to drop the coverage in this situation and save the $250 annual premium.

Raising your OTC deductible to $100 will help reduce your overall premium.

Uninsured motorist coverage Unfortunately, an astoundingly high percentage of the people driving on our highways do not carry appropriate automobile insurance. Suppose that one of these people collides with you, damaging your car and injuring you. You sue to recover the costs you have experienced, only to discover that the person who hit you has no insurance, nor does he have any assets from which to recover your costs. Without uninsured motorist coverage, you will wind up footing the bill for all the costs you incur from the accident, even though the wreck was not your fault.

This coverage provides you with protection if your vehicle is struck by an uninsured (or underinsured) motorist. I recommend that you carry the same limits as under the liability section of your policy. However, if you absolutely have to reduce coverage somewhere in order to reduce your premiums, this would be one area where you could consider lower limits.

If you utilize all of the recommended limits and deductibles as outlined in this section, you will probably be able to increase your coverage substantially and incur only a minor increase in your premium.

UMBRELLA LIABILITY COVERAGE

An umbrella liability policy begins coverage where your homeowners and automobile liability coverages end. In our litigious society, liability costs incurred for an accident that is your fault can run very high. People often try to retire early by winning liability cases when they are injured in any way in an accident. Unfortunately, people frequently sue for exorbitant amounts, and they often win.

Let me give you a poignant example. I have a friend who was involved in a very minor auto accident. She was stopped behind a school bus on an exit ramp, waiting for the traffic signal to change. When the light turned green and the bus started, it rolled backward slightly, its tailpipe denting the very center of the hood of my friend's car. The damage to the car was negligible, but, due to the location of the dent, she was not able to close the hood of her car. The policeman who worked the accident issued her a ticket for stopping too close behind the bus. She fought the ticket in traffic court, but lost the case. The judge ruled that the accident was her fault. Shortly thereafter, my friend was served papers notifying her that the bus driver was suing her for whiplash. Eventually the bus driver dropped the frivolous lawsuit, but this exemplifies how litigious our society has become.

Assume that you are in an auto accident for which you are at fault. You are sued for a total of $1 million by the three other people who were in the vehicle you struck, and the court finds that you are liable. The liability coverage in your auto policy covers your expenses up to $300,000. You are personally responsible for paying the other $700,000. Umbrella liability coverage would start at the $300,000 provided by your auto liability coverage and would cover your court settlement up to $1 million. Actually, these policies are normally written for a *minimum* of $1 million and can go much higher than that.

Umbrella liability policies require that you have certain limits of coverage on your underlying homeowners and auto insurance policies. For most umbrella policies, the limits I have recommended on your homeowners and auto policies will meet the required levels. However, your property and casualty insurance agent will make sure that you comply with all the appropriate limits when you purchase the umbrella coverage. Normally, boats and motor homes can also be covered under an umbrella policy, assuming you have the appropriate levels of liability coverage on them.

ACCIDENT AND HEALTH COVERAGE

Health insurance has become a major political topic due to the steep climb in medical costs in recent years. There are many types of health insurance, and there are different types of coverage within each policy. Most of what I will discuss in this section is normally found in a single policy. However, for our discussion, I will separate the coverages into their individual components.

BASIC BENEFITS

The basic benefits in most health insurance policies cover a few major categories of expenses. These are:

1. HOSPITAL EXPENSES—These expenses cover all the miscellaneous items supplied by the hospital. Unfortunately, these items are not supplied at Wal-Mart prices. I remember an incident that happened when Lisa delivered our first baby. After the delivery, we were presented with a "gift" basket by the hospital. We thought this was very nice, until we got the bill for this "gift" basket (they didn't even ask us if we wanted it!). They charged us twenty-four dollars for a small package of diapers that sold for ten dollars at Wal-Mart. I could go on and on, but you get the point.

Typically, hospital expenses also include such things as daily room and board, and various hospital services, such as use of the operating room, anesthetics, drugs (you know, those ten-dollar aspirins), use of their medical equipment, etc.

Increasing your deductible in this area is often very effective in reducing your overall premium.

2. SURGICAL BENEFITS—These benefits are applied to the charges of the operating surgeon(s). The various type of surgical procedures are normally subject to limits, shown in a schedule of benefits within the policy. You are responsible for costs over the schedule limits.

Some policies define their limits in terms of specific dollar amounts. Other policies use a standard known as UCR, which stands for "usual, customary, and reasonable," in order to determine appropriate benefit levels for various surgical procedures. Under this methodology, the insurance company determines what are the customary charges in a geographical area for a wide variety of surgical procedures. These "customary" charges become the amounts covered by the insurance company.

3. REGULAR MEDICAL BENEFITS—Regular medical benefits cover doctors' expenses for other than surgical procedures.

LIMITATIONS OF BASIC COVERAGES

When you are shopping for health insurance policies, there may be certain limitations inherent in some policies of which you want to be aware. First, certain expenses may not be covered. One of the main items that falls in

Insurance companies may apply the UCR standard to a wide variety of doctors' expenses other than just surgical procedures.

this category is maternity expenses. If you are at a time in your life where you are anticipating starting a family, or growing an existing one, this type of coverage would likely be important to you. Study the policy to determine exactly what is covered and what is not covered. Make sure that you are comfortable with what you find.

Second, see how benefits are determined. Are they based on what are usual and normal charges for a given area, or are they based on specific dollar limits? If they are based on normal charges for an area, then, as the normal charges rise, so will the level of the benefits. This gives you a built-in inflation hedge. On the other hand, if benefits are based on a specific dollar amount, these limits may not keep pace with actual expenses during a period of rapidly rising costs. If this is the case, find out how often limits are updated and on what basis.

MAJOR MEDICAL BENEFITS

Major medical expense policies will cover most types of medical expenses up to very high limits, often $1 million or higher.

Generally, most indemnification types of health insurance policies will combine the basic benefits coverage and the major medical coverage into one policy. It is unusual to see the two types of coverage actually split into two policies.

Health insurance is one area where the use of higher deductibles may result in substantial savings in premium costs. Also, most health insurance policies have a co-insurance provision. Normally, under this provision, the insurer will pay 80 percent of the covered expenses over the deductible, either in total or up to a certain limit.

For instance, let's say that John has a condition that requires surgery. The usual, customary, and reasonable charge for the type of surgery needed by John in his geographical area is $4,500. John's surgeon charges $5,000 for the procedure, but John knows his surgeon is one of the best in this field and feels that the extra expense is justified. John's policy has a $500 annual deductible, of which he has used $0 so far this year. It also has an 80/20 co-insurance provision. How much will John's surgery cost him for just the surgeon's fee?

First, John must begin by satisfying the annual deductible, which would be $500 out of his pocket. Next, the insurance company will pay 80 percent of the UCR cost for the surgery above the deductible amount. The UCR cost for the surgery is $4,500. Subtract from that amount the $500 to fulfill John's deductible, and the insurance company will pay 80 percent of the remaining $4,000, which amounts to $3,200. John pays the remaining $800 of this expense. Finally, John is fully responsible for the $500 his surgeon charges over and above the usual and customary charges for the surgery. So, John's total cost for this surgery will be $1,800, and the portion of the bill for which the insurance company is responsible totals $3,200.

HMO'S, PPO'S

In recent years, the traditional indemnification type of health insurance policy has been hit with competition from Health Maintenance Organizations (HMO's) and Preferred Provider Organizations (PPO's). In an HMO situation, a corporation becomes an individual's primary health care provider. Doctors no longer own their private practices. Instead, they are employees of the HMO and are paid on a salary basis. Normally, an HMO will employ general practitioners as well as specialists.

Patients are limited to using doctors employed by the HMO. Referrals are made to outside physicians only when the HMO does not employ a doctor in the specialty required to meet a patient's needs. Otherwise, patients must generally foot the bill themselves if they seek the services of an outside doctor.

In return for agreeing to limit their choice of doctors, the insured can generally save money on their health care needs. In return for their monthly premium, instead of paying a percentage of the costs for their medical treatments, patients pay a small set fee for each treatment. The same applies to prescribed drugs.

Surveys have shown that the level of care provided varies greatly among HMO's on a national basis. Check out any HMO thoroughly before joining. The dark side of HMO's is that they are profit-making organizations that have agreed to meet essentially all of their clientele's medical needs for what is virtually a set fee. The primary way to increase profits in such situations is to increase volume, i.e., for each doctor to see more patients in the same amount of time, which requires spending less time with each patient. While this may theoretically be accomplished by eliminating unnecessary procedures, it can also result in a compromised level of care.

PPO's are basically a referral network. Doctors maintain their own practices and are responsible for their own overhead. When they join a PPO, they agree to accept a set fee for treatments provided to referred patients. Patients insured by the PPO pay monthly premiums as with traditional health insurance and HMO's. They still pay a portion of their medical expenses, but this is a smaller percent when they use doctors who are members of the PPO. Patients may still be insured when they use doctors outside the PPO, but they bear a higher percent of the cost of their treatment when they choose to do so.

The landscape for available health care options is changing rapidly. I am confident that competition and the free enterprise system will eventually result in the best combination of quality care versus cost of care. It will be interesting to see what emerges over the next five to ten years.

DISABILITY INCOME INSURANCE

Disability income insurance replaces a breadwinner's income in the event of a loss of income due to a disabling accident or illness. Obviously, one of the main determinants of the premium level will be the level of benefit provided by the policy. Most insurance companies will provide you with total coverage of up to 60 to 70 percent of your income. They will normally subtract from this amount any coverage provided to you by other disability income policies you carry, whether they are private policies of other insurance companies or a group insurance plan offered by your employer.

In addition to the amount of the disability benefit, there are three key factors that determine the size of the premium:

1. WAITING PERIOD—The *waiting period*, also known as the *elimination period*, is the length of time between when you become disabled and when you make a claim for income on your policy. There is a trade-off between the length of the elimination period and the level of premiums that you pay. Most occurrences of disabilities last for a very short while. If the insurance company had to process claims and pay benefits for every very short-term disability, it would cause premiums to skyrocket. Once again, the insurance company makes a deal with its policyholders: if the policyholders will insure themselves for the very short-term disabilities and only use the insurance company for long-term disabilities, then it will reward the policyholders with lower premiums. Therefore, lengthening the time of your waiting period will reduce your premiums.

The difference in premiums between a one-month waiting period and a three-month waiting period is sizable. On the other hand, the difference in premiums for switching from a six-month waiting period to a twelve-month waiting period is not as significant. From the policies I have reviewed, six-month waiting periods appear to provide the optimal trade-off between benefits and premiums. This assumes that you would be able to survive financially for six months without an income. If this is not the case, you may be forced to choose a shorter elimination period initially. Be diligent, however; if you can increase your liquid assets so that you can lengthen your waiting period to six months, you will save on your disability income insurance premiums.

2. LENGTH OF BENEFIT PERIOD—The benefit period is the number of months or years that the insurance company will pay the disability benefit once the waiting period is over. Most insurance companies offer one-year, five-year, and "to age sixty-five" benefit periods. The longer the benefit period, the higher will be the premiums. Since the objective is to pay out of pocket for smaller incidents and to buy insurance for protection against catastrophes, I recommend the "to age sixty-five" benefit period.

3. OCCUPATION CLASSIFICATION—As one might expect, disability insurance premium rates will vary based on one's occupation. Thus, the old insurance adage: "The greater the risk, the higher the premium." A construction

worker is obviously more likely to incur a disabling on-the-job accident than a secretary. The higher disability premiums for a construction worker reflect the greater risks inherent in his or her job.

MISCELLANEOUS PROVISIONS

There are certain provisions within disability income policies with which you want to be familiar, including the following:

Guaranteed renewable, noncancelable With your automobile insurance policy, if you make an excessive number of claims, your insurance company may drop you as a customer or raise your rates. You do not want the insurance company providing your disability income policy to have these same options available.

Guaranteed renewable, noncancelable means that the insurance company cannot raise your rates or drop your coverage unless it takes the same action for an entire class of insureds. For instance, if you make an above average number of claims, it will not be able to single you out to raise your rates. However, it may discover that, as a group, male doctors living in Georgia are making a substantially higher than average number of claims. As a result, it may raise the rates for that entire group of insureds.

Social Security offset *Social Security offset* is another provision that will help reduce your disability insurance premiums.

Social Security offers a disability income benefit to those who qualify. Our friends, the actuaries, can predict very precisely, over a large group of people, how many individuals who become disabled will qualify for these benefits. They can also predict with great accuracy the average benefit level received.

The Social Security offset provision is a voluntary option in disability policies. This provision states that if you become disabled and make a claim on your policy, any income provided by Social Security will be used to offset the income paid by the insurance company. If you do not qualify for Social Security benefits, then your disability policy will continue paying you full benefits.

For example, let's say that Dexter is involved in an auto accident and becomes disabled. After a six-month waiting period he makes a claim on his disability policy. His policy pays him a monthly benefit of $3,000 and contains a Social Security offset provision. Dexter applies for Social Security disability benefits and, after a waiting period, is informed that he is qualified to receive benefits of $600 per month. Once Social Security begins paying Dexter the $600 monthly income, his insurance company reduces the monthly benefit it pays by the same $600, thereby keeping Dexter's total monthly income at $3,000.

On the other hand, if Dexter did not qualify for Social Security benefits, his insurance company would continue paying him the full $3,000 per month he had been receiving. Since the companies can predict approximately how many policyholders will qualify for Social Security benefits, and they can estimate how much money this will save them, they can afford to grant policyholders a reduction in their premium for including this provision in their policies.

If saving on premiums is a priority, and for most people it is, adding this provision to your policy is an excellent way to accomplish that.

Definition of disability One very important factor in any disability policy is how the insurance company defines "disability." Obviously, the tighter the definition of a qualifying disability, the lower is the likelihood that a policyholder will be able to collect on a claim. Therefore, you want the most liberal definition of disability available.

Disability is commonly defined as *the inability to perform the essential functions of your job,* during the first two years of a disability. After this two-year period, a disability is typically defined as *the inability to perform the essential functions of any job for which you are reasonably suited due to your education and experience.*

Some definitions of disability require that you be under the constant care of a physician. This is restrictive simply because your physician may have released you from his or her care, there being nothing else the doctor can do for you, and yet you are unable to perform the functions of your job.

Other definitions of disability may state that you are not disabled if you can perform any job for which you are reasonably qualified and that exists anywhere in the national economy, even if such a job is not available in your geographic region. Obviously this, too, is a very restrictive definition of disability.

Partial disability This, to me, is an important provision of a disability insurance policy. It states that if you go back to work on a part-time basis and earn only a percentage of your predisability level of income, then the insurance company will still pay you partial benefits. If the insurance company does not do this, you may lose your disability income benefits, even though you are earning only half the income you were earning prior to becoming disabled.

Suppose that Jill earns $5,000/month as a salesperson. She becomes disabled and makes a claim on her disability income policy. After a year, she returns to her job, but she can work only half as many hours as she did prior to her disability. As a result, she earns only half the level of her predisability income. With the partial disability benefit provision in her policy, Jill would continue to receive half the disability income that she was receiving from the insurance company. This benefit helps a person bridge the income gap as he or she recovers from a disability.

> **KEY POINT**
>
> **Most disability insurance policies require that you experience a period of total disability before they will pay you income benefits for a partial disability.**

LIFE INSURANCE

A life insurance policy pays a lump sum of cash to the beneficiaries upon the death of the insured. Life insurance serves three primary purposes. First, it provides for estate liquidity. When a person dies, depending on the size of the estate, there may be considerable estate taxes due. The estate taxes must be paid out of the assets of the deceased person's estate. If the estate does not have adequate liquid assets with which to pay the taxes, then assets will have to be sold from the estate to raise the liquid funds. Obviously, the heirs may not want to liquidate assets from the estate for a number of reasons. In these situations, a life insurance policy naming the deceased person's estate as the primary beneficiary could provide the estate with the needed liquid funds.

The second purpose of life insurance is to provide a lump sum of money that can be invested to generate a stream of income for the survivors. Many times the person who dies leaves survivors who were dependent on them for income. This is not true just for one-wage-earner families. Two people may have been able to live fine on their individual incomes before they were married, but after getting married they developed a lifestyle that requires two incomes. The absence of a breadwinner can cause serious financial hardships for the survivors.

The third purpose of a life insurance policy is to provide for lump sum monetary needs of the surviving family, such as paying off debts owed, children's education expenses, and a daughter's future wedding. Having life insurance proceeds set aside for these special expenses reduces the income needs of the surviving family.

THE COST OF INSURANCE

How do insurance companies determine the cost of insurance, i.e., the appropriate level of premiums to charge policyholders? Look at Exhibit 14-2. Remember our friends the actuaries. Actuaries can predict very accurately how many people of a certain gender will die at any given age during a given year and, therefore, how many claims will be made. The higher the risk group into which a person falls, the higher the premium he or she will pay.

Here are some general principles. Fewer younger people die than older people. Therefore, the younger a person is, the lower is the life insurance premium he or she will pay. Women live longer than men. Women, therefore, pay lower life insurance premiums than men at any given age. Actuaries have determined that across a large group of people, those who smoke cigarettes have a lower life expectancy than nonsmokers. Smoking cigarettes, therefore, increases your life insurance premiums. You will also pay higher premiums if you engage in any dangerous activities that could result in death by accident, such as hang gliding, auto racing, spelunking, etc.

Exhibit 14-2 focuses on the age issue. At early ages, premiums go up very little from year to year because, at young ages, the risk of dying goes up very little from year to year. However, as one gets older, insurance premiums go up faster from one year to the next because of the increased sta-

EXHIBIT 14-2   COST OF LIFE INSURANCE

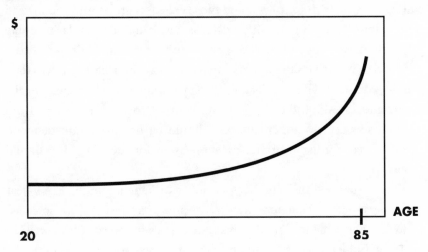

$

AGE

20   85

tistical likelihood of death. At some point, premiums increase exponentially. This is the concept of term insurance. Term insurance is pure insurance protection.

Insurance buys you time. Your eventual objective is to be able to provide for your financial needs from your own assets. You want to reach the point where you are financially independent, and your own assets will provide an adequate income for survivors at your death. When you have achieved this, you are self-insured, and the only reason you *might* need life insurance is for estate liquidity purposes. However, you will not reach this point of financial independence overnight. It will take time. If a breadwinner dies before these goals have been achieved, then life insurance will make up for the gap. In other words, life insurance buys the time that the decedent would have otherwise had to save and accumulate assets for achieving financial independence.

When you are young, your need for life insurance is typically high. You may have a large mortgage. The education expenses for all your children lie ahead of you. Your savings are probably low because you have had only a short time to accumulate assets. If a breadwinner dies during this time of life, his or her spouse and children would have large financial needs for which the life insurance proceeds would need to provide.

As time goes by, your need for life insurance should decrease. Your children graduate from college, and those expenses are behind you instead of in front of you. The mortgage decreases as you make regular monthly payments on it. Your children leave home and are no longer financially dependent on you (that's the way it's supposed to work, at least). Also, as time goes by, you should be steadily increasing your net worth by systematically saving and investing, thereby insuring yourself to a greater extent from your own assets. By retirement, you should be financially independent, and your need for life insurance, except possibly for estate liquidity, should go away.

The actual cost of insurance per dollar of benefit goes up every year that a person ages. Therefore, the cost of pure term insurance, also called annually renewable term (ART) insurance, goes up every year as well. As people get older, because of the reasons discussed above, they should be able to reduce the amount of life insurance they carry on themselves. Their assets steadily increase, while their need for insurance gradually decreases. When their assets equal their needs, they no longer need life insurance. As people reduce the amount of their life insurance coverage, even though the cost per dollar of benefit is rising, the net cost should remain fairly steady. A higher premium for less life insurance should keep the total premium costs at about the same level.

Some people do not like the fact that premiums increase periodically with term insurance. An alternative for those people is permanent insurance. With permanent insurance, the premiums remain steady for the life of the policy instead of rising every year. How can the insurance companies accomplish this?

Exhibit 14-3 provides the answer. When the insured is young, and the cost of insurance is very low, the life insurance company charges the insured a premium higher than the cost of insurance. The extra premium is placed into a savings account, which, by the way, grows on a tax-deferred basis. This tax-deferred savings account earns interest and grows each year as the insured makes his premium payments.

At some point in time, the cost of the insurance exceeds the premiums being paid. When this occurs, the insurance company begins dipping into the cash value of the policy to pay the insurance expense that is above the

EXHIBIT 14-3 PERMANENT LIFE INSURANCE

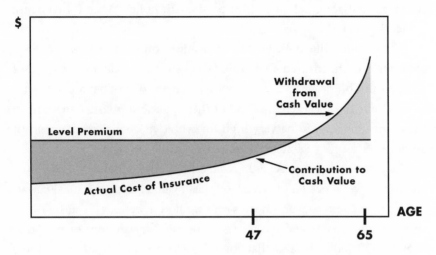

premium being charged. At first, the amount taken from the cash value is less than the interest being earned, so the cash value continues to grow. In later years, the extra premium amount being taken from the cash value equals the interest earned, and the cash value stops growing. Finally, as the cost of insurance continues to increase, the extra premium being removed from the cash value exceeds the interest earnings, and the cash value starts to shrink. When the cash value finally disappears, the policy lapses and no more coverage is provided. It used to be standard practice for insurance companies to set the premiums at a level that caused the policy to lapse at the policyholder's age 100.

TYPES OF LIFE INSURANCE

With this background information as a foundation, let's talk about the various types of life insurance policies and the evolution that has taken place in recent years in the insurance industry.

WHOLE LIFE INSURANCE

A whole life insurance policy is a permanent insurance policy as described above. For many years it was the primary type of insurance policy marketed, with comparatively little term insurance being sold. Quite frankly, one reason for this is because the commissions earned by the selling insurance agent are much higher for permanent policies than for comparable term policies.

With whole life policies, the insurance company makes numerous guarantees to the insured, including (1) The interest rate to be earned, (2) The amount of the cash value at any given age, and (3) That the policy will stay in force until a certain age. All of these guarantees cost something, so the premiums tend to be very high for whole life policies relative to the amount of insurance actually acquired.

Let's say that you purchase a whole life policy providing $100,000 in coverage. Over a period of years, your cash value builds to $50,000. Many people have the mistaken impression that if you were to die at that time, your beneficiaries would receive the $100,000 face amount of the policy plus the $50,000 cash value that you have accumulated, resulting in a total benefit of $150,000. This is a misconception.

The beneficiaries of the deceased individual would receive the $100,000 face amount of the policy and nothing else. So, at that point, the insured has really provided $50,000 of his own $100,000 protection via the cash value he has built up, and the insurance company is really on the hook for only $50,000. This is another reason the insurance company can keep the premium steady: *the amount of coverage that they actually provide declines as the cash value increases.*

TERM INSURANCE

During the 1970s and early 1980s, the expense and inefficiencies of whole life policies became glaringly evident. Cash values offered pitifully low interest rates, while market interest rates were soaring into the double digits. Mutual funds were gaining in popularity and experiencing much higher long-term returns than the rates being paid on life insurance cash values. The industry was ripe for a revolution, and term insurance became the weapon of assault.

The theory behind term insurance was simple: since the cash value in a whole life policy was such a bad investment, buy term insurance instead of whole life insurance. Take the difference between the premiums you would have paid for the whole life policy and the much lower premiums for the term policy and invest it in a mutual fund. Illustrations showed that if mutual funds continued the average rate of return that they had been experiencing, one's cash value would grow much faster, and you were insuring yourself at a much quicker pace than with whole life insurance. As your term insurance premiums increased, you could periodically decrease your amount of coverage and eventually end up with a mutual fund account balance that equaled the face amount of your original term policy. As a general rule, these programs were set up to provide a constant amount of total protection divided between the investment account and the insurance face amount. This concept caught on like wild fire, and it created a tremendous upheaval in the insurance profession.

LEVEL TERM INSURANCE

The concept here is generally the same as for ART insurance, except the premiums are slightly higher at the beginning, but they remain level for various periods of time, such as five years, ten years, etc. Many times, over the time period the premiums remain steady, the total premium paid will be less than the premium for ART insurance.

Let's say that you buy a ten-year level term insurance policy. What happens at the end of ten years? Generally, insurance companies will want you to take another physical at that time to ensure that you have not developed any potentially life-shortening health problems since you first bought the policy. If no medical problems are discovered, then they will renew the policy for another ten years at a higher premium than you paid over the previous ten years. If you saved enough money during the initial ten-year period, you can now afford to reduce the amount of your insurance coverage to keep the premium low. If you do not pass the physical, the policy remains in force, but it becomes an annually renewable term policy.

DECREASING TERM INSURANCE

Decreasing term insurance is annually renewable term insurance. However, instead of the premium increasing every year while the face amount stays the same, the premium remains steady during the life of the policy, and the face amount of the policy declines automatically. This keeps the insured from having to reduce his insurance coverage periodically; it is done automatically for him.

The most common type of decreasing term insurance is mortgage insurance. This policy is designed to liquidate the mortgage balance if the insured dies before the home is paid for. I normally do not recommend mortgage insurance because it is usually more expensive than ordinary term insurance.

UNIVERSAL LIFE INSURANCE

As term insurance began to grow immensely in popularity, insurance companies realized that they needed to develop more competitive permanent insurance products. One of the first new products designed to compete with "buy term and invest the difference" was universal life insurance.

Universal life insurance combined an underlying term policy with a cash value, similar to whole life insurance. However, instead of guaranteeing the interest rate that would be paid on the cash value for the life of the policy, the cash value paid market interest rates, which fluctuated over time. As with whole life policies, the assets in the cash value continued to grow on a tax-deferred basis.

Universal life quickly replaced whole life insurance as the dominant permanent life insurance coverage.

VARIABLE LIFE INSURANCE

Universal life insurance gained in popularity, but many still found fault with it. Even though the cash value paid competitive interest rates, these returns still paled in comparison to those of stock mutual funds in the 1980s and early 1990s. So the insurance industry developed variable life insurance. Variable life insurance is essentially the same concept as universal life insurance, only the cash value can be invested in one or more of several mutual funds.

Over time, new insurance products are being designed to compete more effectively with investments. This is good as long as the insured realizes that what he is gaining in the form of an investment, he is losing in the form of security on his insurance.

The type of life insurance that is appropriate for you is a personal decision. Universal life insurance may make sense for very conservative investors who only use fixed return investments, such as CD's and bonds. For those individuals, the conservative interest-bearing cash value offers a competitive rate of interest and tax-deferred growth.

Variable life insurance makes sense only for more aggressive individuals. The mutual funds in which the cash value is invested will probably offer the highest returns over time of any of the cash value investment options. This type of coverage also offers the least guarantee of value of any of the cash value investments.

I personally prefer the philosophy of buying term insurance and using other types of investments, such as mutual funds, to accumulate wealth. This is in keeping with my philosophy that insurance is a necessary evil, and we should keep our insurance premium costs as low as possible. I think it is wisest to separate our insurance needs from our investment programs.

KEY POINT

All of these comments have been made under the assumption that the policyholder actually needs the insurance. Some life insurance agents and brokers recommend using either universal life or variable life insurance solely as an investment since the cash value grows on a tax-deferred basis. I disagree with this approach. The mutual funds within a variable life policy are typically loaded, plus premium costs are being incurred for insurance coverage that's not needed. I never recommend using life insurance as a stand-alone investment.

DETERMINING YOUR INSURANCE NEEDS

To be a wise consumer of life insurance products, it is essential that you be able to determine how much life insurance you need. Many dollars are wasted on insurance because people really do not know how much insurance they need. If life insurance is being purchased to meet a need, then it should be possible to determine with some level of accuracy what the level of that need is. Once that is accomplished, then it is relatively simple to purchase an appropriate amount of insurance.

There are several factors to be considered in determining how much life insurance coverage is proper for an individual.

FINAL LUMP SUM EXPENSES

When a breadwinner dies, there are certain expenses that must be paid. The first is burial expenses. Gone are the days of inexpensive funerals. The burial plot must be purchased, if that has not already been done. Burial plots are not cheap. Then the funeral itself must be arranged. Just the funeral expenses alone can run in the neighborhood of $5,000. Many funeral companies now allow individuals to arrange and pay for their funerals in advance and guarantee the price of the funerals whenever they actually occur.

There are also administrative expenses involved in probating the estate of the deceased. These costs will vary from state to state. In some states, such as Georgia, where I live, the probate process is relatively inexpensive. Other states charge a percentage of the estate's value to probate it. This can be very expensive. You need to ascertain the costs involved in probating an estate in your state and include that as part of your needs analysis for life insurance purposes.

The third expense is estate taxes. Estate taxes are discussed in more detail in the chapter on estate planning. For larger estates, the estate taxes can be sizable. You must be sure that there will be enough liquid assets to pay these taxes from the estate, or assets will need to be sold in order to pay them.

In addition to financial expenses that are associated with a person's death, you will generally want to liquidate any remaining debts so that they will not be a burden to your surviving family. Establishing an emergency reserve fund of several thousand dollars is a good idea, as well, to handle any unexpected expenses for which you may not have planned.

The final need to be considered is the income need of your survivors. Here, two spouses should have an open and frank discussion concerning the income needs of each if the other were to pass away. It is never easy to discuss these matters, but an open discussion now can save the survivor much heartache and many financial problems later. Perhaps the survivor is employed or would become employed if their spouse were to die. Would the income the survivor could generate be adequate, or would supplementary income need to be provided by life insurance proceeds? Would the survivor even want to join the work force if he or she is not currently employed outside the home?

Income needs should consider more than just normal living expenses. You may not want to plan for your spouse to become rich upon your death, but neither do you want your wife/husband to be financially strapped for the rest of his or her life. Education expenses for surviving children must be taken into consideration as well. Determine what is the necessary lump sum amount that could be invested at a conservative rate of return to generate the required income.

Add all these lump sum needs together, and the difference between that amount and your current level of assets equals the amount of life insurance that is needed.

In Exhibit 14-4, titled "Life Insurance Needs Worksheet," I give an example of how to compute one's life insurance needs, using once again the case of Tom and Mary Sue Smith for our illustration. As usual, blank worksheets are provided at the end of the chapter for your personal use. Complete one worksheet for each spouse.

Let's look at the situation if Tom were to predecease Mary Sue. When you are computing the life insurance needs of a surviving spouse, you make the computation as though the deceased spouse dies today.

Tom and Mary Sue have allocated $6,000 for funeral expenses, $1,000 for probate expenses, over $116,000 for debts to be paid off, and $40,000 to be invested in order to pay the future education costs of their two children. Note that the mortgage balance is included as one of the debts to be

EXHIBIT 14-4

LIFE INSURANCE NEEDS WORKSHEET
TOM AND MARY SUE SMITH

Date: _____

Surviving Spouse: **Mary Sue**

LUMP SUM EXPENSES: PURPOSE	AMOUNT		
Funeral	$ 6,000		
Probate	$ 1,000		
Estate Taxes	$ 0		
Debts	$ 116,582		
Education	$ 40,000		
Other	$		
Other	$		
Other	$		
TOTAL:		$	163,582

INCOME NEEDS:			
Gross annual income needed by surviving spouse	$ 40,000		
Surviving spouse's income	$ 0		
Difference	$ 40,000	(A)	
Interest rate at which money could be invested	6%	(B)	
Lump sum needed to meet income needs (A÷B)		$	666,666
Total lump sum requirement		$	820,248
Available investable assets		$	82,284
LIFE INSURANCE NEED:		$	737,964

paid off. Generally, it makes sense to liquidate the mortgage and reduce the surviving spouse's income need by the amount of the monthly payment. The alternative is to not pay off the mortgage and include the monthly payment as part of the surviving spouse's income needs.

All of the above resulted in a total lump sum expense need of $163,582.

Mary Sue felt that with two children she would like to be able to stop working if Tom were to die. She would need an annual income of $40,000 to live comfortably. If she could earn an average rate of return of 9.5 percent on her invested assets, she could withdraw 6 percent of the balance each year to meet her income needs and reinvest the remaining 3.5 percent to give her a hedge against inflation. That should keep her from ever outliving her income. Dividing $40,000 by .06 (6 percent) yields a needed lump sum of $666,666 to meet Mary Sue's income needs.

Add the $163,582 required for lump sum expenses to the $666,666 needed to meet Mary Sue's income needs in order to obtain a total investable assets requirement of slightly over $830,000. Subtracting Tom and Mary Sue's current liquid asset base of $82,284 yields a total life insurance need on Tom's life of approximately $748,000. I would recommend that he carry $750,000 in total life insurance coverage, giving Mary Sue a little extra for unexpected emergencies. The insurance inventory that the Smiths completed shows that Tom already maintains exactly this amount of life insurance. In his case, the need was met with a group policy through his employer and a second private policy.

In light of the Smiths' current tight cash flow situation, discussed in chapter 4, term insurance would be the most appropriate type of life insurance policy for Tom, which is what he has.

Exhibit 14-5 shows a similar analysis for determining Mary Sue's life insurance needs. The analysis yields a total insurance requirement of $164,631. Let's round this up to $175,000 to give Tom a cushion against unforeseen circumstances that may arise. Since Mary Sue already has a $50,000 term policy, she simply needs to acquire an additional $125,000 in term protection.

EXHIBIT 14-5

LIFE INSURANCE
NEEDS WORKSHEET
TOM AND MARY SUE SMITH

Date: _____

Surviving Spouse: <u>Tom</u>

LUMP SUM EXPENSES: PURPOSE	AMOUNT	
Funeral	$ 6,000	
Probate	$ 1,000	
Estate Taxes	$ 0	
Debts	$ 116,582	
Education	$ 40,000	
Other	$	
Other	$	
Other	$	
TOTAL:		$ 163,582

INCOME NEEDS:			
Gross annual income needed by surviving spouse	$ 40,000		
Surviving spouse's income	$ 35,000		
Difference	$ 5,000	(A)	
Interest rate at which money could be invested	6%	(B)	
Lump sum needed to meet income needs (A÷B)			$ 83,333
Total lump sum requirement			$ 246,915
Available investable assets			$ 82,284
LIFE INSURANCE NEED:			$ 164,631

LIFE INSURANCE NEEDS WORKSHEET

Date: _____

Surviving Spouse: _____

LUMP SUM EXPENSES:

PURPOSE	AMOUNT
Funeral	$ _____
Probate	$ _____
Estate Taxes	$ _____
Debts	$ _____
Education	$ _____
Other	$ _____
Other	$ _____
Other	$ _____
TOTAL:	$ _____

INCOME NEEDS:

Gross annual income needed by surviving spouse	$ _____	
Surviving spouse's income	$ _____	
Difference	$ _____	**(A)**
Interest rate at which money could be invested	_____ %	**(B)**
Lump sum needed to meet income needs (A÷B)		$ _____
Total lump sum requirement		$ _____
Available investable assets		$ _____
LIFE INSURANCE NEED:		$ _____

INSURANCE INVENTORY

LIFE INSURANCE

INSURANCE COMPANY	POLICY NUMBER	INSURED PARTY[1]	OWNERSHIP CODE[2]	BENEFICIARY CODE[2]	FACE AMOUNT	TYPE POLICY	NET CASH VALUE	ANNUAL PREMIUM
					$		$	$
					$		$	$
					$		$	$
					$		$	$
					$		$	$

DISABILITY INCOME INSURANCE

INSURANCE COMPANY	POLICY NUMBER	INSURED PARTY[1]	WAITING PERIOD	BENEFIT PERIOD	MONTHLY BENEFIT PAYMENTS	ANNUAL PREMIUM
					$	$
					$	$
					$	$
					$	$

HEALTH INSURANCE

INSURANCE COMPANY	POLICY NUMBER	TYPE[3]	BENEFIT AMOUNT	DEDUCTIBLE AMOUNT	ANNUAL PREMIUM
			$	$	$
			$	$	$
			$	$	$
			$	$	$

[1]H=Husband W=Wife CH=Child O=Other   [2]H=Husband W=Wife J=Joint O=Other   [3]M=Major Medical D=Dental V=Vision S=Supplemental

INSURANCE INVENTORY

HOMEOWNERS INSURANCE

PROPERTY LOCATION	INSURANCE COMPANY	POLICY NUMBER	DWELLING COVERAGE AMT.	LIABILITY COVERAGE AMT.	MEDICAL COVERAGE AMT.	DEDUCTIBLE AMOUNT	ANNUAL PREMIUM
			$	$	$	$	$
			$	$	$	$	$
			$	$	$	$	$

VEHICLE INSURANCE

VEHICLE	INSURANCE COMPANY	POLICY NUMBER	LIABILITY COVERAGE AMT.	MEDICAL COVERAGE AMT.	COMPREHENSIVE COV. DEDUCTIBLE	COLLISION COV. DEDUCTIBLE	MISCELLANEOUS COVERAGES[4]	ANNUAL PREMIUM
			$	$	$	$		$
			$	$	$	$		$
			$	$	$	$		$
			$	$	$	$		$
			$	$	$	$		$
			$	$	$	$		$

MISCELLANEOUS INSURANCE

TYPE OF INSURANCE	INSURANCE COMPANY	POLICY NUMBER	ITEM INSURED	AMOUNT OF COVERAGE	DEDUCTIBLE AMOUNT	ANNUAL PREMIUM
				$	$	$
				$	$	$
				$	$	$
				$	$	$

[4] T=Towing R=Car Rental U=Uninsured Motorist

## CHAPTER 15

PROTECTING YOUR ESTATE FROM THE TAX AX

"So, Jim," I asked the tall, older gentleman who sat opposite me, "how much did you pay for these wills?"

"Fifty dollars apiece," he said. "My church was holding a silent auction as a fund-raiser. An attorney had donated a will as one of the items to be auctioned. I bid fifty dollars for it and won. I figure I saved a few hundred bucks that way."

"Did he ask to see a financial statement before he prepared it for you?" I asked. This was an important issue because Jim's estate was valued at over $1.2 million.

"No. He just asked me a few questions about how my wife and I wanted to dispense of our assets when we died."

"It's a good thing you haven't needed these wills," I said.

"Why is that, other than the fact I'm glad I haven't died yet?" Jim asked.

"Because the couple of hundred bucks you saved by not having proper wills prepared would have cost your heirs almost a quarter million dollars!"

Jim was shocked, but what I told him was absolutely true. Jim's efforts to save a few dollars almost cost his heirs hundreds of thousands of dollars. Estate planning, properly performed and executed, is a tool that can save families a tremendous amount of taxes upon a person's death. Improper estate planning, on the other hand, can be very costly.

What is estate planning, and why is it such an essential part of a total financial plan?

WILLS

The primary goals of estate planning are to pass your assets to your heirs according to your wishes and to do so in a tax-efficient manner. The main vehicle used to execute your estate plan is a carefully designed will.

If a person dies without a will, the individual is said to have died *intestate.* In that situation, the intestate laws of the state in which the deceased lived dictate how his or her assets will be divided among living relatives, unless the deceased had special trusts set up that spell out how to distribute the assets outside of a will and the probate process. Generally, intestate laws will not distribute your assets according to your desires, so you are wise to prepare a will in which you give specific instructions as to how your estate should be handled.

A will also allows you to perform tax planning for your estate. Most people are not aware of this fact, but the highest tax rates in our country are not income tax rates, but estate tax rates, which can go as high as 60 percent on very large estates. Proper planning can shield some or all of one's estate from taxation, saving potentially thousands (or even hundreds of thousands) of dollars in estate taxes.

PROBATE

When a person dies, his or her estate must be probated. *Probate* is the process of executing the instructions in one's will or distributing one's assets according to the state's intestate laws. It also involves settling any financial matters regarding the estate, such as filing estate tax and estate income tax returns, paying debts, etc. The person responsible for performing these duties, referred to as either the executor (if a male) or the executrix (if a female), is named in the will itself. More than one person may be named to act as co-executors/co-executrixes.

If a will has not been prepared, most jurisdictions require that reports be submitted to the court on a periodic basis that give a clear accounting of how the estate assets have been handled. Normally, under such circumstances, the law places certain bonding requirements on the executor as well. Both stipulations are typically waived in one's will, saving time for the executor and money for the estate.

The cost of the probate process itself will vary greatly from state to state. In some states, such as Georgia, the cost is a relatively low fixed fee. Other states charge higher fees, and a few even charge a percentage of the estate's value. Obviously, this latter arrangement can be very expensive, especially for larger estates. In those situations, a living trust may be a more appropriate estate planning vehicle than a will. While a discussion on such trusts is beyond the scope of this book, an abundance of excellent reading material is available on the subject.

Depending on the circumstances and the choices the executor makes, there may be other significant fees involved in probating the estate. For example, it is advisable in most situations to retain the services of an attorney to aid in the process. This ensures that all the necessary legal procedures will be followed. Also, the deceased may be liable for income taxes on income earned in the year of his or her death (death is no excuse to not pay taxes!). Income taxes may also be due on income the estate has generated during the probate process. Preparing the required tax returns may necessitate the hiring of an accountant familiar with estate tax law.

OTHER IMPORTANT DOCUMENTS

At the time an attorney prepares your will, he or she will usually recommend that you prepare a couple of other documents as well. The first is a *power of attorney*. A power of attorney gives someone whose judgment you trust the legal right to conduct your financial affairs in the event you are unable to do so.

The authority to act on behalf of another, granted in a power of attorney, is vested once all the appropriate individuals sign it. Normally, however, this authority is not actually used until the person for whom the power of attorney was written becomes incapable of carrying on his own affairs. This is why you want to make sure that the power of attorney is a *durable* power of attorney. A *nondurable* power of attorney becomes invalid in the event the person granting the power becomes incapacitated. The powers granted in a durable power of attorney endure beyond one's incapacity, which is the reason for establishing the power to begin with. Normally this authority is given to a spouse or a child.

One example hits especially close to home. During the summer and fall of 1995, both of my parents experienced incapacitating health problems simultaneously. As a result, they were temporarily unable to carry on the day-to-day duties of running a household and arranging for their health care needs. My brother and I were forced to shoulder these responsibilities in their stead. Fortunately, my parents had signed a durable power of attorney. Registering the POA at my parents' bank allowed my brother and me to sign checks drawn from their account, enabling us to carry on their financial affairs until they were once again able to do so.

Establishing a durable power of attorney also eliminates the need for guardianship proceedings in the event of one's incapacity. For instance, let's say an elderly parent becomes incapable of making financial decisions, and it becomes necessary for you to pay your parent's bills and carry on other of his or her financial activities. If your parent has not signed a durable power of attorney, then you must go through court proceedings to be named as your parent's legal guardian in order to perform those duties. Not only is this time consuming, but it can also cost thousands of dollars once all the expenses are tallied. This whole ordeal can be avoided with the use of a durable power of attorney.

Another document your attorney will likely discuss with you is a *durable power of attorney for health care* (DPAHC). A DPAHC allows you to appoint someone else to make health care decisions for you if you are not able to make those decisions for yourself. It is similar to a living will, but is broader in scope.

Medical technology has progressed to the point that doctors can sometimes keep a person alive for many years in what is known as a "persistent vegetative state." Making medical decisions for such a person, who is not able to communicate his will, can be gut wrenching for those involved. The DPAHC is designed to ease this burden a little by giving a trusted individual the authority to act on the prestated wishes of the affected person. It is a neutral document that allows someone to state their desire to be allowed to die under such circumstances or to be kept alive regardless of how hopeless their situation is.

In some circles, the durable health care power of attorney is controversial. At issue is whether giving someone else the right to let you die is tantamount to giving them the right to kill you. Carefully consider the implications of the DPAHC when deciding if it fits into your financial plan.

These are tough decisions, and it may be very unpleasant for some to talk about death. However, I believe you should think about these issues ahead of time and state your desires in writing, whether to live at any cost, or to be allowed to die. This will give those who must make these decisions for you, in the event you are unable to do so, some assurance that your particular wishes will be carried out.

TRUSTS

A trust is an account set up for the benefit of someone, into which are placed various assets. The terms of the trust spell out how the assets are to be used for the benefit of the trust's beneficiary(-ies). The trustee, named in the will as the person in charge of administering the trust, makes the decisions on how the terms of the trust are to be carried out.

For instance, suppose you have a minor child. Your will might establish a trust for the benefit of the child into which her portion of the inheritance is placed. Perhaps the terms of the trust state that once the child reaches the age of majority, the assets of the trust will be distributed directly to her. While the assets are in the trust, however, someone must decide how the money is to be invested. Someone must determine if the child needs principal or income from the trust for personal reasons, such as medical expenses or educational purposes. The trustee makes these decisions and executes them on behalf of the trust's beneficiary. An institution such as a bank or trust company can be named as the trustee, but it is more common to name a trusted friend or relative.

Another type of trust, discussed in more detail in the next section, is a credit shelter trust. These are established specifically for the benefit of surviving spouses and are used as much for tax planning purposes as they are for providing for a spouse's needs.

ESTATE TAX PLANNING

Estate taxes are taxes levied on the value of a person's estate upon his or her death. These taxes are distinct from and unrelated to income taxes.

> **KEY POINT**
>
> Speaking of minor children, you need to decide who will act as their guardian in the event that both of their parents die before they reach the age of majority. The guardian assumes the legal role of the child's parents until the child becomes an adult. One of the most important decisions we can make as Christian parents is who will raise our children if we are not here to do so. Stating in your will whom you want to assume the role of guardian makes the decision legal. If you do not state this in your will, then the courts will name the guardian(s) for your minor children. At that point, your wishes may be irrelevant.

As stated earlier, the will is the primary vehicle where instructions are given for dividing one's estate among heirs in the most tax-efficient manner. An alternative method is to use a living trust, where instructions are executed outside a will and the probate process, to perform estate tax planning. I will only be discussing wills in this book as the tax planning vehicle, though the principles would be similar for a living trust.

Two key laws form the cornerstone of most estate tax planning. The first law states that individuals can pass 100 percent of their estate assets to their spouse tax-free. This law does not shield these assets from estate taxes indefinitely, however, as they may be subject to taxation upon the spouse's death.

The second law states that, beginning in 1999, individuals can exempt $650,000 of their estate from estate taxes. This $650,000 will gradually increase to $1 million by 2006 and can be bequeathed to anybody, not just a spouse, and still escape federal estate taxation.

The biggest part of tax planning for most estates is using these two laws to shield the maximum amount of assets from taxation. Under the 1997 Tax Act, this maximum figure eventually climbs to $2 million for a married couple.

The first step, then, in the tax planning process is to determine the fair market value of your estate. To accomplish this, you must prepare an accurate financial statement showing both the value and owner of all your assets and liabilities. The forms provided in chapter 3 of this book will prove helpful in this regard.

In order to prepare the proper type of will for an individual or a couple, an attorney must know what your full financial picture looks like. If your attorney does not have a complete picture of your assets and liabilities, then she may prepare the wrong kind of will for you.

What do I mean by the right kind of will and the wrong kind of will? Let me explain.

There are two primary types of wills, a *simple will,* and a *tax planning will.* Because the law allows an individual to exempt up to $650,000 of their estate from taxes, there is no need to do any tax planning for a single person's or married couple's estate with assets less than this amount; the whole estate is sheltered from taxes by one personal exemption. A will that includes no provisions for tax planning is called a simple will.

This type of will normally directs that upon a person's death, all of the individual's assets should pass directly to the spouse or other appropriate heirs. Since simple wills are less expensive than tax planning wills, it is not prudent to have a tax planning will prepared until the size of your estate justifies the extra cost.

On the other hand, if your estate is large enough to warrant a tax planning will, do not try to save money by having only a simple will prepared. This mistake could unnecessarily cost your heirs a tremendous amount in estate taxes. I have seen two cases during my career as a financial planner in which attorneys prepared the wrong kinds of wills for clients. In both cases the estates were worth about $1.2 million. With estates of this size, the blunders would have needlessly cost each client's heirs almost a quarter million dollars in estate taxes had the problem not been corrected.

The first instance was the case of Jim, related at the opening of this chapter. In the second situation, a well-known attorney in town who had a general law practice, i.e., he did not specialize in estate planning, prepared the will. As I read through this client's will, I was puzzled at what I saw. The estate tax laws changed dramatically in the early 1980s. Knowing that this client's will had been prepared two years after the change occurred, some of the provisions looked strange to me. My suspicions were confirmed when I read the will over the phone to an estate planning attorney. The will had been prepared according to the prior tax laws.

The only way your attorney can know which type of will to prepare for you is to see a financial statement. Frankly, if your lawyer does not ask you for one in the process of preparing your will, I would find another attorney. This is rudimentary, akin to a doctor obtaining your medical history before treating you.

One thing that is critical at this juncture is to review in whose name your assets are owned. Assets that are owned only in your name are part of your estate. Assets that are only in your spouse's name are part of your spouse's estate. Assets that are jointly owned with another person are normally owned in a manner called *joint with right of survivorship.*

KEY POINT

Assets owned in the form of joint with right of survivorship pass to the full ownership of the second owner upon the death of the first owner and become part of the second owner's estate. *This supersedes instructions in the will.* In other words, you cannot direct in your will that your half of a jointly owned asset be inherited by anyone other than the joint owner. It becomes the full property of the second owner outside the provisions of the will.

As we move through an explanation of tax planning for an estate, I will demonstrate why the proper titling of assets is such a critical matter. Suffice it to say that you should review all your major assets to see how they are titled for ownership purposes.

CATEGORIES OF ASSETS

There are various categories of assets that may be included in your estate. Each category of assets has its own idiosyncrasies that affect how it will be treated for estate planning purposes.

TANGIBLE ASSETS

First to be considered are tangible assets. As the name implies, these are physical assets that can be touched. Examples would be clothing, furs, jewelry, other personal assets, and your residence.

It is important, in the preparation of your will, to decide if you have any specific personal bequests. Perhaps you want your overall estate to be divided between certain heirs in a specific manner, but you want a particular diamond ring to go to your niece. Items often bequeathed specifically are jewelry, personal belongings, and valuables of various types. These items should be identified in the will as clearly as possible, and you should name the individuals specifically whom you desire to receive them.

One's residence is normally one of the largest assets in their estate. It is especially important to review how your residence is titled, particularly for older couples who have lived in the same house for many years. Most people just assume their residence is owned jointly; in many cases it is not.

LIFE INSURANCE

Next for consideration is the face amount of any life insurance policies on which you are named as the insured and the owner. When you prepared your net worth statement in an earlier chapter, only the total *cash value* of your life insurance policies was included as an asset. For estate planning purposes, you want to include the total *face amount* of all life insurance policies you own, since this is the value included in the estate for tax purposes. Normally, the face amount of a life insurance policy is much greater than its cash value.

This alone causes many individuals' estates to be much larger than they imagine. It is not unusual at all for individuals to carry $1 million or more in term life insurance coverage. This full amount would be included in the value of their estate.

Life insurance proceeds are received income tax-free by the beneficiaries, but not estate tax-free. When a life insurance policy is acquired, a beneficiary of the proceeds is named. Generally, the owner of the policy is the person who is insured, though sometimes a trust or other third party might be named as the owner. When the insured dies, the proceeds go directly to the beneficiary, outside the provisions of the will and irrespective of the status of the probate process. If the will does give any instructions as to who should receive the proceeds, its instructions are ignored. The beneficiaries like this arrangement because they do not have to wait for the will to be probated in order to receive the proceeds. Neither do they pay any income taxes on the proceeds. However, the full face amount of the insurance policy is counted as an asset in the owner's estate upon the insured's death.

Sometimes an estate is large enough that a substantial amount of estate taxes will be due on it, but there are not enough liquid assets in the estate to pay those taxes. This situation might occur, for instance, if a significant portion of one's estate consists of real estate. In such situations, individuals will often acquire a life insurance policy and name the estate as the beneficiary. This is done to provide the estate with enough liquid funds to pay the estate taxes. Upon the policyholder's death, the insurance company will write a check for the face amount of the policy *to the decedent's estate.* The proceeds will then be subject to the provisions of the will and the probate process.

A typical arrangement in the wills of a married couple is for each partner to direct that, upon their death, all of their assets should pass to their spouse. Upon the death of both spouses, the assets are to be divided evenly among their children. A question that I am frequently asked is, "Should minor children ever be named as beneficiaries of a life insurance policy?"

Normally, when people acquire a life insurance policy, they will name either their spouse or their estate as the primary beneficiary. Life insurance policies also allow you to name one or more *contingent beneficiaries.* Upon the death of the policyholder, the proceeds are distributed to the primary beneficiary. If the primary beneficiary is not living at the time of the policyholder's death, the proceeds will be distributed instead to the contingent beneficiary. The question of naming a minor child as a beneficiary usually applies to the contingent beneficiary position.

If a minor is named as a beneficiary of an insurance policy, the minor will have full privileges of ownership of these funds immediately upon reaching the age of majority. Many parents feel that it is a better idea to give children money over time instead of all at once, especially if the children are young. To accomplish this, you might establish a trust for the children. The trust's terms might dictate that one third of its assets be distributed to the child at age twenty-five, half the remaining assets will be given to them at age thirty, and the final portion is to be distributed to the child at their age thirty-five. This allows the child to learn from experience how to handle a larger amount of assets responsibly with the first distribution, without the entire inheritance being at stake. In these circumstances the trust, not the child, would be named as the beneficiary.

A more common method of accomplishing this same objective is to establish the trust in your will. The trust will not be established unless both parents die while the child is still a minor. The terms of the trust will be spelled out in the will as well. In this situation, the life insurance policy would name the estate as the beneficiary, and the proceeds would be placed into the trust according to the terms of the will.

KEY POINT

There is no rule that restricts you to naming only one beneficiary of a life insurance policy. You may name several beneficiaries and several contingent beneficiaries. On the application for the policy, simply list each beneficiary and the percentage of the proceeds (or the dollar amount) each is to receive.

One final word of caution: if you have been divorced, review the beneficiary designations on all your life insurance policies. A relatively common occurrence is for a policyholder to name his or her spouse as the primary beneficiary of the proceeds, divorce, remarry, and then forget to change the beneficiary designation on the life insurance policy. Years later the policyholder dies, and the first spouse receives the life insurance proceeds.

RETIREMENT PLANS

Next, all of your retirement plans should be included. Normally, these will be such types of assets as 401(k)'s, 403(b) tax sheltered annuities, IRA's, and miscellaneous other types of plans.

A phenomenon that has changed the landscape of estate tax planning in recent years is that of companies buying out their employees' pension plans with a lump sum payment. This lump sum takes the place of monthly pension payments and is normally rolled into the recipient's Individual Retirement Account upon the person's retirement. Why do corporations do this? To rid the liability of the pensions from their balance sheets. They feel that it is better to take a one-time charge for the lump sum payment than to carry a pension liability for an indeterminable number of years. The full amount of this lump sum, which is often six figures, is now included in the recipient's estate for tax purposes. When you add this amount to 401(k) plans, it is not unusual for blue-collar employees to retire with $250,000 to $500,000 in company retirement accounts.

Let's say that Alice has worked at Acme Widget, Inc., for thirty years. When she retires, she can expect to receive a monthly pension of $2,000. The company offers her a lump sum payment of $250,000 in lieu of a monthly pension. She accepts the lump sum offer and rolls the proceeds into an IRA account at a discount brokerage firm. Formerly, the pension would not be a consideration for estate taxes, since it disappeared upon her death. Now, however, the $250,000 would be included as part of her estate.

Another consideration here is similar to one discussed under the section on life insurance. When individuals establish retirement plans, they name beneficiaries and contingent beneficiaries of the plan's assets. While many of the same factors must be considered regarding retirement plan beneficiaries as for insurance policy beneficiaries, income tax issues add a whole new layer of complexity. When your will is prepared, your attorney can help guide you through the maze of issues that must be addressed.

Once again, if you are divorced, review the beneficiary designations on all of your retirement plans. Chuck Hampton, a well-respected estate planning attorney in Atlanta, tells the story of a dentist who was married for ten years, divorced, remarried, and then died ten years later. When he died, he had a $250,000 balance in his retirement plan. Unfortunately (at least for his second wife), after he remarried, he never changed the beneficiary of his retirement plan from his first wife to his second wife. His first wife was the legal recipient of the $250,000. Did she disclaim it and let the second wife have it? What do you think? Actually, she did agree to split the proceeds with the second wife. Legally, however, she was not required to do even this.

INVESTMENTS

Fourth, any investments that you own outside of a retirement plan should be included as estate assets. Examples would include shares of stocks, bonds, and mutual funds.

When an individual dies, any investments they own are counted as assets in their estate and are valued as of the day of their death (an alternate valuation date of six months after the decedent's death is also allowed; for the sake of our discussion, we will assume that the date of death is used). If the investments are publicly traded, it is a relatively easy matter to ascertain their value. Simply check the newspaper for that day to find the price of the security.

Investments that are not publicly traded present their own set of problems. If the decedent was self-employed and owned shares of stock in his privately held company, it is a much more difficult matter to place a value on the stock. The value of the stock of a privately held corporation is a very subjective matter, and it will generally be given different valuations based on the purpose of the appraisal. If a business owner is going to the bank to get a loan, their business is worth a million dollars. If the business is being valued for estate tax purposes, it is worthless.

Chuck Hampton tells of another instance some years ago when he was preparing a will for a client. The individual owned a business and derived an annual income of $200,000 from it. As Chuck was reviewing the client's assets, he asked him what he felt his business was worth. The client replied, "Thirty thousand dollars." Chuck asked why he felt the business was worth such a small amount. The client replied that since he originally invested $30,000 to start the business, that was its value. Chuck offered to buy the business from him on the spot for $60,000, letting the client double his money. The client's response was predictable. "I would never sell my business for sixty thousand dollars," he said. Chuck explained that was exactly the point. The IRS would take the position, and rightfully so, that any business that generates an annual income of $200,000 for the owner is worth a lot more than $30,000.

So how does the IRS determine the value of a privately owned business? It actually uses several techniques, including requiring the estate to hire a professional appraiser. When estimating the value of a business for estate planning purposes, try to be as realistic as possible.

Another similar situation involves illiquid limited partnership units. It is very difficult to obtain an accurate value for these since the partnerships generally do not perform appraisals on the underlying properties until they are sold. The general partner may be able to provide an acceptable price per unit. Recent sale prices of the units on a secondary market may also provide an adequate price.

CASH EQUIVALENTS

Finally, include any cash and cash equivalent accounts, such as checking accounts, savings accounts, and money market accounts as assets in your estate.

STEP-UP IN BASIS

Before I cover the issues involved in estate tax planning, I want to discuss one other concept, which is more relevant to the heirs than to the estate of the deceased. It is called a *step-up in basis.*

When you buy an asset, say a stock, and then you sell it later for an amount greater than its purchase price, you pay a tax on the gain in value that you experienced. This gain is called a *capital gain,* and the tax you pay is called a *capital gains tax.* The price at which you bought the asset is called your *tax basis,* which is the cost from which the gain will be computed.

When a person dies, her heirs receive a step-up in the tax basis of assets purchased by the decedent. This means that the tax basis for the heir becomes the value of the asset at the time of the decedent's death, *not the cost at which the decedent originally purchased the asset.*

Let me illustrate this concept. Assume that William purchased 100 shares of ABC stock in 1955, and paid a total of $500 for this stock. William dies in 1998, and the stock is worth $15,000. William's son, James, inherits the stock from his father. James follows the stock market very closely and determines that there are other investments that he would rather own than stock in the ABC Company. James sells the stock for $16,000 two years after his father's passing. On how much of a capital gain will James have to pay tax? Only $1,000.

Had William sold the stock just prior to his death for $15,000, he would have had to pay tax on a gain of $14,500. At a capital gains tax bracket of 20 percent, the tax owed would have been $2,900. James's inheritance would have been reduced by the amount of the tax. Instead, James *inherited* the stock with a tax basis of $15,000, the value of the stock on the day his father died, rather than the $500 that his father originally paid for the stock. Understanding the concept of receiving a step-up in basis can be important for tax planning considerations.

A classic example of what can happen when the step-up in basis is not properly utilized was the case of Alex, a gentleman who came into my office about three months ago. Alex's mother had recently passed away, having been ill for several years prior to her death. Just before being admitted into a nursing home three years before she died, Alex's mother had gifted her house to him and his sister. Her intention in gifting the house was for them to rent it out, thus providing income to help defray her nursing home expenses. She had purchased the house many years ago for about $10,000.

When an asset is gifted to someone, that person receives the asset with the same tax basis as the person who made the gift. The stepped-up basis is applicable only to assets that are inherited, not gifted. When Alex's mother gifted the house to him and his sister, they received her $10,000 cost basis in the house. The house is now listed for sale at a price of $85,000. The entire gain of $75,000 will be subject to taxation as a capital gain in the year in which the house is sold. This whole taxable gain could have been avoided had Ed's mother let them inherit the house instead of gifting it to them. The tax savings would have been about $15,000.

CASE ANALYSIS: JOE AND BARBARA DIXON

To demonstrate the concepts involved in estate tax planning, let's look at the estate of Joe Dixon and his wife Barbara, found in Exhibit 15-1. Note that each is the owner of a $300,000 term life insurance policy.

EXHIBIT 15-1

DIXONS' ESTATE
ASSETS

FIXED	CURRENT VALUE	OWNERSHIP CODE[1]
Checking	$ 5,000	J
Savings	$	
Money Market	$ 10,000	J
CD's	$ 15,000	W
Municipal Bonds	$	
Corporate Bonds	$	
Treasury Bonds	$	
Bond Funds	$	
Annuity	$	
Other—Personal	$ 40,000	J
Other	$	
Other	$	
TOTAL FIXED	**$ 70,000**	

VARIABLE	CURRENT VALUE	OWNERSHIP CODE[1]
Common Stocks	$ 45,000	J
Stock Mutual Funds	$ 150,000	J
Limited Partnerships	$	
Business Interests	$	
Real Estates		
(Direct Ownership)	$ 140,000	J
Other	$ 175,000	401(k)-H
Other	$ 120,000	401(k)-W
Other	$	
TOTAL VARIABLE	**$ 630,000**	

TOTAL ASSETS	**$ 700,000**	

[1]H=Husband, W=Wife, J=Joint, IRA, 401(k), OR=Other Retirement OT=Other

Life Insurance (Face Amount):	Amount	Owner
Term Life Insurance	$300,000	H
Term Life Insurance	$300,000	W

SETTLING THE DIXONS' ESTATE WITH NO TAX PLANNING

If we split jointly held assets equally between Joe and Barbara, Joe's estate, including the face amount of his life insurance policy, has a total value of $670,000. You would subtract the balance of any of Joe's liabilities from the value of his assets to arrive at a net estate valuation figure. For the sake of our illustration, let's assume that Joe and Barbara have no outstanding debts. Barbara's estate is valued at $630,000.

Exhibit 15-2 examines Joe's tax situation, assuming he never did any estate tax planning. Joe had a simple will prepared, which is what I call an "all to spouse" will. Joe's will directed that all his assets be given directly to his wife upon his death. Barbara's will passes all her assets to their children.

Remember that 100 percent of an individual's estate may be given to their spouse free of any estate taxes. So, upon Joe's death, all $670,000 of his estate went to his wife. What was the tax bill for this transfer of assets? $0.

By the way, I am not being sexist by examining the Dixons' situation with Joe passing away first. Statistically, husbands pass away before their wives in the majority of cases.

The situation is different upon the death of Barbara. Barbara's estate is now worth $1.3 million. The first $650,000 of asset value is shielded from estate taxes by Barbara's personal exemption. The IRS subtracts this amount from the value of Barbara's estate, leaving her with a taxable estate of $650,000. The taxes due on $650,000 total $258,500. Estate tax brackets are progressive. The greater the value of the estate, the higher the effective tax bracket.

Over a quarter million dollars due on a $1.3 million estate is bad enough, but what will make the Dixons' children really want to cry is when they realize that *this entire estate tax is a gift to Uncle Sam!* The whole amount of estate tax could have been avoided with a little tax planning that may have cost as little as $800 to $1,000.

SETTLING THE DIXONS' ESTATE WITH TAX PLANNING

Now let's take another look at Joe's estate and see what a difference a little tax planning could have made. Exhibit 15-3 outlines the scenario.

Without tax planning, Joe took advantage of the law that lets him pass 100 percent of his estate to Barbara tax-free. But, he failed to use any of his $650,000 exemption to reduce their total estate tax burden. If we could find a way to use his exemption as well as Barbara's, then we could shelter the entire estate from taxes.

One way this could be accomplished would be for Joe to give $650,000

EXHIBIT 15-2

ESTATE TAX CONSEQUENCES
OF SIMPLE WILL

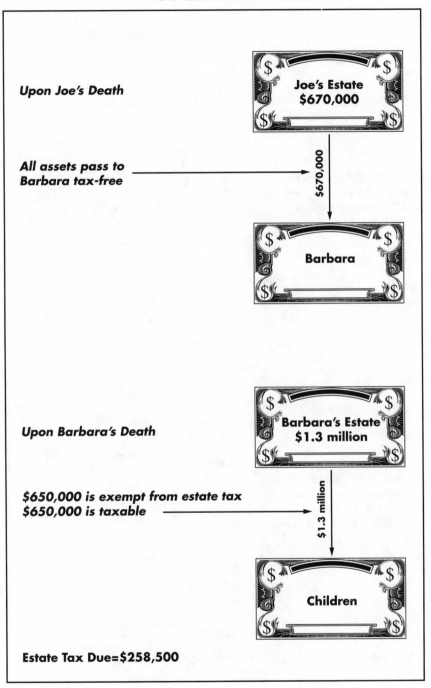

Upon Joe's Death

Joe's Estate $670,000

All assets pass to Barbara tax-free

$670,000

Barbara

Upon Barbara's Death

Barbara's Estate $1.3 million

$650,000 is exempt from estate tax
$650,000 is taxable

$1.3 million

Children

Estate Tax Due=$258,500

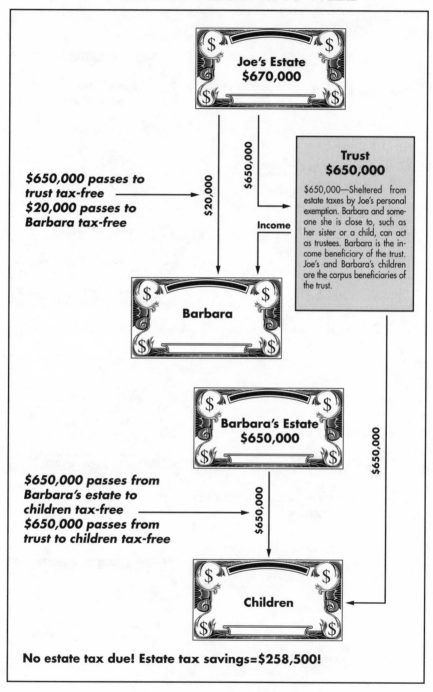

EXHIBIT 15-3

ESTATE TAX CONSEQUENCES
OF TAX PLANNING WILL

**Joe's Estate
$670,000**

**Trust
$650,000**

$650,000—Sheltered from estate taxes by Joe's personal exemption. Barbara and someone she is close to, such as her sister or a child, can act as trustees. Barbara is the income beneficiary of the trust. Joe's and Barbara's children are the corpus beneficiaries of the trust.

*$650,000 passes to
trust tax-free
$20,000 passes to
Barbara tax-free*

$20,000

$650,000

Income

Barbara

**Barbara's Estate
$650,000**

$650,000

*$650,000 passes from
Barbara's estate to
children tax-free
$650,000 passes from
trust to children tax-free*

$650,000

Children

No estate tax due! Estate tax savings=$258,500!

to the children upon his death. His exemption would shelter this entire amount from estate taxes, and only $20,000 would pass to Barbara and become part of her estate. Her $650,000 exemption would then shelter all her assets from taxation.

This solution saves taxes, but it creates another problem—$650,000 of assets that could be used to provide income to Barbara for the rest of her life will be passed on to the children instead. Can't you hear Barbara when Joe tells her of his plan? She would rather let the kids pay the estate taxes than do without $650,000 that she helped accumulate. Frankly, I agree with her.

So, what's the solution? Instead of passing $650,000 to the children, Joe should pass these assets into a trust, called a *credit shelter trust* or *bypass trust*. The trust will be set up so that Barbara can receive the income generated by the investments in the trust. This way, she can still realize the benefit from assets that she has worked hard to help accumulate. The terms of the trust will state that the principal of the trust, known as the corpus, will pass to the children *upon Barbara's death*. Barbara is the income beneficiary of the trust; the children are the principal, or corpus, beneficiaries. Because Barbara never receives the principal of the trust, the $650,000 is never counted as part of her estate. It is sheltered from taxes by Joe's exemption.

Here's what happens when Joe dies. His estate is worth $670,000. His will dictates that $650,000 passes to the trust. Joe's $650,000 exemption shelters this entire amount from taxation. The money in the trust is placed in an income producing investment, such as bonds or mutual funds. Each year Barbara withdraws all the income produced by the investments for her personal benefit.

Two questions arise at this point. First, can Barbara have access to the principal in the trust if she needs it? The answer is yes, under limited circumstances. The trust can make provisions for Barbara to encroach on the principal if the trustee(s) determines that her need is legitimate and complies with the terms established by the trust. This brings us to the second question: Who should serve as the trustee(s) of this trust?

Trustees should be sympathetic to Barbara's needs, yet knowledgeable about financial matters. What better candidate for the job is there than Barbara herself? No one. Would that be legal? Actually, the law does allow Barbara to serve as a trustee, so long as she is not the sole trustee. So, Joe could name Barbara as one trustee and then appoint another co-trustee who will also be very sympathetic to Barbara's needs, such as a sister, or a child.

Once the $650,000 has passed to the trust, the remaining $20,000 of Joe's estate goes directly to Barbara. When she dies, the assets in the trust are distributed to the children, free of estate taxes. Her $650,000 exemption shelters her full estate, which also gets passed to the children. This leaves a taxable estate of $0. The estate tax savings using this technique equals $258,500!

In 1999, up to $1.3 million of a married couple's estate can be sheltered from estate taxes using these techniques. By 2006, this amount will have increased to $2 million.

EQUALIZING THE ESTATES

As discussed earlier, when you have a tax planning will prepared, which assets are owned by which spouse becomes a critical issue. An easy mistake for a married couple to make is to establish the appropriate trusts in their wills to avoid estate taxes, but then jointly own all of their assets. Since the title of ownership takes precedence over the will, all the assets will pass to the full ownership of the joint owner (the surviving spouse) at the time of the first spouse's death, *outside the will.* This will result in there being no assets remaining with which to fund the credit shelter trust. The entire amount of the decedent's estate becomes part of the surviving spouse's estate, and the decedent has wasted his entire $650,000 exemption.

Avoiding this situation requires the use of a technique called *equaliz-*

ing the estates. This involves changing some or all of the assets from joint ownership and placing them into the name of one spouse or the other. The object is to bring the values of both individuals' estates to a level that would fully utilize each spouse's exemption.

For example, in Joe and Barbara's situation, regardless of what the will states, Barbara will become the sole owner of $390,000 of jointly owned assets upon Joe's death. When this amount is added to the $435,000 in assets already titled in her name (including the life insurance policy she owns), Barbara's estate would be valued at $825,000. Only $475,000 would be available from Joe's estate to fund the credit shelter trust. This wastes $175,000 of his allowable exemption, unnecessarily costing his heirs $66,250 in estate taxes.

Joe and Barbara need to transfer some of the assets they own jointly into the individual ownership of one or the other. For example, they could place the mutual funds and $25,000 of the common stocks into Joe's name. All the other jointly owned assets could be transferred to Barbara's name. Then, when Joe dies, his estate would be valued at $650,000, exactly the amount needed to take full advantage of his personal exemption. If Barbara passes away first, the value of her estate would also be $650,000, allowing her to take full advantage of her exemption as well.

Keep in mind that all this is just Estate Planning 101. More advanced techniques used by professional estate planners can shelter substantially larger amounts from estate taxes. The key is to take the time to have a will prepared and to consult with a professional who can help you plan your estate matters.

TRUE WEALTH

## CHAPTER 16

GIVING IS WHAT LIVING IS ALL ABOUT

Normally, when stewardship is taught, it is taught only in regard to our responsibility to give of our finances to the Church. After studying the biblical concept of stewardship, I have found it to be much more comprehensive in scope. Stewardship involves *faithfully managing everything that God has placed in our charge for the furtherance of His kingdom on the earth.*

While charitable giving is but one aspect of biblical stewardship, it is, nevertheless, an important responsibility given to us by God. It is not something that we just flippantly decide whether or not we will do. Giving is a powerful principle of God, designed to be a blessing to both the giver and the recipient of the gift. It is the natural action of a generous heart that desires to express the love of God within it.

If there is one thing I have learned about God, it is that God is good! The Bible says in I Corinthians 13:5 that "love does not seek its own." I John 4:8 tells us that "God is love." Since God is love, and love does not seek its own, then God does not seek His own. That means that God, in all His dealings with us and in all the instructions that He has given to us, is not seeking His own benefit, but rather our good. This means that any instructions He has given us with regard to giving is meant for our blessing.

In Philippians 4, Paul was talking to the church at Philippi about giving. In verse 17 he made this statement, "Not that I seek the gift itself, *but I seek for the profit which increases to your account*" (emphasis mine). Paul, having the attitude of God as a writer of scripture, was inspired by the Holy Spirit to let us know that it is not the gift itself that God is after. God does not need our money. *What God is after is the profit that comes into our lives as a result of the gifts that we give.* This profit comes to us both in this life and in the life to come.

In I Corinthians 16:2, with regard to the collection that Paul was taking up for the poor saints in Jerusalem, he wrote, "On the first day of every week let each one of you put aside and save, as he may prosper, that no collections be made when I come." Giving is to be performed by each of us, in accordance with the level of abundance we have experienced, so that it is not a burden on any one person. God has meant for giving to be a blessing, not a burden.

It makes sense that God wants us to be able to continually increase our level of giving. The more we give, the more the Church is able to minister to people. But to give more, we must prosper in a greater measure. What I have discovered is that the principles of stewardship were not given to us to squeeze more money out of us. Rather, God gave them to teach us His principles of promotion and blessing!

LEGALISM IN GIVING

Paul wrote in I Corinthians 13:3 "And if I give all my possessions to feed the poor, and if I deliver my body to be burned, *but do not have love,* it profits me nothing" (emphasis mine).

I commented earlier that many Bible teachers have made giving out to be something that should be treated like a debt. Christians have often been taught that they will be blessed financially as they fulfill this debt to God. As a result, many Christians give in order to pay what they perceive to be their obligation to God. Their giving is performed in a legalistic manner, and their heart is not involved. They are simply performing their duty. Paul makes it very plain in the above scripture that if our giving does not flow from a heart of love, *it profits us nothing.* In other words, a person receives no blessing when he gives from an attitude of fulfilling a debt to God. *The only attitude that pleases God is when we give from love and a desire to bless others.*

Normally, when a legalistic approach to our giving is taught, the scripture used is the following passage from the book of Malachi:

Malachi 3:8 "Will a man rob God? Yet you are robbing Me! But you say, 'How have we robbed Thee?' In tithes and offerings."

9   "You are cursed with a curse, for you are robbing Me, the whole nation of you!"

10 "Bring the whole tithe into the storehouse, so that there may be food in My house, and test Me now in this," says the Lord of hosts, "if I will not open for you the windows of heaven, and pour out for you a blessing until it overflows."

11 "Then I will rebuke the devourer for you, so that it may not destroy the fruits of the ground; nor will your vine in the field cast its grapes," says the Lord of hosts.

I have heard numerous sermons in which well-meaning ministers have exhorted the listeners to give financially, telling them that if they didn't pay their debt to God, that debt being 10 percent of their income, they were *cursed financially*. Under the Old Covenant this was true. The tithe was given as a commandment to the Israelites as part of the Law of Moses. If they did not fulfill this commandment, they were indeed cursed. In fact, they were cursed if they did not fulfill any of the commandments of the Law. The tithe was only one commandment that, if not fulfilled, would result in their being cursed. It was not a singularly special commandment.

James tells us in chapter 2, verse 10 "For whoever keeps the whole law and yet stumbles in one point, he has become guilty of all." Galatians 3:10 quotes an Old Testament scripture and tells us that for those living under the Law, ". . . Cursed is everyone who does not abide by all things written in the book of the Law, to perform them." Under the Old Covenant, of which the book of Malachi is a part, the Israelites were cursed if they did not keep *all* of the laws of God, not just the law of the tithe.

Under the New Covenant, which the Bible tells us is a better covenant, based on better promises, Jesus Christ has removed the curse from us. If you believe that failing to tithe will produce a curse in your life, then, according to the scriptures that we read in James and Galatians, you must also believe that failing to fulfill any other part of the Law will also produce a curse in your life. If we could earn righteousness and avoid the curse by keeping the Law, then why would Jesus have needed to die on the cross?

As a New Testament believer, you are free from the curse because you are free from the Law. Galatians 3, beginning in verse 13, states "Christ redeemed us from the curse of the Law, having become a curse for us . . ." 14 "in order that in Christ Jesus the blessing of Abraham might come to the Gentiles . . ." Christ redeemed all of His people from the curse that would come upon us for breaking any provision of the Law. The curse that would have been placed on you for failing to conform to God's standard in any area of life fell upon Jesus at the cross on your behalf, Christ "having become a curse *for us*" (emphasis mine). My point is that you are not cursed if you do not tithe.

I am not saying that you should not give 10 percent of your income to the Lord. However, I am telling you that not tithing will not cause a financial curse to come upon you. I will also tell you that if you give 10 percent of your income to the Lord just to keep a curse from coming upon you, not because you want to give that much from your heart, then your giving will not "profit you." You might be giving, but if you "do not have love," it "profits you nothing." You will experience a greater blessing from God by giving a lesser amount of money that you can give cheerfully than you will by giving 10 percent of your income to fulfill the Law and keep a curse from coming on you!

WHY GIVE?

What, then, should be the motivation for our financial giving? I can find four primary biblical motivations for charitable giving:

1. BECAUSE WE LOVE PEOPLE—John 3:16 states, "For God so loved the world, that He gave His only begotten Son, that whoever believes in Him should not perish, but have eternal life."

In giving His Son to die on the cross for the sins of mankind, God gave us the most valuable gift that could have been given. Valuable, not only because of the benefit it provided us but because of the personal cost incurred by God in giving it. What motivated God to give such a gift? A sense of indebtedness, or obligation? No, but rather the love that He had for us compelled Him to give of what He had in order to meet our most pressing need.

God desires that, as we grow in our relationship with Him, we become more and more like Him. If love for others was what prompted God to give, then should it not be our primary motivation for giving as well? As we mature spiritually, we should become less attached to our possessions—remember, they do not belong to us anyway—and more concerned with meeting the needs of others. Love gives. If our hearts are filled with God's love, then we will not be able to help but give.

What is our first motivation for giving? We give because we love people!

2. So that we can be a blessing to others—Part of the reason that God blesses us in the first place is so we can be a blessing to others. In Genesis 12, God made a covenant with Abraham. Verse 2 tells us that part of the covenant was ". . . And I will bless you, . . . and so you shall be a blessing." Part of our covenant with God is that not only will He bless us but we will bless others as well. We can not bless others, however, unless we are first blessed ourselves.

3. To preach the gospel and establish God's covenant on the earth— I think we need to be practical and realize that it takes money to preach the gospel. It takes money to pay the salaries of pastors who shepherd the flock. Paul made it clear that those who preach the gospel full-time should make their living from the gospel. This principle does not apply only to pastors, but to anyone who ministers the gospel on a full-time basis, such as missionaries who preach the gospel overseas and apostles who start new churches.

There are numerous ways to get the gospel message out to a lost and dying world. Many of these methods, such as Christian radio and television, cost money. The huge Billy Graham crusades, which have resulted in the salvation of untold thousands, and possibly millions, have been made possible by the faithful financial support of believers who were determined that the gospel would be spread.

The fact is that it takes money to reach the lost. If we are committed to spreading the gospel, then we have no choice but to support it with our finances.

4. IT IS A BIBLICAL PRINCIPLE OF FINANCIAL BLESSING—There is a force of financial blessing that is released in our lives by the giving of our money. Paul addresses this very directly in the book of II Corinthians, chapter 9. In the first five verses, Paul is discussing arrangements for a collection that is to be taken, apparently for the relief of impoverished saints living in Jerusalem. It is obvious from the comments he makes that he is referring to a financial gift. Then, beginning in verse 6, he says, "Now this I say, he who sows sparingly shall also reap sparingly; and he who sows bountifully shall also reap bountifully."

THE SEED PRINCIPLE OF GIVING

The implications of this verse are obvious. Paul compares the giving of finances to the act of a farmer planting seed. The planting of a seed should ultimately result in the harvesting of an amount of fruit far greater than the amount of seed that was planted. The only inference that can possibly be made from such an analogy is that our giving is the planting of financial seed. This planting of seed opens the door for a financial harvest to be returned to us at some point in the future.

Can a farmer who skimps on the amount of seed he plants reasonably expect a bountiful harvest? No! He will experience a sparse harvest instead. But the farmer who invests in his field by planting a bountiful volume of seed has every right to expect that the harvest will be bountiful as well.

Paul applies this same principle to our giving. Those who give sparsely relative to their income can expect a sparse financial blessing from their giving. Those who give generously will experience a bountiful harvest of financial blessing in their lives. *Our level of harvest will be directly related to our level of giving.*

Will the harvest that we receive be a financial harvest? Is it possible that our giving of finances will result in a harvest that is not financial? While a giving heart may express itself in many ways and, therefore, plant seeds in many areas, giving financially is the planting of a financial seed. Therefore, it is biblical to expect a financial harvest. Observe the following verses:

Genesis 1:11 Then God said, "Let the earth sprout vegetation, plants yielding seed, and fruit trees bearing fruit after their kind, with seed in them, on the earth"; and it was so.

12 And the earth brought forth vegetation, plants yielding seed after their kind, and trees bearing fruit, with seed in them after their kind; and God saw that it was good.

In these verses, God put into motion a law that is inviolable: seeds produce fruit after their own kind. If you plant an orange seed, you will produce an orange tree every time. You will never bring forth a peach tree by planting an orange seed; an orange tree will always be produced from an orange seed. If you plant financial seeds, to not receive financial fruit would be a violation of this law.

Our attitude toward out giving is every bit as important as the level of our giving. Paul goes on to say in verse 7 of II Corinthians 9, "Let each one do just as he has purposed in his heart; not grudgingly or under compulsion; *for God loves a cheerful giver*" (emphasis mine). To give grudgingly means that we will do it, but we would rather not. To give under compulsion means that we feel we must do it, or something bad will happen to us if we do not. To give under compulsion means that our gift is not given from a heart of love and desire. Neither of these wrong attitudes is pleasing to God. God loves when we give cheerfully because only then are we reflecting His character from our heart. God has a giving heart, and He wants us to have giving hearts as well.

KEY POINT

Remember, God blesses a *lifestyle* of giving. Determining in your heart, in advance, your level of giving allows you to discuss the matter with God during a time when you can best hear from God and are the least subject to emotions or circumstances.

Other scriptures confirm Paul's message of the financial blessing that is released by giving. Luke 6:38 states, "Give, and it will be given to you; good measure, pressed down, shaken together, running over, they will pour into your lap. For whatever measure you deal out to others, it will be dealt to you in return." This is a law. God has spoken it and it cannot be repealed. When we give, it *will* be given back to us.

Proverbs 11, beginning in verse 24, says, "There is one who scatters, yet increases all the more, And there is one who withholds what is justly due, but it results only in want. 25 The generous man will be prosperous, And he who waters *will himself be watered*" (emphasis mine).

Often the laws of God's kingdom run counter to the thoughts of our natural mind. For instance, the above verse says that a principle of prosperity is to be generous, giving of your resources to meet the needs of others. The natural mind rebels at such a notion. The unspiritual person thinks that the way to prosper is to hoard every penny he can and that to give money away only *decreases* his net worth, not *increases* it. He thinks that giving material possessions away is a waste of his valuable resources. Yet, God tells us that greater financial blessings will come to us if we are generous with our money than if we hoard our possessions for our own selfish use.

HOW MUCH SHOULD WE GIVE?

One final comment about giving. In II Corinthians 9:7, which we have already discussed, Paul tells us to give as we have purposed in our hearts. He has already told us that our level of reaping will be directly related to our level of giving. A question naturally arises, being, "How much should we give?" Obviously, we need money to live on, and, yet, the greater amount that we give, the greater will be the financial blessings returned to us.

In the scripture in Genesis we read earlier, the Bible tells us that God placed the seed in the fruit. The fruit was to be eaten, and the seed was to be planted for future harvests. As we plant financial seed and give, fruit will be obtained as a result. In the harvest that is a result of our giving will be both fruit for personal consumption and more seed for planting. You must determine in your heart and decide for yourself what level of seed is to be planted. The Bible does give us some guidelines, however.

I Corinthians 16:2 tells us to give as we have prospered. This statement implies that the amount of money we give should correspond to the amount of income we earn. A logical way to implement this principle would be to give a specific percentage of our income.

We should all pray and make deliberate decisions as to the level that we can give cheerfully and not grudgingly or under compulsion. We should also make it our goal to increase our giving over time. Two things in particular should cause this to happen.

First, if we give as we prosper, then the more we prosper, the more we can give. If we have based our level of giving on a certain percentage of our income, then this will happen automatically.

Second, when we determine our level of giving, we set the percentage of our income that we give based on what we can give cheerfully. As we mature spiritually, we should begin to feel God's heart on matters more deeply. We should also grow in our reliance on God's promises. It seems to me, then, that our desire to give would increase over time, as should our ability to trust God and to believe His Word concerning our giving. The natural outcome of this line of reasoning is that the percentage of our income that we give should increase over time as well. Each year as you determine your level of giving, set a goal by faith to increase the percentage of your income that you give. Be free with your giving. It is a gift of love to begin with. Don't let it ever become a burden. Make it a *faith goal* to increase your level of giving each year.

TRUE WEALTH

As important as money is, it will never fulfill the void that people have inside them. Ever since Adam fell, and sin entered the world, man has been seeking to find fulfillment in external things. He has tried to rebuild the Garden of Eden by his efforts, looking to find satisfaction in pleasures, possessions, and status.

True wealth is internal, not external. It is found only in a personal relationship with Jesus Christ. Nothing else will satisfy the inward yearnings of our souls. The more we try to find fulfillment in external things, the more we become in bondage to them. True wealth can be found only in unity with God through His Son Jesus Christ.

I hope from this book you understand that God loves you and wants you to be blessed. But be wise enough to understand that money will never fulfill you. You will never achieve your financial potential until you are free enough from your money to give it away to meet the needs of others. Until you reach that point, you will be a slave of your possessions. There is a joy in life that you can experience only by giving of yourself and your possessions to help others. No, God does not bless you just so you can give to others, but *giving is the very heart of God.* Only by developing a lifestyle of giving can you be totally free from the love of money, and capable of truly achieving your financial potential!

Coupling a lifestyle of giving with the other financial principles taught in this book is a powerful combination. Prepare your plan, be diligent to faithfully execute it, and you will be well on your way to *achieving your financial potential!*

ENDNOTES

1. CFP® and Certified Financial Planner® are federally registered marks owned by the Certified Financial Planner Board of Standards, Inc.
2. Used with permission. ©1998 Ibbotson Associates, Inc. All rights reserved. [Certain portions of this work were derived from copyrighted works of Roger G. Ibbotson and Rex Sinquefield.]
3. Ibid.
4. Ibid.
5. Inflation measure used was CPI-U, the Consumer Price Index for all urban consumers. Source: U.S. Bureau of Labor Statistics, Monthly Labor Review and Handbook of Labor Statistics, periodic. *http://stats.bls.gov:80/news-rels.htm*
6. Used with permission. ©1998 Ibbotson Associates, Inc. All rights reserved. [Certain portions of this work were derived from copyrighted works of Roger G. Ibbotson and Rex Sinquefield.]
7. Ibid.
8. Reprinted by permission of Standard and Poor's Ratings Services, a division of The McGraw-Hill Companies, Inc., ©1998.
9. Morningstar, Inc., 225 West Wacker Drive, Chicago, IL 60606, (312) 696-6000. To subscribe, call (800) 735-0700. Also view Morningstar on-line at http://www.morningstar.net.
10. Used with permission. ©1998 Ibbotson Associates, Inc. All rights reserved. [Certain portions of this work were derived from copyrighted works of Roger G. Ibbotson and Rex Sinquefield.]

INDEX

SCOTT A. KAYS, C.F.P.

President, Kays Financial Advisory Corporation
President, Scott Kays Ministries, Inc.

Scott Kays is a respected expert in the field of financial planning. He is the President and Founder of Kays Financial Advisory Corporation, an Atlanta-based money management firm registered with the Securities and Exchange Commission as an investment advisor. He graduated from the Georgia Institute of Technology with a 4.0 G.P.A., obtaining a bachelor of science degree in management. He is also a graduate of the College for Financial Planning in Denver, Colorado, and he obtained the Certified Financial Planner designation in 1986.

Mr. Kays is a member of American MENSA, the national high IQ society. He is also a member of the International Association for Financial Planning and has served on the board of directors for the Georgia chapter. Mr. Kays has been honored in the Cambridge *Who's Who Registry of Business Leaders* and the Marquis *Who's Who in Finance and Industry*.

Mr. Kays authors the **KFAC Market Newsletter,** a quarterly commentary on the economy and various financial markets. He has frequently hosted investment seminars for such major corporations as IBM, AT&T, Bell-South, Cox Enterprises, and Puritan/Churchill Chemical Company, and he has been a guest on "Praise the Lord," a nationally televised talk show.

In addition to his investment advisory credentials, Mr. Kays is a committed Christian and respected Bible teacher. He committed his life to Christ at the age of fifteen, and acknowledged the call of God to teach the Bible at the age of seventeen. He served as the associate pastor for a nondenominational church in Atlanta from 1989–1992 and for Woodstock United Methodist Church from 1994–1996. He has also served on the board of directors of Global Christian Ministries, a national interdenominational ministerial fellowship.

To contact Mr. Kays, write him at Kays Financial Advisory Corporation, 1640 Powers Ferry Road, Building 30, Suite 200, Marietta, GA 30067, or visit KFAC's website at www.scottkays.com.